Brit

From its launch in 1768 in Edinburgh, Scotland, 15 editions and constant revisions of the printed encyclopædia have contained contributions from the greatest names in science, mathematics, literature, history, religion, philosophy and the arts. Since the 1990s it has been the most respected continuously updated, worldwide encyclopædia online. More than 4,000 expert contributors, backed by a staff of professional fact-checkers and editors, ensure that Britannica's text and visual resources are clear, current and correct.

Contributors

Jonathan Mirsky has taught Chinese, Chinese History and Literature at Cambridge University, the University of Pennsylvania, and Dartmouth College. From 1993 to 1998 he was East Asia editor of *The Times* (London) based in Hong Kong. He has also written for the *Observer*, the *Economist*, and the *Independent*. He is a regular writer for the *New York Review of Books*, the *Times Literary Supplement*, the *International Herald Tribune*, and *The Spectator*. In 1989 Dr Mirsky was named British newspapers' International Reporter of the Year for his coverage of the Tiananmen uprising. In 1999 he was a Shorenstein Fellow at Harvard. In 2002 he was the I. F. Stone Fellow in the Graduate School of Journalism at the University of California, Berkeley.

Dorothy-Grace Guerrero is a Senior Research Associate of Focus on the Global South, a special project of Chulalongkorn University Social Research Institute in Bangkok.

Frances Wood is head of the Chinese Department at the British Library. She is also the author of, among other books, *Did Marco Polo Go to China?*, *The Silk Road* and *The First Emperor of China*.

THE **Britannica**® GUIDE TO

MODERN
CHINA

A comprehensive introduction to the
the world's new economic giant

ROBINSON

Britannica®

Constable & Robinson Ltd
3 The Lanchesters
162 Fulham Palace Road
London W6 9ER
www.constablerobinson.com

Encyclopædia Britannica, Inc.
www.britannica.com

First published in the UK by Robinson,
an imprint of Constable & Robinson Ltd, 2008

ISBN 978-1-84529-801-2

Printed and bound in the EU

1 3 5 7 9 10 8 6 4 2

CONTENTS

Part 4 Culture

Part 5 Places

LIST OF ILLUSTRATIONS AND MAPS

Illustrations

The Great Goose Pagoda *Werner Forman/Corbis*
The Great Wall *Frans Lemmens/Zefa/Corbis*
Bank of China Tower *Corbis*
Beijing National Stadium *CSPA/Newsport/Corbis*

Maps

All maps © Encyclopædia Britannica Inc.

INTRODUCTION

The Central Country
Jonathan Mirsky

Zhonghuo. The name says it all: China, the "Central Country". Nowadays, China may be central only in name, but its claim to be first, most, and largest arouse expectations, fears, and hopes that it will make the twenty first century its own.

For what other country and head of state could London literally be turned red? That is what happened during a recent exhibition of Chinese art from the imperial collection at the Royal Academy. On the night of the opening, central London was illuminated from the Thames to the West End by red floodlights. When China's President Hu Jintao and Queen Elizabeth visited the show to view the Manchu emperor's favourite objects the building was closed all day to the public; Mr Hu and his royal host had the place to themselves for 50 minutes.

And why not? What country, after all, could have given the world such engineering marvels as the Great Wall or the world's highest railway (to Tibet) or is said to have invented the compass, gunpowder, block- and movable-type printing, paper, porcelain, and silk weaving—all inventions, one might say, that should be known by every school-child. And how about winnowing machines, wheelbarrows, non-choking harnesses for draught animals, the crossbow, the kite, the suspension bridge, watertight compartments in ships, fore and aft sails, canal lock gates, and deep borehole drilling? All these, too, the Chinese assert they invented, and their claims are echoed in many quarters.

Size matters. Within its borders China embraces the world's largest population. More striking still, there have always been more Chinese, including non-Hans (ethnic minorities), than any other people—already fifty million in the first century after the birth of Christ. Today, China's army is the world's largest, as is its civil service, and there are more cities in China with populations of a million or more than in any other country. And if surviving after birth and leading a long life are signs of a successful society, Chinese live-birth rates and longevity now exceed those in most developing countries and are nearly the equal of developed countries.

China is usually described as the world's oldest continuous civilization; unlike Egypt and Greece, many of the basic elements of Chinese culture, especially the written language and the habits and manners of its people, remain intact today. These characteristics have survived not only the invasions of non-Chinese peoples, notably the Mongols and Manchus, but during those long occupations the conquerors themselves adopted many Chinese habits and institutions. Nor, despite the humiliations of the unequal treaties of the nineteenth century, has China proper— excluding Hong Kong and Taiwan—ever been colonized. Some Western influences have in their time been harsh, but somehow, what may be called the "China magic" has succeeded in turning much Western influence to China's advantage, while many traditional values have been retained, especially in the country- side. Starbucks and Vuitton may be objects of desire but many up-to-date Chinese prefer traditional remedies to foreign drugs.

Such cultural continuities and adaptations have always marked the Chinese and their rulers, especially the government formed after the communist triumph in 1949. Communism, a Western notion, was transfigured in China; and while it is nowadays a cliché to say that the country is no longer communist (in the Cold War sense of the term), its basic political organization and authority can still be recognized, to use the Chinese term, as "socialism with Chinese characteristics".

Indeed, two things are made plain in the education of the youngest Chinese school child—that the Communist Party saved China and there can be no other leading group, and that Chinese civilization is the oldest and finest. As for the non-Han Chinese living within China's borders, some 55 identified ethnic minorities, it is emphasized that their best hopes for the future lie in the adoption of Han culture.

While there is considerable disagreement about the extent, and cost, of the transformation, China's economic rise since 1980 has been breathtaking. As this book shows, the standard of living in the largest cities has risen significantly, foreign businesses have flooded into the country, and, more recently, China's investment in foreign banks and other institutions has been unrivalled by any other developing country. Many urban Chinese now dress, read, travel internally and abroad, pray, and employ themselves in ways unthinkable 20 years ago.

Beijing has broken out of its previous stand-alone foreign policy and now participates in a myriad of international organizations and activities. It has been a major player during international crises such as North Korea's development of nuclear weapons and the crackdown on internal opposition in Myanmar (Burma). After the re-absorption of Hong Kong in 1997, Beijing kept its word to guarantee the policy of "One China Two Systems"—political dissent and the opposition press have not been erased and when Hong Kong people resisted the imposition of a new sedition law with enormous demonstrations, Beijing withdrew the proposed legislation. Despite China's threats to invade Taiwan (long considered to be part of China), Beijing fulminated but stayed its hand when Taiwan's leaders proposed formal independence from the mainland.

It is undeniable, therefore, that China, poor and undeveloped in 1949 despite its historic cultural achievements, has transformed itself into an economic and military near-superpower, tourist destination, and seat-holder at the top level of international discourse and diplomacy. Yet this does not present the full complexity of a country in transition.

The astonishing speed at which this transformation has taken place has given rise to a new theory of development that accords with China's self-image of a country that can become modern and internationally significant, meet the needs and desires of its people, and define human rights and democracy in its own way. Although Beijing has signed most international treaties on human rights, it defines these rights, in its own words, as the guarantee of stability, food, clothing, and shelter to its vast population. Chinese democracy, the party insists, is not based on the "Westminster model", but on the gradual introduction of elections at the village, and eventually, town and county levels and on the government's constant "consultation" with many interest groups about the direction of policies that the regime determines are in the national interest. Thus, the Chinese government considers advice from foreigners on expanding rights to be an "affront to Chinese sovereignty".

For some China-watchers, these innovations in governing should be praised rather than condemned. Some foreign experts go further, contending that if outsiders criticize how China is ruled and organized, it will only make China's rulers defensive and regard themselves as besieged in a hostile environment. (This picture of China, including its cultural accomplishments and political achievements, is amply outlined in the following chapters.) What is equally plain is that in some negative aspects, China is also "biggest", "first" and "most". These aspects, too, have their impact on the Chinese people and on China's relations with the rest of the world.

China's population today exceeds 1.3 billion and, by necessity, its growth is now limited. But the costs of such limitations have been high. The One-Child family policy, implemented in 1980, was the most unpopular of any program since 1949. Ruthlessly enforced, the policy repudiated not only the fundamental cultural preference for male heirs but also the practical fact that retired rural Chinese, with no means of support, expected their married sons to care for them—while their married daughters devoted themselves to their husbands' families. Where there was only a single married male child, one of the pairs of in-laws, it was feared, would languish without support. After the promulgation of the policy, desperate couples either killed newborn girls, placed them for adoption, or, as scans of fetuses became widely available, opted to abort unborn females. The result has been a widening gap in the gender ratios. In some parts of China as many as 118 male babies now survive for every 100 females.

Another aspect of the modern face of the Chinese government is the continued suppression of dissent. The harsh treatment of dissidents, while moderated in recent years, continues. The protests in Beijing's Tiananmen Square in 1989 and similar manifestations in dozens of other Chinese cities were merely the most dramatic example of the regime's attitude to opposition—many activists from that event still remain in prison. Chinese critics of the regime once deemed "counter-revolutionary" are now termed "criminal" and remain subject to detention. A new form of surveillance is scanning the Internet, in which Chinese security officials can search for suspect words such as "democracy" in emails and blogs.

The Chinese economic miracle, made possible by a policy of unbridled industrial growth, has had its consequences. The Chinese environment is now among the most polluted in the world, and China may have overtaken the United States into first place for emission of dangerous hydrocarbons. Some half dozen of the world's most polluted rivers are Chinese and more than a dozen Chinese cities are at the top of the world's pollution black list. There are reports that tens of thousands of Chinese children die each year from breathing poisonous air and drinking poisonous water.

In international developments, as noted above, China has played a positive role in attempting to persuade its neighbour, North Korea, to abandon that country's development of nuclear weapons. It is suggested, without substantial evidence, that in 2007 Beijing also advised the authorities in Myanmar to heed international calls to cease the oppression of the Buddhist clergy there. Elsewhere, China has continued to insist that urging countries such as Zimbabwe to adhere to international standards of human rights is to infringe their sovereignty. Indeed, in its accelerating search for sources of oil, China has struck deals with authoritarian regimes in Africa and the Middle East while remaining silent on the treatment of their citizens. In this regard, China also has been a leading international supplier of weapons to oppressive regimes, with China's riposte that developed countries such as the United States, Britain, and France have been far from innocent in this regard.

In international commerce, China is now a major exporter of manufactured goods, the low prices of which attract consumers around the world. However, two dark clouds hover over this picture. First, conditions in Chinese factories (as well as in many other industrial enterprises in the country, notably coal mines) are considered by many to be unsatisfactory, with complaints that workers live in substandard accommodations and are badly paid. The other blight is the periodic breakdown of quality control that can lead to the use of faulty components or deadly ingredients. Such occurrences have precipitated massive recalls of such products as toys, pet food, and cosmetics.

In sum, China is now on a path in which, within an orderly but admittedly corrupt society, market reforms are aimed at satisfying popular demands for economic progress. So far, this has been largely successful, despite the growing disparity between the urban relatively affluent and the rural poor who have gained little from the reforms. But in the face of tens of thousands of annual demonstrations reported in the official press, both by underpaid and endangered industrial workers and by peasants oppressed by local officials, the regime has avoided further scenes comparable to the events of 1989 or even large-scale police suppression of local outbursts.

After the disorders of the Mao years, especially the Cultural Revolution of 1966–76, the Chinese Communist Party appears, for the moment at least, to have convinced many Chinese that the alternative to party rule is *luan,* or chaos. Beijing has also persuaded many in the international community that, despite developments in Taiwan and Hong Kong, "Chinese don't want democracy". In 1919, during the May Fourth Movement, patriotic Chinese came to believe that China could be saved by "Mr Science" and "Mr Democracy". 'Mr Science' has long since entered the scene. But some years ago, Roderick MacFarquhar, a professor of government at Harvard University, warned the Communist Party School in Beijing that Mr Democracy "still waits at the door. Until he is invited in, Chinese will be subjects not citizens".

If these tactics and strategy succeed, if widespread corruption remains within some sort of bounds, and if no riot or demonstration suddenly spills into the kind of national uprising that overthrew the Manchus in 1911, Beijing will have formed a new kind of society. The international community watched the televised events of 1989 in horror, and Beijing was forced to ride out a period of foreign condemnation. The great powers, however, want a stable China, an economically successful state, and a regime in Beijing that will play by the pragmatic rules that govern the international scene. As an American policy-maker recently remarked "We like to know and trust the guy at the other end of the phone when we call Beijing".

For the moment, then, China's leaders fear their people's capacity for uprisings and disorder but believe with some reason that "stability" can be sustained with a regular diet of material goods. Still, these leaders, who are Mao Zedong's heirs, also have their eyes on history. Lucian Pye, a long-time professor of political science at the Massachusetts Institute of Technology and one of the shrewdest observers of the Chinese scene, has observed that historians write relatively little about economic reformers: "The big chapters are reserved for those leaders who brought political freedom and security to their people".

The Perils of China's Explosive Growth
Dorothy-Grace Guerrero

China in the early twenty first century is a far cry from the country that in the 1950s Swedish Nobel Prize-winning economist Gunnar Myrdal predicted would remain mired in poverty. In anticipation of the 2008 Olympic Summer Games, Beijing has undergone a massive makeover that showed how fast change can happen in a country of some 1.3 billion people. New subway lines were constructed, and the fast-disappearing *hutongs* ("residential alleyways") gave way to still more skyscrapers. China is now the world's fourth-largest economy and third-largest trading country. It accounts for approximately 5 per cent of world gross domestic product (GDP) and has recently graduated in status to a middle-income country. Beijing has also emerged as a key global aid donor. In terms of production, China supplies more than one-third of the world's steel, half of its cement, and about a third of its aluminium.

China's achievements in poverty reduction from the post-Mao Zedong era, in terms of both scope and speed, have been impressive: about 400 million people have been lifted from poverty. The standard of living for many Chinese is improving, and this has sparked widespread optimism that the government's goal of achieving an overall well-off, or *xiaokang*, society is possible in the near future.

The figures that illustrate China's remarkable economic achievements, however, conceal huge and outstanding challenges that, if neglected, could jeopardize these very gains. Many local and foreign-development analysts agree that China's unsustainable and reckless approach to growth has put the country, and the world, on the brink of environmental catastrophe. China is already coping with limited natural resources that are fast disappearing. In addition, not everyone is sharing in the benefits of such growth—about 135 million people, or one-tenth of the population, still live below the international absolute poverty line. There is a huge inequality between the urban and rural population, as well as between the poor and the rich. The increasing number of protests (termed "mass incidents" in China) is attributed to both environmental causes and experiences of injustice. If these social problems remain, it could imperil the "harmonious development", or *hexie fazhan*, project of the government and eventually erode the Chinese Communist Party's continued monopoly of political power.

The Challenge of Environmental Sustainability

China consumes more coal than the United States, Europe, and Japan combined and is about to surpass, or has already surpassed, the United States as the world's biggest emitter of greenhouse gases. Beijing is also the biggest emitter of sulfur dioxide, which contributes to acid rain. Chinese scholars blame the increase in emissions on rapid economic growth and the fact that China relies on coal for 70 per cent of its energy needs. More than 300,000 premature deaths annually are attributed to airborne pollution. The changing lifestyle of the increasing number of middle-class families also contributes to the problem. In Beijing alone, 1,000 new cars are added to the roads every day. Seven of the ten most polluted cities in the world are located in China.

The UN's 2006 Human Development Report cited China's worsening water pollution and its failure to restrict heavy polluters. At that time more than 300 million people lacked access to clean drinking water. About 60 per cent of the water in China's seven major river systems was classified as being unsuitable for human contact, and more than one-third of industrial wastewater and two-thirds of municipal wastewater were released into waterways without any treatment. China had about 7 per cent of the world's water resources and roughly 20 per cent of its population. In addition, this supply is severely regionally imbalanced—about four-fifths of China's water is situated in the southern part of the country.

The Pearl River Delta and Yangtze River Delta, two regions well developed owing to recent export-oriented growth, suffer from extensive contamination from heavy-metal and persistent organic pollutants. The pollutants emanate from industries outsourced from the developed countries and electronic wastes that are illegally imported from the United States. According to an investigation of official records conducted by the Institute of Public and Environmental Affairs (IPE), a domestic environmental non-governmental organization, more than 30 multinational corporations (MNCs) with operations in China have violated water-pollution-control guidelines. These MNCs included Pepsi-Co Inc., Panasonic Battery Co., and Foster's Group Ltd. The IPE's data was based on reports by government bodies at local and national levels.

China is beginning to realize, however, that its growth path is not cost-free. According to the State Environmental Protection Administration and the World Bank, air and water pollution is costing China 5.8 per cent of its GDP. Though the Chinese government carries the responsibility for fixing the overwhelming environmental consequences of the country's breakneck growth, help, if offered, from the transnational companies and consumers from industrialized countries that benefit greatly from China's cheap labour and polluting industries could also be utilized in the challenging clean-up task.

When the Chinese government began setting targets for reducing energy use and cutting emissions in 2004, the idea of adopting a slower growth model and the predictions about the looming environmental disaster were not, at first, received with enthusiasm. By 2007, however, targets had been established for shifting to renewable energy, for employing energy conservation, and for embracing emission-control schemes. The target was to produce 16 per cent of energy needs from alternative sources (hydroelectricity and other renewable sources) by 2020.

The Social Justice Challenge

Inside China, people are more concerned about issues related to widespread inequality than about opportunities to showcase their country to the world. The Gini coefficient (which indicates how inequality has grown in relation to economic growth) has increased in China by 50 per cent since the late 1970s. Less than 1 per cent of Chinese households control more than 60 per cent of the country's wealth. This inequality is more pronounced when seen in urban versus rural per capita income. In the countryside, life generally is harsh, and most people are poor. The ratio of urban versus rural per capita income grew from 1.8:1 in the early 1980s to 3.23:1 in 2003. (The world average was between 1.5:1 and 2:1.) Added to the problem of low income, Chinese rural residents also shoulder disproportionate tax burdens while having less access to public services, such as education and health care. Recently, the government has abolished a number of taxes to help address poverty in the countryside.

The temporary migration from rural areas to the cities of some 100 million to 150 million Chinese peasants is not an easy transition. The rural migrant workers keeping factories and construction sites running have been denied access to urban housing and to urban schooling for their children. Women migrant workers face triple discrimination for being poor un-skilled labour, female, and rural in origin. The anger and bitter-ness behind the riots and protests in the countryside (there are reportedly tens of thousands of these each year) are not so much about poverty as they are about fairness. Agricultural land in China is communally owned. (In theory, each village owns the land around it, and each family holds a small tract of land on a long-term lease.) Since the mid-1980s, however, urbanization has claimed some 25,000 square miles (65,000 square km) of farm-land; people have seen their land taken from them and then turned into homes bought for large sums by the new rich, and they have witnessed local officials lining their own pockets. Meanwhile, they have received little compensation in return and have spent years away from home living tenuous hand-to-mouth existences as factory or construction workers. Many are cheated of their wages by unscrupulous bosses. Given the reports of mass public protests, it is evident that many in China are clamouring for a more equitable distribution of China's bounty from its more than two decades of growth.

PART I

CONTEXT

CHINA—FACTS AND FIGURES

Official name: Zhonghua Renmin Gongheguo (People's Republic of China).

Form of government: single-party people's republic with one legislative house (National People's Congress).

Chief of state: President.

Head of government: Premier.

Capital: Beijing (Peking).

Official language: Mandarin Chinese.

Official religion: none.

Monetary unit: 1 renminbi (yuan).

Demography

Population (2007): 1,317,925,000.

Density (2007): persons per sq mile 356.6, persons per sq km 137.7.

Urban–rural (2007): urban 43.9%; rural 56.1%.

Sex distribution (2007): male 51.52%; female 48.48%

Age breakdown (2004): under 15, 19.3%; 15–29, 22.1%; 30–44, 27.2%; 45–59, 19.0%; 60–74, 9.6%; 75 and over, 2.8%.

Population projection: (2010) 1,338,959,000; (2020) 1,408,064,000.

Ethnic composition (2000): Han (Chinese) 91.53%; Chuang 1.30%; Manchu 0.86%; Hui 0.79%; Miao 0.72%; Uighur 0.68%; Tuchia 0.65%; Yi 0.62%; Mongolian 0.47%; Tibetan 0.44%; Puyi 0.24%; Tung 0.24%; Yao 0.21%; Korean 0.15%; Pai 0.15%; Hani 0.12%; Kazakh 0.10%; Li 0.10%; Tai 0.09%; other 0.54%.

Religious affiliation (2005): nonreligious 39.2%; Chinese folk-religionist 28.7%; Christian 10.0%, of which unregistered Protestant 7.7%, registered Protestant 1.2%, unregistered Roman Catholic 0.5%, registered Roman Catholic 0.4%; Buddhist 8.4%; atheist 7.8%; traditional beliefs 4.4%; Muslim1.5%.

Major urban agglomerations (2005): Shanghai 14,503,000; Beijing 10,717,000; Guangzhou 8,425,000; Shenzhen 7,233,000; Wuhan 7,093,000; Tianjin 7,040,000; Chongqing 6,363,000; Shenyang 4,720,000; Dongguan 4,320,000; Chengdu 4,065,000; Xi'an 3,926,000; Harbin 3,695,000; Nanjing 3,621,000; Guiyang 3,447,000; Dalian

3,073,000; Changchun 3,046,000; Zibo 2,982,000;
Kunming 2,837,000; Hangzhou 2,831,000; Qingdao
2,817,000; Taiyuan 2,794,000; Jinan 2,743,000; Zhengzhou
2,590,000; Fuzhou 2,453,000; Changsha 2,451,000;
Lanzhou 2,411,000.

Households. Average household size (2004) 3.6, of which
urban households 3.0, rural households 4.1.

Vital statistics
Birth rate per 1,000 population (2006): 12.1 (world avg.
20.3).
Death rate per 1,000 population (2006): 6.8 (world avg.
8.6).
Natural increase rate per 1,000 population (2006): 5.3
(world avg. 11.7).
Total fertility rate (avg. births per childbearing woman;
2005): 1.72.
Life expectancy at birth (2005): male 70.9 years; female
74.3 years.

National economy
Gross national product (2006): US$ 2,641,846,000,000
(US$ 2,035 per capita).
Budget (2004). Revenue: Y 2,639,647,000,000.
Expenditures: Y 2,848,689,000,000 (economic
development 27.8%, of which agriculture 8.3%; social,
cultural, and educational development 26.3%;
administration 19.4%; defence 7.7%; other 18.8%).
Public debt (external, outstanding; 2005): US$
82,853,000,000.

Foreign trade

Imports (2004): US$ 561,229,000,000 (machinery and apparatus 41.7%, of which transistors/microcircuits (2003) 12.7%, computers and office machines (2003) 5.9%, machines specialized for particular industries (2003) 5.0%; mineral fuels 8.6%; professional and scientific equipment 7.4%; plastics and related products 5.0%; organic chemicals 4.2%; iron and steel 4.2%.

Major import sources: Japan 16.8%; Taiwan 11.5%; South Korea 11.1%; United States 8.0%; Germany 5.4%; Malaysia 3.2%; Singapore 2.5%; Russia 2.2%; Hong Kong 2.1%; Australia 2.1%.
Exports (2004): U.S.$ 593,326,000,000 (machinery and apparatus 41.8%, of which computers and office machines (2003) 14.3%, telecommunications, sound recording and reproducing equipment (2003) 10.3%, electrical machinery [including microcircuits] (2003) 9.9%; wearing apparel and accessories 11.3%; iron and steel incl. finished products 4.2%; chemicals and chemical products 4.1%; transport equipment 3.5%).

Major export destinations: United States 21.1%; Hong Kong 17.0%; Japan 12.4%; South Korea 4.7%; Germany 4.0%; The Netherlands 3.1%; United Kingdom 2.5%; Taiwan 2.3%; Singapore 2.1%; France 1.7%.

Military

Total active duty personnel (March 2006): 2,255,000 (army 71.0%, navy 11.3%, air force 17.7%).
Military expenditure as percentage of GDP (2005): 2.0%; per capita expenditure US$ 34.

Internet resources for further information:
National Bureau of Statistics of China
  http://www.stats.gov.cn/english
Embassy of The People's Republic of China
  http://www.china-embassy.org

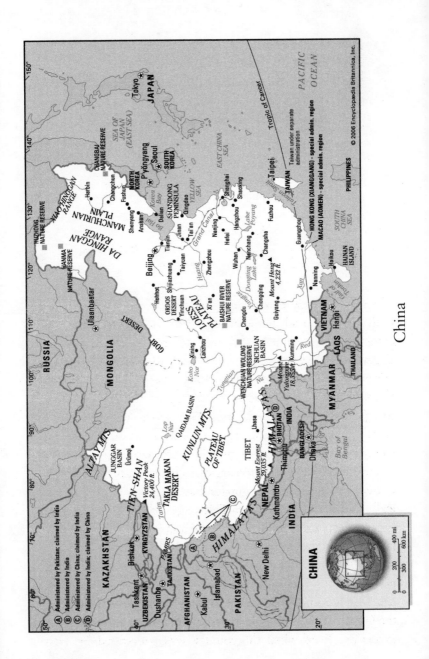

China

I

OVERVIEW

China is a highly diverse and complex country in terms of both physical and human geography. Its topography encompasses the highest and one of the lowest places on Earth, and its relief varies from nearly impenetrable mountainous terrain to vast coastal lowlands. Its climate ranges from extremely dry, desert-like conditions in the north-west to tropical conditions in the south-east; China has the greatest contrast in temperature between its northern and southern borders of any country in the world.

With more than 4,000 years of recorded history, China is one of the few existing countries that also flourished economically and culturally in the earliest stages of world civilization. Indeed, despite the frequent political and social upheavals that have ravaged the country over its long history, China is unique among nations in its longevity and resilience as a discrete politico-cultural unit. Much of China's cultural development has been accomplished with relatively little outside influence, the introduction of Buddhism from India constituting a major exception. Even when the country was penetrated by such "barbarian" peoples as the Manchu, these groups soon became largely absorbed into the fabric of Han Chinese culture.

This relative isolation from the outside world over the centuries enabled Chinese culture to develop and blossom, but it also left China ill-prepared to cope with that world when, from the mid-nineteenth century, it was confronted by technologically superior foreign nations. There followed a century of decline and decrepitude, as China found itself relatively helpless in the face of a foreign onslaught. The trauma of this external challenge became the catalyst for a revolution that began in the early twentieth century against the old regime and culminated in the establishment of a communist government on the mainland in 1949, one that has held power ever since. This event reshaped global political geography, and China has since come to rank among the most influential countries in the world.

The largest nation in Asia, China stretches for about 3,250 miles (5,250 km) from east to west and 3,400 miles (5,500 km) from north to south. Its land frontier is about 12,400 miles (20,000 km) in length, and its coastline extends for some 8,700 miles (14,000 km). The country is bounded by Mongolia to the north; Russia and North Korea to the north-east; the Yellow Sea and the East China Sea to the east; the South China Sea to the south-east; Vietnam, Laos, Myanmar (Burma), India, Bhutan, and Nepal to the south; Pakistan to the south-west; and Afghanistan, Tajikistan, Kyrgyzstan, and Kazakhstan to the west. In addition to the 14 countries that border directly on it, China also faces South Korea and Japan, across the Yellow Sea, and the Philippines, which lie beyond the South China Sea.

The most remarkable feature of China's relief is the vast extent of its mountain chains; the mountains, indeed, have exerted a tremendous influence on the country's political, economic, and cultural development. A rough estimate is that about one-third of the total area consists of mountains. The topography is marked by many splendours. Mount Everest (Qomolangma Feng; 29,035 feet [8,850 metres] high), situated on the border between China and Nepal, is the highest peak in the world. By contrast, the lowest part of the Turfan Depression in the Uygur Autonomous Region of Xinjiang—Lake Ayding—is 508 feet (155 metres) below sea level. The coast of China contrasts greatly between south and north. To the south of Hangzhou Bay, the coast is rocky and indented, with many harbours and offshore islands. To the north, except along the Shandong and Liaodong Peninsulas, the coast is sandy and flat.

China's physical relief has dictated its social development in many respects. The civilization of Han Chinese originated in the southern part of the Loess Plateau, in the region of present-day Xi'an, and from there it extended outward until it encountered the combined barriers of relief and climate. Thus, for a long time the ancient political centre of China was located along the lower reaches of the Huang He (Yellow River).

Because of topographical barriers, however, it was difficult for the central government to gain complete control over the entire country, except when an unusually strong dynasty was in power. For centuries the Sichuan Basin—an isolated region in south-western China, about twice the size of Scotland, well protected by high mountains and self-sufficient in agricultural products—was an independent kingdom. A comparable situation arose in the Tarim Basin in the north-west.

It is therefore possible to divide China into three major topographical regions: the eastern, north-western, and south-western zones. The eastern zone is shaped by the rivers, which divide into two plains. The north-western region is arid and eroded by the wind, and forms an inland drainage basin. The south-west is a cold, lofty, and mountainous region containing intermontane plateaus and inland lakes.

The Country

The Northeast Plain (also known as the Manchurian Plain and the Sungliao Plain) is located in China's north-east, the region formerly known as Manchuria. It is bordered to the west and north by the Da Hinggan (Greater Khingan) Range and to the east by the Xiao Hinggan (Lesser Khingan) Range. An undulating plain split into northern and southern halves by a low divide rising from 500 to 850 feet (150 to 260 metres), it is drained in its northern part by the Sungari River and tributaries and in its southern part by the Liao River. Its basic landscapes are forest-steppe, steppe, meadow-steppe, and cultivated land. Its soils are rich and black, and it is a famous agricultural region. The river valleys are wide and flat with a series of terraces formed by deposits of silt. During the flood season the rivers inundate wide areas, further enriching the soil with minerals and nutrients.

To the south-east of the Manchurian Plain is a series of ranges comprising the Changbai, Zhangguangcai, and Wanda Mountains (in Chinese these are collectively known as the Changbai Shan or "Forever White Mountains"). These mountains are broken up by occasional open valleys. In some parts the scenery is characterized by rugged peaks and precipitous cliffs. The highest peak is the volcanic cone of Mount Baitou (9,003 feet [2,744 metres]), which has a beautiful crater lake at its snow-covered summit. As one of the major forest areas of China, the region is the source of many valuable furs and popular medicinal herbs.

Comparable in size to the Northeast Plain, most of the

North China Plain is monotonously flat. It was formed by enormous sedimentary deposits brought down by the Huang He and the Huai River from the Loess Plateau. This vast plateau of some 154,000 square miles (400,000 square km) forms a unique region of loess-clad hills and barren mountains between the North China Plain and the deserts of the west. In the north the Great Wall of China forms the boundary, while the southern limit is the Qin Mountains in Shaanxi province. This range, a high and rugged barrier extending from Gansu to Henan, constitutes the greatest chain of mountains east of the Plateau of Tibet. Geographers use a line between the Qin Mountains and the Huai River to divide China into north and south.

The Sichuan Basin is one of the most attractive geographical regions of China. It is surrounded by mountains, which protect against cold northern winds. The lack of arable land has led to farmers cultivating the slopes of the hills, on which they have built terraces that frequently cover the slopes from top to bottom.

South-eastern China is bordered by a rocky shoreline backed by picturesque mountains. The higher peaks may reach elevations of some 5,000 to 6,500 feet (1,500 to 2,000 metres). The rivers are short and fast-flowing and have cut steep-sided valleys. The chief areas of settlement are on narrow strips of coastal plain where rice is produced. Along the coast there are numerous islands, where the fishing industry is well developed.

East of Yichang, in Hubei province, lie a series of plains along the Yangtze River (Chang Jiang). The plains are particularly wide in the delta area and in places where the Yangtze receives its major tributaries—including large areas of low-lands around Dongting, Poyang, Tai, and Hongze lakes, which are all hydrologically linked with the Yangtze. Here rivers, canals, and lakes form a dense network of waterways. The surface of the plain has been converted into a system of flat terraces, which descend in steps along the slopes of the valleys.

The Nan Mountains (Nan Ling) are composed of many ranges running from north-east to south-west. These ranges form the watershed between the Yangtze to the north and the Pearl (Zhu) River to the south. The main peaks along the watershed are above 5,000 feet (1,500 metres), and some are more than 6,500 feet (2,000 metres). But a large part of the land to the south of the Nan Mountains is also hilly; flatland does not exceed 10 per cent of the total area. The Pearl River delta is the only extensive plain in this region and is also the richest part of South China. The coastline is rugged and irregular, and there are many promontories and protected bays, including those of Hong Kong and Macau. The principal river is the Xi River, which rises in the highlands of eastern Yunnan and southern Guizhou.

To the south-west of the country the Yunnan-Guizhou Plateau comprises the northern part of Yunnan and the western part of Guizhou. Yunnan is more distinctly a plateau and contains larger areas of rolling uplands than Guizhou, but both parts are distinguished by canyonlike valleys and precipitous mountains.

The Plateau of Tibet, a great upland massif, occupies about one-quarter of the country's area. A large part of the plateau lies at elevations above 13,000 to 16,500 feet (4,000 to 5,000 metres). The border ranges of the plateau (the Kunlun Mountains and the Himalayas) are even higher, with individual peaks rising to heights of 23,000 to 26,000 feet (7,000 to 8,000 metres) and higher. As a rule, the interior (i.e. Tibet-side) slopes of these border mountains are gentle, while the exterior slopes are precipitous. The plateau's eastern and southern periphery is the source of many of the world's great rivers, including the Yangtze, Huang He, Mekong, Salween, Indus, and Brahmaputra. Only in the low valleys, chiefly along the Brahmaputra valley, are there centres of human settlement.

North of the Plateau of Tibet and at a much lower elevation lies the Tarim Basin. It is hemmed in by great mountain ranges: the Tien Shan (Tian Shan; "Celestial Mountains") on the north, the Pamirs on the west, and the Kunlun Mountains on the south. Glacier-fed streams descend from these heights only to lose themselves in the loose sands and gravels of the Takla Makan Desert, which occupies the centre of the basin. The Takla Makan is one of the most barren of the world's deserts. Only a few of the largest rivers—such as the Tarim and Hotan (Khotan)—cross the desert, but even their flow is not constant, and they have water throughout their entire courses only during the flood period.

North of the Tarim Basin is another large depression, the Junggar (Dzungarian) Basin. It is enclosed by the Tien Shan on the south, while to the north-east it is cut off from Mongolia by the Altai Mountains. The surface of the basin is flat, with a gentle slope to the south-west. The larger portion of the land lies at elevations between about 1,000 and 1,500 feet (300 and 450 metres), and in the lowest part the elevation drops to just below 650 feet (200 metres). In general the main part of the basin is covered by a broad desert with barchans (crescent-shaped sand dunes that move); only in certain parts are dunes retained by vegetation.

The Chinese (eastern) part of the Tien Shan consists of a complex system of ranges and depressions divided into two major groups of ranges: the northern and the southern. The groups are separated by a strip of intermontane depressions that itself is broken up by the interior ranges. Ancient metamorphic rock constitutes the larger portion of the ranges in the interior zone; Paleozoic (i.e. about 250 to 540 million years old) sedimentary and igneous sedimentary beds form its northern and southern chains, while Mesozoic (about 65 to 250 million years old) sandstones and conglomerates fill the inter-montane depressions in the interior zone and constitute the foothill ridges. The height of the main Chinese chains of the Tien Shan is between 13,000 and 15,000 feet (4,000 and 4,600 metres), with individual peaks exceeding 16,000 feet (4,900 metres); the interior chains reach 14,500 feet (4,400 metres). In the western part, where precipitation is adequate, large glaciers are formed, reaching a length of more than 20 miles (32 km). Large rivers with heavy flows, such as the Ili (Yili) River and its tributaries, begin their courses there, and the predominantly alpine meadow-steppe is one of the best grazing lands of China.

The People

One-fifth of humanity is of Chinese nationality. Additionally, some 55 million ethnic Chinese live outside the country. China is composed of a large number of ethnic and linguistic groups. The Han (Chinese), the largest group, outnumber the minority groups or minority nationalities in every province or auton-omous region except Tibet and Xinjiang, and their numbers there are growing far faster than those of the native peoples. The Han, therefore, form the great homogeneous mass of the Chinese people, sharing the same culture, the same traditions, and the same written language. For this reason, the general basis for classifying the country's population is largely linguis-tic rather than ethnic.

Some 55 minority groups are spread over approximately three-fifths of the country's total area. Where these minority groups are found in large numbers, they have been given some semblance of autonomy and self-government. The government takes great credit for its treatment of these minorities; it has advanced their economic well-being, raised their living standards, provided educational facilities, promoted their national languages and cultures, and raised their literacy levels, as well as introduced a written language where none existed previously. However, some minorities (e.g. Tibetans) have been subject to varying degrees of repression.

Of the 50-odd minority languages, only 20 had written forms before the coming of the communist regime in 1949; and only relatively few written languages (e.g. Mongolian, Tibetan, Uighur, Kazakh, Dai, and Korean) were in everyday use. Other written languages were used chiefly for religious purposes and by a limited number of people. Several major language families are represented in China. By far the largest groups are speakers of Sino-Tibetan and Altaic languages, with considerably smaller numbers speaking Indo-European, Austroasiatic, and Tai languages.

The Sino-Tibetan language family is by far the most prominent and within this family, Han Chinese is the most widely spoken language. Although unified by their tradition— the written ideographic characters of their language as well as many other cultural traits—the Han speak several mutually unintelligible dialects and display marked regional differences.

By far the most important Chinese tongue is Mandarin, or *putonghua*, meaning "ordinary language" or "common language". There are three variants of Mandarin. The first of these is the northern variant, of which the Beijing dialect, or Beijing *hua*, is typical and which is spoken to the north of the Qin Mountains–Huai River line. As the most widespread Chinese tongue, it has officially been adopted as the basis for a national language. The second is the western variant, also known as the Chengdu or Upper Yangtze variant, which is spoken in the Sichuan Basin and in adjoining parts of south-western China. The third is the southern variant, also known as the Nanjing or Lower Yangtze variant, which is spoken in northern Jiangsu and in southern and central Anhui. Some authorities also recognize a fourth north-western variant, used in most of north-western China. Related to Mandarin are the Hunan, or Xiang, language, spoken by people in central and southern Hunan, and the Gan dialect. The Huizhou language, spoken in southern Anhui, forms an enclave within the southern Mandarin area.

Less intelligible to Mandarin speakers are the dialects of the south-east coastal region, stretching from Shanghai to Guangzhou (Canton). The most important of these is the Wu language, spoken in southern Jiangsu and in Zhejiang. This is followed, to the south, by the Fuzhou, or Northern Min, language of northern and central Fujian and by the Xiamen-Shantou (Amoy-Swatow), or Southern Min, language of southern Fujian, eastern-most Guangdong, and Taiwan. The Hakka language of southern-most Jiangxi and north-eastern Guangdong has a rather scattered pattern of distribution. Probably the best known of these southern dialects is Yue, particularly Cantonese, which is spoken in central and western Guangdong, Hong Kong, and in southern Guangxi—a dialect area in which a large proportion of overseas Chinese originated.

In addition to the Han, the Manchu and the Hui (Chinese Muslims) also speak Mandarin and use the Chinese writing system. The Hui, firm adherents of Islam, are descendants of Persian and Central Asian Muslims who travelled to China as merchants, soldiers, and scholars and intermarried with several Chinese nationalities. They are intermingled with the Han throughout much of the country and are distinguished as Hui only in the area of their heaviest concentration, the Autonomous Region of Ningxia. Other Hui communities are organized as autonomous prefectures (*zizhizhou*) in Xinjiang and as autonomous counties (*zizhixian*) in Qinghai, Hebei, Guizhou, and Yunnan. Increasingly, the Hui have been moving from their scattered settlements into the area of major concentration, possibly in order to facilitate intermarriage with other Muslims.

The Manchu claim that they are descendants of the Manchu warriors who invaded China in the seventeenth century and founded the Qing dynasty (1644–1911/12). Manchu is virtually a dead language—though it is closely related to Sibo (or Xibe), which is still vital—and the Manchu have been completely assimilated into Han Chinese culture. They are found mainly in North China and the north-east, but they form no separate autonomous areas above the commune level.

The Zhuang (Zhuangjia) are China's largest minority group. Most of them live in the Zhuang Autonomous Region of Guangxi. They are also found in national autonomous areas in neighbouring Yunnan and Guangdong. They depend mainly on rice cultivation for their livelihood. In religion the Zhuang are animists, worshipping particularly the spirits of their ancestors. Members of the Buyi (Zhongjia) group are concentrated in southern Guizhou, where they share an autonomous prefecture with the Miao (Hmong) group. The Dong people are settled in small communities in Guangxi and Guizhou; they share with the Miao group an autonomous prefecture set up in south-east Guizhou in 1956.

Tibetans are distributed over the entire Qinghai–Tibetan highland region. Outside Tibet, Tibetan minorities are found in five Tibetan autonomous prefectures in Qinghai, two in Sichuan, and one each in Yunnan and Gansu. The Tibetans still maintain their tribal characteristics, but few of them are nomadic. Though essentially farmers, they also raise livestock and, like other tribal peoples in the Chinese far west, hunt to supplement their food supply. The major religion of Tibet is Buddhism, with a theocracy under the Dalai Lama ruling from the seventeenth century until the Chinese army asserted control in 1959. Many of the Yi (Lolo) are concentrated in two autonomous prefectures—one in southern Sichuan and another in northern Yunnan. They raise crops and sometimes keep flocks and herds.

The Miao-Yao (Hmong-Mien) peoples, with their major concentration in Guizhou, are distributed throughout the central south and south-western provinces and are found also in some small areas in eastern China. They are subdivided into many rather distinct groupings. Most of them have now lost their traditional tribal practices through the influence of the Han, and it is only their language that serves to distinguish them. Two-thirds of the Miao are settled in Guizhou, where they share two autonomous prefectures with the Dong and Buyi groups. The Yao people are concentrated in the Guangxi-Guangdong-Hunan border area.

In some areas of China, especially in the south-west, many different ethnic groups are geographically intermixed. Because of language barriers and different economic structures, these peoples all maintain their own cultural traits and live in relative isolation from one another. The Han are active in the towns and fertile river valleys of some of these locales, while the minority peoples continue to base their livelihood on more traditional forms of agriculture or on grazing their livestock on hillsides and mountains. The vertical distribution of these peoples is in zones—usually the higher they live, the less complex their way of life. In former times they did not mix well with one another, but now, with highways penetrating deep into their settlements, they have better opportunities to communicate with other groups and have benefited from improved living conditions.

While the minorities of the Sino-Tibetan language family are thus concentrated in the south and south-west, the second major language family—the Altaic—is represented entirely by minorities in north-western and northern China. The Altaic family falls into three branches: Turkic, Mongolian, and Manchu-Tungus. The Turkic language branch is by far the most numerous of the three Altaic branches. The Uighur, who are Muslims, form the largest Turkic-speaking minority. They are distributed over chains of oases in the Tarim and Junggar basins of Xinjiang and mainly depend on irrigated agriculture for a livelihood. Other Turkic minorities in Xinjiang are splinter groups of nationalities living in neighbouring countries of Central Asia, including the Kazakhs and the Kyrgyz, all being adherents of Islam. The Kazakhs and Kyrgyz are pastoral nomadic peoples who still show traces of tribal organization. The Kazakhs live mainly as herders in north-western and northern Xinjiang (notably in the Ili River region), tending flocks in summer pastures and retiring to camps in the valleys during the winter. The Kyrgyz are high-mountain pastoralists and are concentrated mainly in the western-most part of Xinjiang.

The Mongolians, who are by nature a nomadic people, are the most widely dispersed of the minority nationalities of China. Most of them are inhabitants of the Inner Mongolia Autonomous Region. Small Mongolian and Mongolian-related groups of people are scattered throughout the vast area from Xinjiang through Qinghai and Gansu and into the provinces of the north-east (Jilin, Heilongjiang, and Liaoning). In addition to the Inner Mongolia Autonomous Region, Mongolians are established in two autonomous prefectures in Xinjiang, a joint autonomous prefecture with Tibetans and Kazakhs in Qinghai, and several autonomous counties in the western area of the north-east. Some Mongolians retain their tribal divisions and are pastoralists, but large numbers practise sedentary agriculture, and others combine crop growing with herding. Those who depend on animal husbandry travel each year around the pastureland—grazing sheep, goats, horses, cattle, and camels—and then return to their point of departure. A few engage in hunting and fur trapping to supplement their income.

A few linguistic minorities in China belong to neither the Sino-Tibetan nor the Altaic language family. The Tajiks of westernmost Xinjiang are related to the people of Tajikistan, and their language belongs to the Iranian branch of the Indo-European family. The Kawa people of the border area adjacent to Myanmar (Burma) speak a tongue of the Mon-Khmer branch of the Austroasiatic family. Speakers of languages in the Tai family are concentrated in southern Yunnan, notably in two autonomous prefectures—one whose population is related most closely to the Thai of northern Thailand and another whose Tai speakers are related to the Shan people of Myanmar (Burma). The Li of Hainan Island form a separate group whose dialects are related to the Tai and Austronesian languages. They share with the Miao people a district in the southern part of the island. A significant number of Koreans are concentrated in an autonomous prefecture in eastern Jilin along the North Korean border.

Town and Country

Modern China is a nation of vast cities, some of the largest on earth. Many of them, such as Xi'an, are quite ancient; others, such as Beijing, began to grow with the establishment of government centres hundreds of years ago; still others, such as Shanghai and Guilin, have become major metropolises only in the last century. But even with the greatness of its cities, with a combined population estimated to reach 1.4 billion by 2020, far more Chinese live in the countryside than in the towns.

An overwhelming majority of rural settlements in China consist of sizable compact (nucleated) villages, except in mountainous and hilly terrain where such compaction is not possible. The formation of such rural settlements is related not only to the increasing population and to a long historical background but also to water supply (the practice of drilling deep wells, for instance) and to defence (especially, in former days, against attack by bandits). Many of the large villages have no urban atmosphere at all, even with populations of several thousand. Frequent markets may be held between such settlements to enable the peasants to barter their agricultural produce. Animals and people live in close proximity in Chinese villages, which accounts for the great number of zoonotic diseases that originate there, including most modern strains of influenza.

On the North China Plain, villages are fairly evenly distributed and are connected with one another by footpaths and cart tracks. Houses are built close together and are mostly made of sun-dried brick or pounded earth. Many of the market towns or even large villages are surrounded by walls. The number and length of the streets depend on the town's size and the nature of the terrain; some streets are merely narrow lanes.

Rural landscapes of central and southern China are dominated by rice fields. The Yangtze River delta has almost every type of human settlement, from the single farmstead to the fairly large market town. Villages to the south and east of Lake Tai in Jiangsu province are generally located 1 to 2 miles (1.6 to 3 km) apart, and since the 1980s many of these have been developed into small towns. Villages in central China, particularly on the lower Yangtze, are larger than those of North China; many have a few shops that serve not only the villagers but also the dispersed residents nearby. In the centre of dozens of such villages is a market town, which collects rural produce and distributes manufactured goods. Communication among the villages is mainly by boat, along the dense network of waterways. The most elegant structures in the landscape are the numerous stone bridges that span streams and canals. In the Chengdu Plain of the Sichuan Basin, a large part of the population lives in isolated farmsteads or scattered hamlets, surrounded by thickets of bamboo and broad-leaved trees.

Cave dwellings are another distinctive feature of the Chinese rural landscape. They are common on the Loess Plateau and particularly in northern Shaanxi, western Shanxi, and south-eastern Gansu, where the loess cover is thick and timber is scarce. A cave dwelling has the advantage of being naturally insulated, making it cooler in summer and warmer in winter.

The economic reforms initiated in China from the late 1970s had a profound impact on rural settlement. Improvements in agricultural productivity created a vast pool of surplus labour. Many of these rural workers went to the cities in search of factory jobs, but a large number stayed behind, where they engaged in a growing system of rural industrial production termed "township enterprise". Usually engaged in light manufacturing for both domestic and export markets, these enterprises helped transform thousands of villages into partially urbanized towns and raised the standard of living for millions of peasants. The new towns thus served as a link between the city and the countryside and became a significant factor in the rapidly growing rural economy.

Urbanization and industrialization often have been closely related in China. The first major post-1949 urbanization push began in the mid-1950s, as the government intensified its efforts to convert the country into an industrial power. Urban growth accelerated even more rapidly from the mid-1980s, with China's serious entry on to the global economic stage.

Thus, the rapid development of modern manufacturing industries and of communications in China produced a dramatic change in the urban landscape. Many new towns and cities have been built around manufacturing and mining centres. In the remoter areas of China, the first appearance of railways and highways contributed to the rapid growth of some entirely new towns, such as Shihezi in northern Xinjiang and Shiquanhe in western Tibet. Among larger cities, Ürümqi (Urumchi; capital of Xinjiang), Lanzhou (capital of Gansu), and Baotou (in Inner Mongolia) are examples where expansion has been extremely rapid. Lanzhou lies midway between south-eastern and north-western China. Baotou, formerly a bleak frontier town of traders, artisans, and immigrant farmers, has become one of the country's largest steel centres.

Some two-fifths of China's population is urban, up from less than one-fourth in 1975. While the urban–rural proportion is relatively low compared with more highly industrialized countries, it represents an enormous number of people—comparable to the total population of North America. Some four dozen cities have populations of more than 1,000,000, and the populations of several other dozen are between 500,000 and 1,000,000. The distribution of China's large cities mirrors the national population distribution, with heavy concentrations in the eastern coastal provinces, lesser but still significant numbers in the central provinces, and considerably fewer in western regions.

The Population

Historical records show that as long ago as 800 BCE, in the early part of the Zhou dynasty, China was already inhabited by about 13.7 million people. Until the last years of the Western Han dynasty, about 2 CE, comparatively accurate and complete registers of population were kept, and the total population in that year was given as 59.6 million.

During the later years of the Northern Song dynasty, in the early twelfth century, when China was already in the heyday of its economic and cultural development, the total population began to exceed 100 million. Later, uninterrupted and large-scale invasions from the north reduced the country's population. When national unification returned with the advent of the Ming dynasty, the census was at first strictly conducted. The population of China, according to a registration compiled in 1381, was quite close to the one registered in 2 CE.

From the fifteenth century onward the population increased steadily, growth being interrupted by wars and natural disasters in the mid-seventeenth century and slowed by the internal strife and foreign invasions in the century that preceded the communist takeover in 1949. During the eighteenth century China enjoyed a lengthy period of peace and prosperity, characterized by continual territorial expansion and an accelerating population increase. In 1762 China had a population of more than 200 million, and by 1834 that population had doubled. It should be noted that during that period the amount of cultivable land did not increase concomitantly, and land hunger became a growing problem from that time on.

Great population movements have been a recurring theme throughout Chinese history. Typically, some disastrous event such as famine or political upheaval would depopulate an area already intensively cultivated, after which people in adjacent crowded regions would move in to occupy the deserted land. A peasant rebellion in Sichuan in the 1640s caused great loss of life, and people from neighbouring Hubei and Shaanxi then entered Sichuan to fill the vacuum; this migration pattern continued until the nineteenth century.

Three centuries later the Taiping Rebellion caused another large-scale disruption of population. Many people in the lower Yangtze valley were massacred by the opposing armies, and the survivors suffered from starvation. After the rebellion was defeated, people from Hubei, Hunan, and Henan moved into the depopulated areas of Jiangsu, Anhui, and Zhejiang, where farmland was lying abandoned and uncultivated. Similar examples include the Nian Rebellion in the Huai River region in the 1850s and 1860s, the Muslim rebellions in Shaanxi and Gansu in the 1860s and 1870s, and the great Shaanxi and Shanxi famine of 1877–78.

The most significant internal population movement in modern Chinese history was that of the Han to Manchuria (now known as the Northeast). Even before the Qing (Manchu) dynasty was established in 1644, Manchu soldiers had launched raids into North China and captured Han labourers, who were then obliged to settle in Manchuria. An imperial decree in 1668 closed the area to further Han migration, but this ban was never effectively enforced. By 1850, Han colonizing settlers had become dominant in Manchuria. The ban was later partially lifted, partly because the Manchu rulers were harassed by disturbances in China proper and partly because the Russian Empire continually tried to invade sparsely populated and thus weakly defended Manchuria. The ban was finally removed altogether in 1878, but settlement was encouraged only after 1900.

The influx of people into Manchuria was especially pronounced after 1923, and incoming farmers rapidly brought a vast area of virgin grassland under cultivation. About two-thirds of the immigrants entered Manchuria by sea, and one-third came overland. Because the region's winter weather was so severe, migration in the early stage was highly seasonal, usually starting in February and continuing through the spring. After the autumn harvest a large proportion of the farmers returned south. As Manchuria developed into the principal industrial region of China, however, large urban centres arose there, and the nature of the migration changed. No longer was the movement primarily one of agricultural resettlement; instead it became essentially a rural-to-urban movement of interregional magnitude.

After 1949 the new government's efforts to foster planned migration into interior and border regions produced notice-able results. Although the total number of people involved in such migrations is not known, it has been estimated that by 1980 between one-fourth and one-third of the population of such regions and provinces as Inner Mongolia, Xinjiang, Heilongjiang, and Qinghai consisted of recent migrants, and migration had raised the proportion of Han in Xinjiang to about two-fifths of the total. Efforts to control the growth of large cities led to the resettlement in the countryside of some 20 million urbanites after the failure of the Great Leap Forward and of nearly the same number of urban-educated youths in the decade after 1968. However, most of these "rusticated youths" subsequently returned to the cities.

The economic reforms begun in the late 1970s have un-leashed a tidal wave of both rural-to-urban and west-to-east migration, reversing trends of the previous three decades. This has further exacerbated the country's uneven population dis-tribution, bringing enormous influxes to the urban areas of the eastern provinces and further depleting the population in the western regions. However, tens of millions of rural people who go to the cities to find jobs also return home for periods of time during the year. These individuals have tended to group themselves according to their native area for mutual benefit, much as ethnic groups have done in other major world cities. However, the unregulated influx of so many migrants and the instability of their lives and work have put considerable strain on the host cities, notably the environment and public security.

In cities and the countryside alike, sanitation and medical care greatly improved after 1949. Epidemics were brought under control, and subsequent generations enjoyed progressively better health. Public hygiene also improved, and, as a result, the death rate declined faster than the birth rate, and the population growth rate increased. China's population reached 1 billion in the early 1980s and had surpassed 1.3 billion early in the twenty first century.

The continually growing population has been a major problem for the government. In 1955–58, with the country struggling to obtain an adequate food supply and saddled with a generally low standard of living, the authorities sponsored a major birth-control drive. A second attempt at population control began in 1962, when the main initiatives were programmes promoting late marriages and the use of contraceptives. The outbreak of the Cultural Revolution in 1966 interrupted this second family-planning drive, but in 1970 a third and much stricter programme was initiated. The attempt this time was to make late marriage and family limitation obligatory, and it culminated in 1979 in efforts to implement a policy of one child per family. Those efforts were redoubled in 2000, but it appears that in most rural areas there is still widespread resistance to the one-child policy. Overall it has been successful, though, in China's cities, but with an unintended consequence that the Chinese characterize as the "little emperor/empress" phenomenon: a single child pampered by two parents and four grandparents, a scenario that does not fit well with the egalitarian, self-sacrificing ideals of the communist state of old. The policy has also had another effect, largely in the countryside, where baby girls are killed to make room for baby boys, who are considered to be more useful economically. The result is a population imbalance; it is believed that there are at least 40 million more men than women in China today.

Other developments affected the rate of population growth more than the first two official family-planning campaigns, notably the disastrous effects of Chinese leader Mao Zedong's Great Leap Forward economic programme of 1958–60. The policies of the Great Leap caused a massive famine in China, the death rate surpassed the birth rate, and by 1960 the overall population was declining. By 1963 the country was recovering from the famine, and, even though the second birth-control campaign had already begun, a soaring birth rate produced an annual population growth rate of more than 3%, the highest since 1949.

Since 1970, however, when the third family-planning programme was launched, state efforts have been much more effective. China's population growth rate is now among the lowest for a developing country, although, because its population is so huge, annual net population growth is still considerable.

PART 2

HISTORY

2

THE RISE OF THE REPUBLIC (1912–49)

For more than 3,500 years, China was ruled by a succession of dynasties whose heads enjoyed absolute power, unimpeded by independent judiciaries or other formal means of checking the exercise thereof. The reigning emperor was supported by a vast Confucian bureaucracy populated by scholars and administrators, who were true servants of the imperial state and were able to exercise only limited decision-making on their own. Even so, official corruption was epidemic, as were social ills such as poverty and hunger. The closing years of the Qing dynasty, the nation's last, were marked by the rise of many nationalist, reformist, and revolutionary organizations dedicated to establishing popular rule in China.

In 1912, the 268-year rule of the Qing dynasty ended, its downfall hastened by the pressure of foreign intervention as well as internal demands for change. During the first half of the twentieth century, the old order in China gradually disintegrated, and turbulent preparations were made for a new society. Foreign influences undermined the traditional governmental system, nationalism became the strongest activating force, and civil wars and Japanese invasion tore the vast country apart and held back its modernization.

The man at the centre of this change was Sun Yat-sen, sometimes called the father of modern China. Sun was born to a family of poor farmers in Xiangshan, in the South China province of Guangdong. In 1879 his brother Sun Mei, who had earlier emigrated to Hawaii as a labourer, brought him to Honolulu where, as a student at a British missionary school for three years and at an American school, Oahu College, for another year, he first came into contact with Western influences.

Although not trained for a political career in the traditional style, Sun was nevertheless ambitious and was troubled by the way China, which had clung to its traditional ways under the conservative Qing dynasty, suffered humiliation at the hands of more technologically advanced nations. Forsaking his medical practice in Guangzhou (Canton), he went north in 1894 to seek his political fortunes. In a long letter to Li Hongzhang, governor general of Zhili, he set forth his ideas of how China could gain strength. With this scant reference, Sun went to Hawaii in October 1894 and founded an organization called the Revive China Society (Xingzhonghui), which became the forerunner of the secret revolutionary groups Sun later headed.

Taking advantage of China's defeat in the Sino-Japanese War (1894–95) and the ensuing crisis, Sun went to Hong Kong in 1895 and plotted for an uprising in Guangzhou, the capital of his native province. When the scheme failed, he began a 16-year exile abroad.

The year 1903 marked a significant turning point in Sun's career; from then on, his following came increasingly from the educated class, the most prestigious and influential group in China. In 1904 he was able to establish several revolutionary cells in Europe, and in 1905 he became head of a revolutionary coalition, the United League (Tongmenghui), in Tokyo. For the next three years the society propagandized effectively through its mouthpiece, "People's Journal" (*Minbao*).

The rise in Sun's fortune increased many of his difficulties. The United League was very loosely organized, and Sun had no control over the individual members. Worse still, all the revolts Sun and the others organized ended in failure. The members fell into despair, and outside financial contributions declined. In 1907 the Japanese government gave him a sum of money and asked him to leave the country. A year later French Indochina, where Sun had hatched several plots, banned him completely. Hong Kong and several other territories were similarly out of his reach. In the circumstances, Sun spent a year in 1909–10 touring Europe and the USA.

Returning to Asia in June 1910, he left for the West again in December after a meeting with other revolutionaries, in which they decided to make a massive effort to capture Guangzhou. This time Sun raised more money in Canada and the USA, but the uprising of April 27 in Guangzhou (known as the March 29 Revolution, because of its date in the Chinese calendar) fared no better than the earlier plots. The possibility of revolutionary success seemed more remote than ever.

But help was to come from the Qing. In 1911 the dynastic rulers decided to nationalize all the trunk railways, thus incurring the wrath of local vested interests. Armed rebellion broke out in the province of Sichuan, and the court exposed itself to further attacks by failing to suppress it. In October of the same year a local revolutionary group in Wuhan, one of many in China by this time, began another rebellion, which, in spite of its lack of coordination, unexpectedly managed to overthrow the provincial government. Its success inspired other provincial secessions.

Sun Yat-sen learned of the revolution from the newspapers while he was in Denver, Colorado. He returned to Shanghai in December and was elected provisional president by delegates meeting in Nanjing (Nanking). Knowing that his regime was weak, Sun made a deal with Yuan Shikai, an Imperial minister who had been entrusted with full power by the court.

Although the revolution of 1911 ushered in a republic, China had virtually no preparation for democracy. A three-way settlement ended the revolution: the Qing dynasty abdicated; Sun Yat-sen relinquished the provisional presidency in favour of Yuan Shikai, who was regarded as the indispensable man to restore unity; and Yuan promised to establish a republican government.

Yuan was from a landed military family of Xiangcheng in Henan province. In his youth he showed a propensity for pleasure-seeking and excelled in physical activity rather than scholarship, although in his maturity he was regarded as a man of remarkable astuteness. In 1912 he appeared to conservatives and revolutionaries alike as the only man who could lead the country to peace and unity. The treasury then was empty; the provinces were in the hands of local warlords; a permanent constitution was still in the making; and the newly elected National Assembly was, to Yuan, too quarrelsome and too cumbersome for the good of the country.

The first years of the republic were marked by a continuing contest between Yuan and the former revolutionaries over where ultimate power should lie. The contest began with the election of parliament (the National Assembly) in February 1913. The Nationalist Party (Kuomintang [KMT], or Guomindang), made up largely of former revolutionaries, won a commanding majority of seats. Parliament was to produce a permanent constitution. Song Jiaoren, the main organizer of the KMT's electoral victory, advocated executive authority in a cabinet responsible to parliament rather than to the president. In March 1913, Song was assassinated; the confession of the assassin and later circumstantial evidence strongly implicated the premier and possibly Yuan himself.

Parliament tried to block Yuan's effort to get a "reorganization loan" (face value US$125 million) from a consortium of foreign banks, but in April Yuan concluded the negotiations and received the loan. He then dismissed three military governors. That summer, revolutionary leaders organized a revolt against Yuan, later known as the Second Revolution, but his military followers quickly suppressed it. Sun Yat-sen, one of the principal revolutionaries, fled to Japan.

Yuan then coerced parliament into electing him formally to the presidency, and he was installed on October 10, the second anniversary of the outbreak of the revolution. By then his government had been recognized by most foreign powers. When parliament promulgated a constitution placing executive authority in a cabinet responsible to the legislature, Yuan revoked the credentials of the KMT members, charging them with involvement in the recent revolt. He dissolved parliament on January 10, 1914, and appointed another body to prepare a constitution according to his own specifications. The presidency had become a dictatorship.

Following the outbreak of the first world war in 1914, Japan joined the side of the Allies and seized the German leasehold around Jiaozhou Bay together with German-owned railways in Shandong. China was not permitted to interfere. Then, on January 18, 1915, the Japanese government secretly presented to Yuan the Twenty-one Demands, which sought in effect to make China a Japanese dependency. Yuan directed the negotiations by which China tried to limit its concessions, which centred on greater access to Chinese ports and railroads and even a voice in Chinese political and police affairs.

At the same time, Yuan searched for foreign support. The European powers, locked in war, were in no position to restrain Japan, and the USA was unwilling to intervene. The Chinese public, however, was aroused. Most of Yuan's political opponents supported his resistance to Japan's demands. Nevertheless, on May 7 Japan gave Yuan a 48-hour ultimatum, forcing him to accept the terms or face defeat.

Japan gained extensive special privileges and concessions in Manchuria (Northeast China) and confirmed its gains in Shandong from Germany. China promised not to alienate to any other power any harbour, bay, or island on the coast of China nor to permit any nation to construct a dockyard, coaling station, or naval base on the coast of Fujian, the province nearest to Japan's colony of Taiwan.

In the wake of the humiliation of these forced concessions, Yuan launched a movement to revive the monarchy, with some modernized features, and to place himself on the throne. The Japanese government began to "advise" against this move in October and induced its allies to join in opposing Yuan's plan. Additional opposition came from the leaders of the Nationalist and Progressive parties, as well as his own military associates. When he called on them for help, all withheld support. On March 22—with the tide of battle running against his forces in the south-west, Japanese hostility increasingly open, public opposition in full cry, and his closest subordinates advising peace—Yuan announced the abolition of the new empire. His opponents, however, demanded that he give up the presidency as well. The revolt continued to spread, with more military leaders or warlords declaring the independence of their provinces. The issue became that of succession should Yuan retire. The president, however, became gravely ill and died on June 6.

Yuan's four years in power had serious consequences for China. The country's foreign debt was much enlarged, and a precedent had been established of borrowing for political purposes. Yuan's defiance of constitutional procedures and his dissolution of parliament also set precedents that were later repeated. Many were disillusioned with the republican experiment; China was a republic in name, but arbitrary rule based on military power was the political reality. The country was becoming fractured into competing military satrapies—the beginning of warlordism.

Events taking place far away reverberated in China as well. In February 1917 the US government severed diplomatic relations with Germany and invited the neutral powers, including China, to do the same. This brought on a crisis in the Chinese government, and parliamentary factions and public opinion were bitterly divided. Sun Yat-sen, now in Shanghai, argued that entering the war could not benefit China and would create additional perils from Japan. Under heavy pressure, parliament voted to sever diplomatic relations with Germany. Yet there remained obstacles to China's entry into war until August 14, 1917.

Meanwhile, in July, Sun Yat-sen, supported by part of the Chinese navy and followed by some 100 members of parliament, attempted to organize a rival government in Guangzhou, in opposition to Beijing. The initial costs of this undertaking, termed the Movement to Protect the Constitution, were probably supplied by the German consulate in Shanghai. On September 1 the rump parliament in Guangzhou established a military government and elected Sun commander-in-chief. Real power, however, lay with military warlords, who only nominally supported Sun. The southern government declared war on Germany on September 26 and unsuccessfully sought recognition from the Allies as the legitimate government.

Although its wartime participation was limited, China made some gains from its entry into the war, taking over the German and Austrian concessions. It was also assured a seat at the peace conference. Japan, however, extended its gains in China. The Beijing government granted concessions to Japan for building railways in Shandong, Manchuria, and Mongolia. These were in exchange for loans amounting to nearly US$90 million, which went mainly to strengthen the Anhui military clique with arms and cash. Japan also made secret agreements with its allies to support its claims to the former German rights in Shandong and also induced the Beijing government to consent to these. In November 1917 the USA recognized that because of "territorial propinquity . . . Japan has special interests in China." This treaty seemed to underwrite Japan's wartime gains.

Important economic and social changes occurred during the first years of the republic. With the outbreak of the war, foreign economic competition with native industry abated, and native-owned light industries developed markedly.

A new intelligentsia had also emerged. The educational reforms and the ending of the governmental examination system during the final Qing years enabled thousands of young people to study sciences, engineering, medicine, law, economics, education, and military skills in Japan. Others went to Europe and the USA. Upon their return they took important positions and were a modernizing force in society.

This intellectual revolution is sometimes referred to as the New Culture Movement. It was led by many of the new intellectuals, who held up for critical scrutiny nearly all aspects of Chinese culture and traditional ethics. Guided by concepts of individual liberty and equality, a scientific spirit of inquiry, and a pragmatic approach to the nation's problems, they sought a much more profound reform of China's institutions.

In September 1915 Chen Duxiu, who had studied in Japan and France, founded the magazine *Xinqingnian* "New Youth" to oppose Yuan's imperial ambitions and to regenerate the country's youth. This quickly became the most popular reform journal, and in 1917 it began to express the iconoclasm of new faculty members at Beijing University (Beida), which Chen had joined as dean of the College of Letters.

Beijing University, China's most prestigious institution of higher education, was being transformed by its new chancellor, Cai Yuanpei, who had spent many years in advanced study in Germany. Cai made the university a centre of scholarly research and inspired teaching. The students were quickly swept into the New Culture Movement.

A proposal by Hu Shih, a former student of the American philosopher John Dewey, that literature be written in the vernacular language (*baihua*) rather than the classical style won quick acceptance. By 1918 most of the contributors to "New Youth" were writing in *baihua*, and other journals and newspapers soon followed suit. Students at Beijing University began their own reform journal, *Xinchao* ("New Tide"). A new experimental literature inspired by Western forms became highly popular, and scores of new literary journals were founded.

This new literary consciousness developed into organized political protest. On May 4, 1919, patriotic students in Beijing protested the decision at the Paris Peace Conference that Japan should retain defeated Germany's rights and possessions in Shandong. Many students were arrested in the rioting. Waves of protest spread throughout the major cities of China. Merchants closed their shops, banks suspended business, and workers went on strike to pressure the government. Finally, the government was forced to release the arrested students, to dismiss some officials charged with being tools of Japan, and to refuse to sign the Treaty of Versailles. This outburst helped spread the iconoclastic and reformist ideas of the intellectual

movement, which became known as the May Fourth Movement. By the early 1920s, China was launched on a new
revolutionary path.

This new revolution was led by the Nationalist Party (KMT)
and the Chinese Communist Party (CCP). The Nationalist
Party had its origins in the earlier United League (Tongmenghui) lead by Sun Yat-sen. Following the establishment of the
Republic in 1912 the party receded until 1919, when Sun and a
small group of veterans were prompted by the patriotic
upsurge to rejuvenate and revive the KMT. The party's publications took on a new life as the editors entered the current
debates on what was needed to "save China". The formation
of an effective party took several years, however. In the spring
of 1922 Sun attempted to launch a northern campaign as an
ally of the Manchurian warlord Zhang Zuolin against Beijing.

The CCP grew directly from the May Fourth Movement. Its
leaders and early members were professors and students who
came to believe that China needed a social revolution and who
began to see Soviet Russia as a model. Chinese students in
Japan and France had earlier studied socialist doctrines and
the ideas of Karl Marx, but the Russian Revolution of 1917
stimulated a fresh interest in keeping with the enthusiasm of
the period for radical ideologies.

Li Dazhao, the librarian of Beijing University, and Chen
Duxiu, Dean of the Faculty of Letters at Beijing University,
were the CCP's cofounders. Inspired by the success of the
Russian Revolution in 1917, Li began to study and lecture on
Marxism, influencing many students who later became im-
portant Communist leaders, including Mao Zedong (then an
impoverished student whom Li had employed as a library
clerk). Since 1915 Chen had been the editor of *Qingnian zazhi*
("Youth Magazine") in Shanghai, later renamed *Xinqingnian*.
In its pages he proposed that the youth of China undertake a

vast intellectual, literary, and cultural revolution to rejuvenate the nation. Many of the young writers who contributed to the monthly were later to become important intellectual and political leaders.

In March 1920 word reached China of Soviet Russia's Karakhan Manifesto, which promised to give up all special rights gained by tsarist Russia at China's expense and to return the Russian-owned Chinese Eastern Railway in Manchuria without compensation. The contrast between this promise and the Versailles award to Japan that had touched off the 1919 protest demonstrations could hardly have been more striking. Although the Soviet government later denied such a promise and attempted to regain control of the railway, the impression of this first statement and the generosity still offered in a more diplomatic second Karakhan Manifesto of September 1920 left a favourable image of Soviet foreign policy among Chinese patriots.

In the same year, on behalf of the international Communist organization, the Comintern, Russia sent Grigory N. Voytinsky to offer assistance to the CCP. Voytinsky met Li Dazhao in Beijing and Chen Duxiu in Shanghai, and they organized the Socialist Youth League, laid plans for the Communist Party, and started recruiting young intellectuals. By the spring of 1921 there were about 50 members in various Chinese cities and in Japan, many of them former students who had been active in the 1919 demonstrations. Mao Zedong, a protégé of Li Dazhao, had started one such group in Changsha.

The CCP held its First Congress in Shanghai in July 1921, with 12 or 13 attendants and with a Dutch Communist, Hendricus Sneevliet (who used his Comintern name, Maring, in China) and a Russian serving as advisers. Maring had become head of a new bureau of the Comintern in China, and he had arrived in Shanghai in June 1921. At the First Congress, Chen Duxiu was chosen to head the party.

The next two years were spent recruiting, publicizing Marxism and the need for a national revolution directed against foreign imperialism and Chinese militarism, and organizing unions among railway and factory workers. By 1923 the party had some 300 members, with perhaps 3,000 to 4,000 in the ancillary Socialist Youth League.

However, the CCP was in serious difficulty. The railway unions had been brutally suppressed, and there were few places in China where it was safe to be a known Communist. In June 1923 the Third Congress of the CCP met in Guangzhou, where Sun Yat-sen provided a sanctuary. After long debate, this congress accepted the Comintern strategy pressed by Maring—that Communists should join the KMT and make it the centre of the national revolutionary movement.

Sun rejected a multiparty alliance but had agreed to admit Communists to his party, and several, including Chen Duxiu and Li Dazhao, had already joined the KMT. Even though Communists would enter the other party as individuals, the CCP was determined to maintain its separate identity and autonomy and to attempt to control the labour union movement.

By mid-1923 the Soviets had decided to financially assist Sun in Guangzhou and to send an old Bolshevik, Mikhail M. Borodin, as their principal adviser to Sun Yat-sen. The Soviet leaders also decided to replace Maring with Voytinsky as principal adviser to the CCP, which had its headquarters in Shanghai. Thereafter three men—Karakhan in Beijing, Borodin in Guangzhou, and Voytinsky in Shanghai—were the field directors of the Soviet effort to bring China into the anti-imperialist camp of "world revolution". The offensive was aimed primarily at the positions in China of Great Britain, Japan, and the USA.

These countries too were moving toward a new, postwar relationship with China. At the Washington Conference (November 1921 to February 1922), China put forth a 10-point proposal, which, after negotiations, became four points: to respect the sovereignty, independence, and territorial and administrative integrity of China; to give China opportunity to develop a stable government; to maintain the principle of equal opportunity in China for the commerce and industry of all countries; and to refrain from taking advantage of conditions in China to seek exclusive privileges detrimental to the rights of friendly countries. The treaty was signed as the Nine-Power Pact on February 6. In the meantime, separate negotiations between China and Japan produced a treaty in which Japan agreed to return the former German holdings in Shandong to China—although under conditions that left Japan with valuable privileges in the province.

For a few years thereafter, Great Britain, Japan, the USA, and France attempted to adjust their conflicting interests in China, cooperated in assisting the Beijing government, and generally refrained from aiding particular Chinese factions in the recurrent power struggles. But China was in turmoil, with regional warlord militarism in full swing.

This time of upheaval saw the re-emergence of the nationalist KMT which held its First National Congress in Guangzhou on January 20–30, 1924. Here Borodin, who had reached Guangzhou in October 1923, began to advise Sun about reorganizing the party. The programme announced goals of broad social reform and a fundamental readjustment of China's international status. The proposed constitution described a centralized organization, modelled on the Soviet Communist Party, with power concentrated in a small, elected group and with a descending hierarchy of geographical offices controlled by executive committees directed from above. Members were pledged to strict discipline and were to be organized in tight cells.

Sun was again designated as leader of the party and had veto rights over its decisions. The congress elected a central executive committee and a central supervisory committee to manage party affairs and confirmed Sun's decision to admit Communists, though this was opposed by numerous party veterans, who feared the KMT itself might be taken over. A few Communists, including Li Dazhao, were elected to the executive committee.

From February to November 1924, Sun and his colleagues had some success in making the KMT's influence felt nationally; they also consolidated the Guangzhou base, although it still depended on mercenary armies. The military academy was set up at Whampoa (Huangpu), on an island south of Guangzhou, and the first group of some 500 cadets was trained. In September Sun began another northern campaign in alliance with Zhang Zuolin against the warlords Cao Kun and Wu Peifu, who now controlled Beijing. The campaign was interrupted, however, when Wu's subordinate, Feng Yuxiang, betrayed his chief and seized Beijing on October 23, while Wu was at the front facing Zhang Zuolin. Feng and his fellow plotters invited Sun to Beijing to participate in the settlement of national affairs, while Feng and Zhang invited Duan Qirui to come out of retirement and take charge of the government. Sun accepted the invitation and departed for the north on November 13. Before he arrived in Beijing, however, he fell gravely ill with incurable liver cancer and died in Beijing on March 12, 1925.

By January 1926 the KMT could claim some 200,000 members. The CCP's membership grew from fewer than

1,000 in May 1925 to about 10,000 by the end of that year.

The two parties now competed for direction of nationalist policy, control of mass organizations, and recruitment of new members. Under Comintern coaching, the CCP strategy was to try to split the KMT, drive out its conservative members, and turn it to an ever more radical course. In August 1925, KMT conservatives in Guangzhou tried to stop the leftward trend. One of the strongest advocates of the Nationalists' Soviet orientation, Liao Zhongkai, was assassinated. In retaliation Borodin, Chiang Kai-shek, and Wang Ching-wei deported various conservatives. A group of KMT veterans in the north then ordered the expulsion of Borodin and the Communists and the suspension of Wang Ching-wei; they set up a rival KMT headquarters in Shanghai.

This event also brought to prominence one of the leading figures of the next stages of the Chinese Republic—Chiang Kai-shek. Chiang was born into a moderately prosperous merchant and farmer family in the coastal province of Zhejiang. From 1909 to 1911 he served in the Japanese army, whose Spartan ideals he admired and adopted. More influential were the youthful compatriots he met in Tokyo; plotting to rid China of the Qing dynasty, they converted Chiang to republicanism and made him a revolutionary.

In 1911, upon hearing of revolutionary outbreaks in China, Chiang returned home and helped in the sporadic fighting that led to the overthrow of the Manchus. He then participated in the struggles of China's republican and other revolutionaries against China's new president and would-be emperor, Yuan. After these excursions into public life, Chiang momentarily lapsed into obscurity. Yet when Sun Yat-sen began to reorganize the Nationalist Party along Soviet lines, Chiang visited the Soviet Union to study Soviet institutions, especially the Red

Army. Back in China, he became commandant of a military academy, established on the Soviet model, at Whampoa near Guangzhou. After Sun's death in 1925, Chiang, with the Whampoa army behind him, became the strongest of Sun's heirs, and met this threat with consummate shrewdness.

Chiang, now commander of the National Revolutionary Army, took steps in March to curb the Communists and to send away several Soviet officers whom he believed were scheming against him. Communists were no longer permitted to hold high offices in the central headquarters. Chiang also demanded Comintern support of a northern military campaign.

Within two months the National Revolutionary Army gained control of Hunan and Hubei, and by the end of the year it had taken Jiangxi and Fujian. By early spring of 1927, revolutionary forces were poised to attack Nanjing and Shanghai, and the political situation was unstable. Hunan and Hubei were swept by a peasant revolt marked by violence against landlords and other rural power holders. Business in the industrial and commercial centre of the middle Yangtze—the Wuhan cities—was nearly paralysed by a wave of strikes. Communists and KMT leftists led this social revolution. In January the British concessions in Hankou and Jiujiang were seized by Chinese crowds. Foreigners and many upper-class Chinese fled from the provinces under Nationalist control. The northern armies began to form an alliance against the southerners.

While conservative Nationalist leaders in Shanghai mobilized against the headquarters in Wuhan, there was a deep rift within the revolutionary camp itself. The climax of the conflict came after Nationalist armies had taken Shanghai and Nanjing in March. Nanjing was captured on March 23, and the following morning some Nationalist soldiers looted foreign properties, attacked the British, US, and Japanese consulates, and killed several foreigners. That afternoon, British and US warships on the Yangtze fired into the concession area, allowing some of the foreign nationals to flee, and others subsequently were evacuated peacefully.

In Shanghai a general strike led by Communists aroused fears that the Chinese might seize the International Settlement and the French concession, now guarded by a large international expeditionary force. Conservative Nationalist leaders, some army commanders, and Chinese business leaders in Shanghai encouraged Chiang to expel the Communists and suppress the Shanghai General Labour Union. On April 12–13, gangsters and troops bloodily suppressed the guards of the General Labour Union, arrested many Communists, and executed large numbers. Similar suppressions were carried out in Guangzhou, Nanjing, Nanchang, Fuzhou, and other cities under military forces that accepted Chiang's instructions. The KMT conservatives then established a rival Nationalist government in Nanjing.

Wang Ching-wei had returned to China via the Soviet Union. Arriving in Shanghai, he refused to participate in the expulsions and went secretly to Wuhan, where he again headed the government. In July, however, the leftist Nationalist leaders in Wuhan, having learned of a directive by Soviet leader Joseph Stalin to Borodin to arrange for radicals to take control of the government, decided to expel the Communists and compel the Soviet advisers to leave. The leftist government thereby lost important bases of support; furthermore, it was ringed by hostile forces and cut off from access to the sea, and it soon disintegrated.

The CCP went into revolt. Using its influence in the Cantonese army, it staged an uprising at Nanchang on August 1 and in October attempted the "Autumn Harvest" uprising in several central provinces. Both efforts failed. In December, Communist leaders in Guangzhou started a revolt there, capturing the city with much bloodshed, arson, and looting; this uprising was quickly suppressed with much slaughter. Between April and December 1927 the CCP lost most of its membership by death and defection. A few score leaders and some scattered military bands then began the process of creating military bases in the mountains and plains of central China, remote from centres of Nationalist power.

The now more conservative KMT resumed its Northern Expedition in the spring of 1928 with a reorganized National Revolutionary Army. In the drive on Beijing it was joined by the National People's Army. In early June they captured Beijing. By the end of the Northern Expedition, the major warlords had been defeated by the Nationalists, whose armies now possessed the cities and railways of eastern China. On October 10 the Nationalists formally established a reorganized National Government of the Republic of China, with its capital at Nanjing; Beijing was renamed Beiping ("Northern Peace").

The most serious immediate problem facing the new government was the continuing military separatism. The government had no authority over vast areas of western China, and even regions in eastern China were under the rule of independent regimes that had lately been part of the Nationalist coalition. Recognition by the foreign powers brought the Nationalist government the revenues collected by the efficient Maritime Customs Service; when the powers granted China the right to fix its own tariff schedules, that revenue increased.

Although the aim of constitutional, representative government was asserted, the Nationalist government at Nanjing was in practice dominated by Chiang Kai-shek. The army and the civil bureaucracy were marked by factional divisions, which

Chiang carefully balanced against one another so that ultimate decision-making was kept in his own hands. The KMT was supposed to infuse all government structures and to provide leadership, but the army came to be the most powerful component of government. Chiang's regime was marked by an increased militarism, which external circumstances reinforced.

Nevertheless, the Nationalists did much to create a modern government and a coherent monetary and banking system and to improve taxation. They expanded the public educational system, developed a network of transportation and communication facilities, and encouraged industry and commerce. Again it was urban China that mainly benefited; little was done to modernize agriculture or to eradicate disease, illiteracy, and underemployment in the villages, hamlets, and small towns. With conscription and heavy taxation to support civil war and a collapsing export market for commercial crops, rural economic conditions grew worse during the Nationalist decade.

During its first few years in power the Nationalist government had some success in reasserting China's sovereignty. The country was in a nationalistic mood, determined to roll back foreign economic and political penetration. Several concession areas were returned to Chinese control, and the foreign powers assented to China's resumption of tariff autonomy. Yet these were merely token gains. Manchuria was a huge and rich area of China in which Japan had extensive economic privileges, possessing part of the Liaodong Peninsula as a leasehold and controlling much of southern Manchuria's economy through the South Manchurian Railway. The Chinese began to develop Huludao, in Liaodong, as a port to rival Dairen (Dalian) and to plan railways to compete with Japanese lines.

Japan held on to Manchuria, which its military leaders regarded as vital. Many Japanese had acquired a sense of mission that Japan should lead Asia against the West. The Great Depression had hurt Japanese business, and there was deep social unrest. In September 1931 a group of Chinese officers set in motion a plot (beginning with the Mukden Incident) to compel the Japanese government to extend its power in Manchuria. The Japanese government was drawn step by step into the conquest of Manchuria and the creation of a regime known as Manchukuo. China was unable to prevent Japan from seizing this vital area. The National Government's policy was to trade space for time in which to build military power and unify the country. Its slogan, "Unity before resistance", was directed principally against the Chinese Communists.

The Japanese occupation of Manchuria and an ancillary localized war around Shanghai in 1932 distracted the Nationalists and gave the Communists a brief opportunity to expand and consolidate. In the meantime, the Communists had created 15 rural bases in central China, and they established a government, the Jiangxi Soviet, on November 7, 1931. Within the Soviet regions, the Communist leadership expropriated and redistributed land and enlisted the support of the poorer classes in other ways.

Between 1930 and 1934 Chiang Kai-shek launched a series of five military encirclement campaigns against the Chinese Communists in an attempt to annihilate their base area (the Jiangxi Soviet) on the Jiangxi–Fujian border in south-eastern China. The Communists successfully fought off the first four campaigns using tactics of mobile infiltration and guerrilla warfare developed by Mao. In the fifth campaign Chiang mustered about 700,000 troops and established a series of cement blockhouses around the Communist positions. The forces suffered heavy losses and were nearly crushed.

On October 15, 1934, the remaining 85,000 troops, 15,000 administrative personnel, and 35 women broke through the Nationalist lines at their weakest points and fled westward. Mao, at the time of the Communists' departure, was not in control of events; Zhu De was the commander of the army, and Zhou Enlai was the political commissar of the party. The first three months of the march were disastrous for the Communists: subjected to constant bombardment from Chiang's air force and repeated attacks from his ground troops, they lost more than half of their army. Morale was low when they arrived in Zunyi, in the south-western province of Guizhou.

The march then headed toward Northwest China, near the safety of the Soviet border and close to the territory occupied by the Japanese in north-eastern China. In June 1935 a force under Zhang Guotao, a longtime Communist leader, joined the main army, and at Maoerkai in western Sichuan a power struggle ensued between Mao Zedong and Zhang. Zhang's group, accompanied by Zhu De, headed toward the extreme south-western part of China. The main body under Mao proceeded toward northern Shaanxi, where the Communist leaders Gao Gang and Liu Zhidan had built up another Soviet area.

Mao arrived at this destination in October 1935 along with only about 8,000 survivors. Along the route some Communists had left the march to mobilize the peasantry; but most of the missing had been eliminated by fighting, disease, and starvation. Among the missing were Mao's two small children and his younger brother, Mao Zetan. Mao's troops joined the local Red Army contingent of 7,000 men, and other units (including that of Zhu De) swelled their total strength by late 1936 to about 30,000 troops. In December 1936 the Communists moved to the nearby district of Yan'an in Shaanxi, where they remained throughout the war with the Japanese.

During the Long March, Mao Zedong rose to pre-eminence in the CCP leadership. In the early 1930s he had engaged in bitter power struggles with other party leaders and actually had found himself in a fairly weak position at the start of the Long March campaigns, but in January 1935 a rump session of the CCP Political Bureau (Politburo) confirmed Mao in the newly created post of chairman.

It was also during the Long March that the CCP began to develop a new political strategy—a united front against Japan. It was first conceived as an alliance of patriotic forces against Japan and the Nationalist government, but, as Japan's pressure on China and the pressure of the Nationalist armies against the weakened Red armies increased, the Communist leaders began to call for a united front of all Chinese against Japan alone. Virtually all classes and various local regimes supported this, and the Communists moderated their revolutionary programme and terminated class warfare in their zone of control in order to pursue the united front against Japan.

Chiang was determined, however, to press on with his campaign against the Communists. He ordered the Manchurian army, and the Northwestern army, to attack the Communist forces in northern Shaanxi. Many officers in those armies sympathized with the Communist slogan "Chinese don't fight Chinese"; they preferred to fight Japan, a sentiment particularly strong in the homeless Manchurian army. The warlord Zhang Xueliang was conducting secret negotiations with the Communists and had suspended the civil war. In December 1936 Chiang Kai-shek flew to Xi'an to order the renewed pursuit of the anti-Communist campaign. There General Zhang detained Chiang on the morning of December 12 (this became known as the Xi'an Incident).

Fearing that China would be plunged into renewed disorder if Chiang were killed, the nation clamoured for his release. The

Soviet Union quickly denounced the captors and insisted that Chiang be freed (the Soviet Union needed a united China opposing Japan, its potential enemy on the east). The CCP leaders also decided that Chiang's release would serve China's interests as well as their own, if he would accept their policy against Japan. Chiang was eventually released on December 25 with the understanding that he would call off the civil war and unite the country against the invader.

The two Chinese parties began protracted and secret negotiations for cooperation, each making concessions. But it was not until September 1937, after the Sino-Japanese War had begun, that the Nationalist government formally agreed to a policy of cooperation with the CCP. For its part, the CCP publicly affirmed its adherence to the realization of Sun Yat-sen's Three Principles of the People, its abandonment of armed opposition to the KMT and of the forcible confiscation of landlords' property, the substitution of democracy for its soviet government, and the reorganization of the Red Army as a component of the national army under the central government.

On July 7, 1937, the Marco Polo Bridge Incident, a minor clash between Japanese and Chinese troops near Beiping finally led the two countries into war. The Japanese quickly took Beiping and captured Tianjin. On August 13 savage fighting broke out in Shanghai. By now the prestige of both nations was committed, and they were locked in a war.

As never before in modern times, the Chinese united themselves against a foreign enemy. China's standing armies in 1937 numbered some 1.7 million men, with a half million in reserve. Japan's naval and air superiority was unquestioned, but Japan could not commit its full strength to campaigns in China.

During the first year of the undeclared war, Japan won victory after victory against sometimes stubborn Chinese

resistance. By late December, Shanghai and Nanjing had fall-
en, the latter city being the site of the infamous Nanjing
Massacre (December 1937–January 1938) perpetrated by
Japanese troops, during which from 100,000 to 300,000
Chinese were killed. However, China had demonstrated to
the world its determination to resist the invader. This gave the
government time to search for foreign support. China found its
major initial help from the Soviet Union. On August 21, 1937,
the Soviet Union and China signed a non-aggression pact, and
the former quickly began sending munitions, military advisers,
and hundreds of aircraft with Soviet pilots. Yet Japanese forces
continued to win important victories. By mid-1938 Japanese
armies controlled the railway lines and major cities of northern
China. They took Guangzhou on October 12, stopping the
railway supply line to Wuhan, the temporary Chinese capital,
and captured Hankou, Hanyang, and Wuchang on October
25–26. The Chinese government and military command
moved to Chongqing in Sichuan, farther up the Yangtze
and behind a protective mountain screen.

At the end of this first phase of the war, the Nationalist
government had lost the best of its modern armies, its air force
and arsenals, most of China's modern industries and railways,
its major tax resources, and all the ports through which
military equipment and civilian supplies might be imported.
However, it still held a vast though largely undeveloped
territory and had unlimited manpower reserves. So long as
China continued to resist, Japan's control over the conquered
eastern part of the country would be difficult.

During the second stage of the war (1939–43), the battle
lines changed only slightly, although there were many engagements of limited scale. Japan tried to bomb Free China into
submission; Chongqing suffered repeated air raids in which
thousands of civilians were killed. But the Chinese would not

submit. Hundreds of thousands migrated to western China to continue the struggle. Students and faculties of most eastern colleges took the overland trek to makeshift quarters in distant inland towns. Factories and skilled workers were re-established in the west. The government rebuilt its shattered armies and tried to purchase supplies from abroad.

In 1938–40 the Soviet Union extended credits for military aid of US$250 million, while the USA, Great Britain, and France granted some US$263.5 million for civilian purchases and currency stabilization. Free China's lines of supply were long and precarious; when war broke out in Europe, shipping space became scarce. After Germany's conquest of France in the spring of 1940, Britain bowed to Japanese demands and temporarily closed Rangoon, Burma (Yangôn, Myanmar), to military supplies for China (July–September). In September 1940 Japan seized control of northern Indochina and closed the supply line to Kunming. The Soviet Union had provided China its most substantial military aid, but, when Germany attacked the Soviet Union in June 1941, this aid virtually ceased. By then, however, the USA had sold China 100 fighter planes—the beginnings of a US effort to provide air protection.

In addition to bombing, the civilian population in Free China endured other hardships. Manufactured goods were scarce, and hoarding drove up prices. The government did not have the means to carry out rationing and price control, though it did supply government employees with rice. The government's sources of revenue were limited, yet it supported a large bureaucracy and an army of more than 3 million conscripts. The government resorted to printing currency inadequately backed by reserves. Inflation grew until it was nearly uncontrollable. Between 1939 and 1943 the morale of the bureaucracy and military officers declined. Old abuses of the Chinese political system reasserted themselves—factional

politics and corruption, in particular. The protracted war
progressively weakened the Nationalist regime.

The war had the opposite effect upon the CCP. The party's
leaders had survived 10 years of civil war and had developed a
unity, camaraderie, and powerful sense of mission. They had
learned to mobilize the rural population and to wage guerrilla
warfare. In 1937 the CCP had about 40,000 members and the
poorly equipped Red Army numbered perhaps 100,000. By
agreement with the Nationalist government, the Red Army
was renamed the Eighth Route Army; Zhu De and Peng
Dehuai served as commander and vice-commander, and Lin
Biao, He Long, and Liu Bocheng were in charge of its three
divisions. The Communist base in the north-west covered
parts of three provinces with an undeveloped economy and
a population of about 1.5 million. Operating within the
general framework of the United Front against Japan, the
leaders of the Eighth Route Army adopted a strategy that used
their experience in guerrilla warfare. They sent small columns
into areas of northern China that the Japanese army had
overrun but lacked the manpower to control; there they
incorporated remnant troops and organized the population
to supply food, recruits, and sanctuaries for guerrilla units
attacking small Japanese garrisons.

Early in the period of united resistance, the Nationalist
government permitted the New Fourth Army to be created
from remnants of Communist troops left in Jiangxi and Fujian
at the time of the Long March. Commanded by General Ye
Ting—with Xiang Ying, a Communist, as chief of staff—this
force of 12,000 officers and soldiers operated behind Japanese
lines near Shanghai with great success. Its strategy included
guerrilla tactics, organizing resistance bases, and recruitment.
This army grew to more than 100,000 in 1940; by then it
operated in a wide area on both sides of the lower Yangtze.

Thus the CCP revitalized itself, recruiting rural activists and patriotic youths from the cities and systematically strengthened its ranks by continuous indoctrination and by expelling dissident and ineffective party members.

Despite Japanese aggression, there were numerous clashes between Communists and Nationalists as their military forces competed for control of enemy territory and as the Communists tried to expand their political influence in Nationalist territory through propaganda and secret organizing. Though both sides continued the war against Japan, each was fighting for its own ultimate advantage. Bitter anticommunist sentiment in government circles found its most violent expression in the New Fourth Army Incident of January 1941.

The government had ordered the New Fourth Army to move north of the Huang He (Yellow River) and understood that its commanders had agreed to do so as part of a demarcation of operational areas. However, most of the army had moved into northern Jiangsu (south of the Huang) and, together with units of the Eighteenth Army Group, was competing with government troops for control of bases there and in southern Shandong. Ye Ting and Xiang Ying stayed at the army's base south of the Yangtze. Apparently believing that Ye did not intend to move northward, government forces attacked the base on January 6, 1941. The outnumbered Communists were defeated, Ye Ting and some 2,000 others were captured, Xiang Ying was killed, and both sides suffered heavy casualties. Ignoring Chiang Kai-shek's order to dissolve the New Fourth Army, the Communist high command named Chen Yi as its new commander and Liu Shaoqi as political commissar.

The danger of renewed civil war caused widespread protest from China's civilian leaders. The People's Political Council, a multiparty advisory body formed in 1938 as an expression of united resistance, debated the issue and later tried to mediate.

In addition, neither the KMT nor the CCP was willing to push the conflict to open civil war. The government deployed many of its best divisions in positions to prevent the Communist forces from further penetration of Nationalist-held territories and to weaken the CCP through a strict economic blockade. Yet the real threat was still from Japan.

By July 1941 the USA knew that Japan hoped to end the undeclared war in China and that Japan was preparing for a southward advance toward British Malaya and the Dutch East Indies, planning to first occupy southern Indochina and Thailand, even at the risk of war with Britain and the USA. One US response was the decision to send large amounts of arms and equipment to China, along with a military mission to advise on their use. The underlying strategy was to revitalize China's war effort as a deterrent to Japanese land and naval operations southward. By December 1941 the USA had sent a military mission to China and had implicitly agreed to create a modern Chinese air force, maintain an efficient line of communications into China, and arm 30 divisions.

Japan's bombing of Pearl Harbor in Hawaii brought the USA into alliance with China, and Great Britain joined the Pacific war as its colonial possessions were attacked. This widening of the Sino-Japanese conflict lifted Chinese morale, but its other early effects were harmful. With the Japanese conquest of Hong Kong on December 25, China lost its air link to the outside world and one of its principal routes for smuggling supplies. By the end of May 1942, the Japanese held most of Burma, having defeated the British, Indian, Burmese, and Chinese defenders. China was almost completely blockaded. For the moment, there was little China's allies could do other than state a willingness to offer China loans.

The solution was found in an air route from Assam, India, to Kunming, in south-west China—the dangerous "Hump" route along the southern edge of the Himalayas. In March 1942 the China National Aviation Corporation (CNAC) began freight service over the Hump, and the USA began a transport programme the next month. But shortages and other difficulties had to be overcome, and not until December 1943 were cargo planes able to carry as much tonnage as was carried along the Burma Road by trucks two years earlier. This was much less than China's needs for gasoline and military equipment and supplies.

China's alliance with the USA and Great Britain was marked by deep conflict. Great Britain gave highest priority to the defeat of its main enemy, Germany. The US Navy in the Pacific had been seriously weakened by the Japanese air attack at Pearl Harbor and required many months to rebuild. During the winter of 1941–42, the grand strategy of the USA and Great Britain called for the defeat of Germany first and then an assault across the Pacific against Japan's island empire. China was relegated to a low position in US strategic planning. The USA aimed to keep China in the war and enable it to play a positive role in the final defeat of Japan on the continent.

Chiang Kai-shek, on the other hand, envisaged a joint strategy by the USA, the British Commonwealth, and China over the whole Pacific area, with China playing a major role. He demanded an equal voice in Allied war planning, which he never received, though US President Franklin D. Roosevelt was generally solicitous. From the fundamentally different outlooks of Chiang, British Prime Minister Winston Churchill, and Roosevelt and because of the divergent national interests of China, the British Commonwealth, and the USA, there followed many controversies that had powerful repercussions in China and led to frustrations and suspicions among the partners.

After Burma fell to the Japanese, controversy developed over whether the principal Chinese and US effort against Japan should be devoted to building up US air power based in China or to reform of the Chinese army and its training and equipment for a combat role. Chiang advocated primary reliance on US air power to defeat Japan. Several high-ranking US generals, on the other hand, emphasized creation of a compact and modernized Chinese ground force able to protect the airfields in China and to assist in opening an overland supply route across northern Burma. Already in India, the USA was training two Chinese divisions from remnants of the Burma campaign, plus artillery and engineering regiments (this became known as X-Force). Also in training were Chinese instructors to help retrain other divisions in China. Both air development and army modernizing were being pushed in early 1943, with a training centre created near Kunming to re-energize and re-equip select Chinese divisions (called Y-Force), and a network of airfields was being built in southern China. This dual approach caused repeated conflict over the allocation of scarce airlift space.

By the end of 1943 the China-based US Fourteenth Air Force had achieved tactical parity with the Japanese over central China, and was beginning to bomb Yangtze shipping, and had conducted a successful raid on Japanese airfields on Taiwan. A second training centre had been started at Guilin to improve 30 more Chinese divisions (Z-Force). However, the campaign to open a land route across northern Burma had run into serious difficulty.

At the first Cairo Conference in November, Chiang met Churchill and Roosevelt for the first time. The Cairo Declaration promised that, following the war, Manchuria, Taiwan, and the Pescadores Islands would be returned to China and that Korea would gain independence. The three allies pledged themselves to "persevere in the . . . prolonged operations necessary to procure the unconditional surrender of Japan". These words, however, concealed deep differences over global strategy. US planners realized that Japan might be approached successfully through the south and central Pacific and that the Soviet Union would enter the war against Japan after Germany's defeat; hence, the importance of China to US grand strategy declined.

Churchill was unwilling to use naval resources, needed for the forthcoming European invasion, in a seaborne invasion of Burma to help reopen China's supply line. Yet Chiang had demanded a naval invasion of Burma as a condition to committing the Y-Force to assist in opening his supply line. Shortly after Cairo, Churchill and Roosevelt agreed to set aside the seaborne invasion of Burma; when Chiang learned of this, he requested enormous amounts of money, supplies, and air support, asserting that otherwise Japan might succeed in eliminating China from the war. The USA did not accede, and Chinese–American relations began to cool.

By 1944 China was in crisis. Japan faced increasing pressure in the Pacific and threats to its supply bases and communications lines in China as well as to nearby shipping. Its response was two-fold—first, to attack from Burma toward Assam to cut the supply lines or capture the airfields at the western end of the Hump and, second, to capture the railway system in China from north to south and seize the eastern China airfields used by the USA.

The British and Indian army defeated the Japanese attack on Assam (March–July 1944) with help from transport planes withdrawn from the Hump. But the Japanese campaign in China, known as Ichigo, showed up the weakness, inefficiency, and poor command of the Chinese armies after nearly seven years of war. Chinese armies nominally numbering several hundred thousand troops were unable to put up effective resistance. Peasants in Henan attacked the collapsing Chinese armies—only recently their oppressors.

The second phase of the Ichigo campaign was a Japanese drive southward from Hankou and north-westward from Guangzhou to take Guilin and open the communication line to the India–China border. By November the Chinese had lost Guilin, Liuzhou, and Nanning, and the Japanese were approaching Guiyang on the route to Chongqing and Kunming. This was the high-water mark of Japan's war in China. Thereafter, it withdrew experienced divisions for the defence of its over-extended empire, and China finally began to benefit from the well-trained X-Force when two divisions were flown in from Burma in December to defend Kunming.

Meanwhile, the Chinese government was involved in a crisis of relations with the USA, which contended that the Chinese army must be reformed, particularly in its command structure, and that lend-lease supplies must be used more effectively. There were also many subsidiary problems. General Joseph Stilwell, the executor of disagreeable US policies in China, had developed an unconcealed disdain for Chiang, whom he nominally served as chief of staff. Stilwell was an effective troop commander, and Roosevelt requested that Chiang place Stilwell in command of all Chinese forces. In the context of Chinese politics, in which control of armies was the main source of power, President Chiang's compliance was inconceivable. He declined the request and asked for Stilwell's recall. Roosevelt agreed, but thereafter his relations with Chiang were no longer cordial. Stilwell was replaced by General Wedemeyer.

The military weakness in 1944 was symptomatic of a gradual deterioration that had taken place in most aspects of Nationalist Chinese public life. Inflation began to mount alarmingly as the government pumped in large amounts of paper currency to make up its fiscal deficits. Salaries of government employees, army officers, teachers, and all those on wages fell far behind rising prices. For most, this spelled poverty amid growing war-weariness.

Dissatisfaction with the government's policies spread among intellectuals. Inflation provided opportunities for some groups to profit through hoarding needed goods, smuggling high-value commodities, black market currency operations, and graft. Corruption spread in the bureaucracy and the armed forces. As the war dragged on, government measures to suppress dissidence grew oppressive. Secret police activity and efforts at thought control were aimed not only against Communists but also against all influential critics of the government or the KMT.

The Communist armies were growing rapidly in 1943 and 1944. According to US war correspondents visiting the Yan'an area in May 1944 and to a group of US observers that established itself there in July, the Communists professed allegiance to democracy and to continued cooperation with the Nationalist government in the war effort. There was convincing evidence that the areas under Communist control extended for hundreds of miles behind Japanese lines in northern and central China.

This situation was the result of many factors. Communist troop commanders and political officers in areas behind Japanese lines tried to mobilize the entire population against the enemy. Party members led village communities into greater participation in local government. They also organized and controlled peasants' associations, labour unions, youth leagues, and women's associations. They linked together the many local governments and the mass organizations and determined their policies. Because of the need for unity against

Japan, the Communist organizers tended to follow reformist economic policies.

The party experimented with various forms of economic cooperation to increase production; one of these was mutual-aid teams in which farmers temporarily pooled their tools and draught animals and worked the land collectively. In areas behind Japanese lines, some mutual-aid teams evolved into work-and-battle teams composed of younger peasants: when danger threatened, the teams went out to fight as guerrillas under direction of the local Communist army; when the crisis passed, they returned to the fields. The party recruited into its ranks the younger leaders who emerged from populist activities.

Thus, it penetrated and to some extent controlled the multitude of villages in areas behind Japanese lines. As the Japanese military grip weakened, the experienced Communist armies and political organizers spread their system of government ever more widely. By the time of the CCP's Seventh Congress in Yan'an (April–May 1945), the party claimed to have an army of more than 900,000 and a militia of more than 2,000,000. It also claimed to control areas with a total population of 90,000,000. These claims were disputable, but the great strength and wide geographical spread of Communist organization was a fact.

The Pacific war (which in China became known as the War of Resistance Against Japanese Aggression) ended on August 14 (August 15 in China), 1945, and the formal Japanese surrender came on September 2. China rejoiced. Yet the country faced enormously difficult problems of reunification and reconstruction and a future clouded by the dark prospect of civil war.

In a little more than four years after Japan's surrender, the CCP and the People's Liberation Army (PLA; the name by

which Communist forces were now known) conquered mainland China and, on October 1, 1949, the People's Republic of
China was established, with its capital at Beijing (the city's
former name restored). The factors that brought this about
were many and complex and subject to widely varying interpretation, but the basic fact was a Communist military triumph growing out of a profound and popularly based
revolution. The process may be perceived in three phases:
(1) from August 1945 to the end of 1946, the Nationalists and
Communists raced to take over Japanese-held territories, built
up their forces, and fought many limited engagements while
still conducting negotiations for a peaceful settlement; (2)
during 1947 and the first half of 1948, after initial Nationalist
success, the strategic balance turned in favour of the Communists; and (3) the Communists won a series of smashing
victories beginning in the latter part of 1948 that led to the
establishment of the People's Republic.

One reason for Communist success was the social revolution
in rural China. The CCP was now unrestrained by the multi-
class alliance of the United Front period. In mid-1946, as civil
war became more certain, the party leaders launched a land
revolution. They saw land redistribution as an integral part of
the larger struggle; by encouraging peasants to seize landlords'
fields and other property, the party apparently expected to
weaken the government's rural class base and strengthen its
own support among the poor. This demanded a decisive attack
on the traditional village social structure. The party leaders
believed that to crack the age-old peasant fear of the local elite
and overcome the traditional respect for property rights required unleashing the hatred of the oppressed. Teams of
activists moved through the villages, organizing the poor in
"speak bitterness" meetings to struggle against landlords and
Nationalist supporters, to punish and often to kill them, and to

distribute their land and property. The party tried to control the process in order not to alienate the broad middle ranks among the peasants, but land revolution had a dynamism of its own, and rural China went through a period of terror. Yet apparently the party gained from the revolutionary dynamism; morale was at fever pitch, and, for those who had benefited from land distribution, there was no turning back.

The year 1948 was the turning point in the civil war. In central China, Communist armies of 500,000 troops proved their ability to fight major battles on the plains and to capture, though not always hold, important towns such as Luoyang and Kaifeng. In northern China they encircled Taiyuan, the capital of Shanxi; took most of Chahar and Jehol, provinces on Manchuria's western flank; and recaptured Yan'an, which had been lost in March 1947. The decisive battles were fought in Shandong and Manchuria, where the forces of Chen Yi and Liu Bocheng and those under Lin Biao crushed the government's best armies. For the government it was a year of military and economic disasters.

In Shandong, despite the departure of Chen Yi's forces, Communist guerrillas gradually reduced the government's hold on the railway from Qingdao to Jinan; they penned up about 60,000 government troops in the latter city, an important railway junction. Instead of withdrawing that garrison southward to Suzhou, the government left it, for political reasons, to stand and fight. Then Chen Yi's forces returned to Shandong and overwhelmed the dispirited Jinan garrison on September 24. This opened the way for a Communist attack on Suzhou, the historic northern shield for Nanjing and a vital railway centre.

Beginning in December 1947, a Communist offensive severed all railway connections into Mukden and isolated the Nationalist garrisons in Manchuria. The government armies went on the defensive in besieged cities, partly out of fear that demoralized divisions would defect in the field. Instead of withdrawing from Manchuria before it was too late, the government tried unsuccessfully to reinforce its armies and to supply the garrisons by air. With the fall of Jinan, Lin Biao launched his final offensive. He now had an army of 600,000, nearly twice the Nationalist force in Manchuria.

He first attacked Jinzhou, the government's supply base on the railway between Jinan and Mukden; it fell on October 17. Changchun fell three days later. The great garrison at Mukden then tried to retake Jinzhou and Changchun and to open the railway line to the port of Yingkou on Liaodong Bay. In a series of battles, Lin Biao's columns defeated this cream of the Nationalist forces. By early November the Nationalists had lost some 400,000 troops as casualties, captives, or defectors.

The government's military operations in the first part of 1948 produced ever larger budget deficits through the loss of tax receipts, dislocation of transportation and productive facilities, and increased military expenditures. Inflation was out of control. In August the government introduced a new currency, the gold yuan, to replace the old notes at the rate of 3,000,000:1, promising drastic reforms to curtail expenditures and increase revenue. Domestic prices and foreign exchange rates were pegged, with severe penalties threatened for black market operations. The people were required to sell their gold, silver, and foreign currency to the government at the pegged rate; large numbers did so in a desperate effort to halt the inflation. In Shanghai and some other places, the government used draconian methods to enforce its decrees against speculators, but it apparently could not control its own expenditures or stop the printing presses. Furthermore, the government's efforts to fix prices of food and commodities brought about an almost complete stagnation of economic activity, except for illicit buying and selling at prices far above the fixed levels. Some army officers and government officials were themselves engaged in smuggling, speculation, and other forms of corruption. Then came the loss of Jinan and news of the threat in Manchuria. During October the final effort to halt inflation collapsed, with shattering effect to morale in Nationalist-held cities. Prices started rocketing upward once more.

Between early November 1948 and early January 1949, the two sides battled for control of Suzhou. Zhu De concentrated 600,000 troops under Chen Yi, Liu Bocheng, and Chen Geng near that strategic centre, which was defended by Nationalist forces of similar size. Both armies were well-equipped, but the Nationalists had superior armour and were unopposed in the air. Yet poor morale, inept command, and a defensive psychology brought another disaster to the Nationalist government. One after another, its armies were surrounded and defeated in the field. When the 65-day battle was over on January 10, the Nationalists had lost some 500,000 men and their equipment. The capital at Nanjing would soon lie exposed.

With Manchuria and most of the eastern region south to the Yangtze in Communist hands, the fate of Tianjin and Beiping was sealed. The railway corridor between Tianjin and Zhangjiakou was hopelessly isolated. Tianjin fell on January 15 after a brief siege, and Beiping surrendered on January 23, allowing a peaceful turnover of China's historic capital and centre of culture.

Thus, during the last half of 1948, the Communist armies had gained control over Manchuria and north-eastern China nearly to the Yangtze, except for pockets of resistance. They had a numerical superiority and had captured such huge stocks of rifles, artillery, and armour that they were better equipped than the Nationalists.

Great political shifts occurred in 1949. Chiang Kai-shek retired temporarily in January, turning over to the vice-president, General Li Tsung-jen, the problem of holding the government together and trying to negotiate a peace with Mao Zedong. Li's peace negotiations (February–April) proved hopeless. The Nationalists were not prepared to surrender; they still claimed to govern more than half of China and still had a large army. General Li tried to secure US support in the peace negotiations and in the military defence of southern China, but the US government, attempting to extricate itself from its entanglement with the collapsing forces of the Nationalist government, pursued a policy of non-involvement.

When peace negotiations broke down, Communist armies crossed the Yangtze virtually unopposed; the Nationalist government abandoned its indefensible capital on April 23 and moved to Guangzhou. In succession, Communist forces occupied Nanjing (April 24), Hankou (May 16–17), and Shanghai (May 25). The Nationalists' last hope lay in the south and west, but Xi'an, a longtime Nationalist bastion and the gateway to the north-west, had fallen to General Peng Dehuai on May 20. During the last half of 1949, powerful Communist armies succeeded in taking the provinces of southern and western China. By the end of the year, only the islands of Hainan, Taiwan, and a few other offshore positions were still in Nationalist hands, and only scattered pockets of resistance remained on the mainland. The defeated Nationalist government re-established itself on Taiwan, to which Chiang had withdrawn early in the year, taking most of the government's gold reserves and the Nationalist air force and navy. On October 1, with most of the mainland held by the PLA, Mao proclaimed the establishment in Beijing of the government of the People's Republic of China.

3

THE PEOPLE'S REPUBLIC (1949–2007)

The communist victory in 1949 brought to power a peasant party that had learned its techniques in the countryside but had adopted Marxist ideology and believed in class struggle and rapid industrial development. Extensive experience in running base areas and waging war before 1949 had given the CCP deeply ingrained operational habits and proclivities. The long civil war that created the new nation, however, had been one of peasants triumphing over urban dwellers and had involved the destruction of the old ruling classes.

When the CCP proclaimed the People's Republic, most Chinese understood that the new leadership would be preoccupied with industrialization. A priority goal of the communist political system was to raise China to the status of a great power. While pursuing this goal, the "centre of gravity" of communist policy shifted from the countryside to the city, but Chairman Mao Zedong insisted that the revolutionary vision forged in the rural struggle would continue to guide the party.

In a series of speeches in 1949, Chairman Mao stated that his aim was to create a socialist society and, eventually, world communism. These objectives, he said, required transforming consumer cities into producer cities to set the basis on which "the people's political power could be consolidated". He advocated forming a four-class coalition of elements of the urban middle class—the petty bourgeoisie and the national bourgeoisie—with workers and peasants, under the leadership of the CCP. The people's state would exercise a dictatorship "for the oppression of antagonistic classes" made up of opponents of the regime.

The authoritative legal statement of this "people's democratic dictatorship" was given in the 1949 Organic Law for the Chinese People's Political Consultative Conference, and at its first session the conference adopted a Common Program that formally sanctioned the organization of state power under the coalition.

Following the communist victory, a widespread urge to return to normality helped the new leadership restore the economy. Police and party cadres in each locality, backed up by army units, began to crack down on criminal activities associated with economic breakdown.

The cost of restoring order and building up integrated political institutions at all levels throughout the country proved important in setting China's course for the next two decades.

Revolutionary priorities had to be made consonant with other needs. Land reform proceeded in the countryside: landlords were virtually eliminated as a class, land was redistributed and, after some false starts, China's countryside was placed on the path toward collectivization. In the cities, however, a temporary accommodation was reached with noncommunist elements. Many former bureaucrats and capitalists were retained in positions of authority in factories, businesses, schools, and governmental organizations.

Once in power, communist cadres could no longer condone what they had once sponsored, and inevitably they adopted a more rigid and bureaucratic attitude toward popular participation in politics. Many communists, however, considered these changes a betrayal of the revolution; their responses gradually became more intense, and the issue eventually began to divide the once cohesive revolutionary elite. That development became a central focus of China's political history from 1949.

During this initial period, the CCP made great strides toward bringing the country through three critical transitions: from economic prostration to economic growth, from political disintegration to political strength, and from military rule to civilian rule. The determination and capabilities demonstrated during these first years provided the CCP with a reservoir of popular support that would be a major political resource for years.

Almost as soon as the revolution had been accomplished, PLA troops—Chinese People's Volunteers—entered the Korean War against UN forces in October 1950. Beijing, threatened by the northward thrust of UN units, attempted to halt them by its threats to intervene. However, Douglas MacArthur, commander of the UN forces, ignored the threats. Only when UN troops reached the Chinese border did Beijing act. By the time hostilities ended in July 1953, approximately two-thirds of China's combat divisions had seen service in Korea.

In the three years of war, a "Resist America, aid Korea" campaign translated the atmosphere of external threat into a spirit of sacrifice and enforced patriotic emergency at home. Regulations for the Suppression of Counter-Revolutionaries (1951) authorized police action against dissident individuals and suspected groups. A campaign against anticommunist holdouts, bandits, and political opponents was also pressed.

War offered a shroud to dress up a rush of internal changes. Under the Agrarian Reform Law of 1950, the property of rural landlords was confiscated and redistributed, fulfilling a promise to the peasants and smashing a class identified as feudal or semi-feudal. The property of traitors, "bureaucrat capitalists" (especially the "four big families" of the Nationalist Party [KMT]—the K'ungs [Kongs], Soongs [Songs], Chiangs [Jiangs], and Ch'ens [Chens]), and selected foreign nationals was also confiscated, helping end the power of many industrialists and providing an economic basis for industrialization. Programs were begun to increase production and to lay the basis for long-term socialization.

These programmes coincided with a massive effort to win over the population to the leadership. Such acts as a marriage law (May 1950) and a trade union law (June 1950) symbolized the break with the old society, while mass organizations and the regime's "campaign style" dramatized the new.

During 1949–50, policy toward the cities focused on restoring order, and rehabilitating the economy. To accomplish these tasks, the CCP tried to discipline the labour force, win over the confidence of the capitalists, and implement drastic fiscal policies so as to undercut inflation. These policies brought such remarkable successes that by late 1950 many urban Chinese viewed the CCP leadership as necessary reformers. Indeed, numerous capitalists believed them to be "good for business".

But, beginning in 1951, the revolutionary agenda of the communists began to be felt in the cities. A Suppression of Counter-Revolutionaries campaign dealt violently with many former leaders of secret societies, religious associations, and the KMT. In late 1951 and early 1952, three major political

campaigns brought the revolutionary essence of the CCP home
to key urban groups. The Three-Antis campaign targeted
communist cadres who had become too close to China's
capitalists. The Five-Antis campaign was aimed at the capitalists themselves and brought them into line with charges of
bribery, tax evasion, theft of state property and economic
information, and cheating on government contracts. Finally,
the thought-reform campaign humbled university professors
and marked a turning point in the move from Western to
Soviet influence in structuring China's university curriculum.

The pressures toward national consolidation and the costly
struggle in Korea had significant consequences. In the several
provinces of Manchuria (now called the Northeast), there was
a growing industrial and military concentration, as well as an
increased presence of Soviet economic advisers.

Gao Gang headed Northeast China and, in addition to his
authoritative regional position, also influenced decisions in
Beijing. He planned the Three-Antis campaign and took the
lead in adapting Soviet techniques to Chinese factory management and economic planning.

Gao promoted these techniques on a national basis when he
moved to Beijing in late 1952 to set up the State Planning
Commission. Working closely with the head of the party's
Organization Department and other senior officials, Gao
allegedly tried to drastically reduce the authority of his potential competitors, notably Liu Shaoqi and Zhou Enlai, both
leading members of party and state organs. The ensuing power
struggle lasted more than a year, reflecting an underlying
fissure in the CCP.

This period saw a marked change in Soviet influence in
China. The officially sanctioned terms of that influence had
been worked out in a visit by Mao to Moscow in December
1949, and were formalized in the Treaty of Friendship,

Alliance, and Mutual Assistance (signed February 14, 1950). The seeds of doubt concerning Soviet willingness to help China had been sown. The applicability of the Soviet model to China and the degree to which its use might become a pretext for Soviet manipulation of China began to be questioned.

Nevertheless, these potential reductions in Soviet influence were counterbalanced by growing Soviet activity in other fields. The Chinese army was reorganized along Soviet lines, with a greater emphasis on heavy firepower and mobility. Soviet texts and propaganda materials flooded the country. The Soviet Union had earlier extended US$300 million in credit (used up by 1953), which was followed by a smaller developmental loan in 1954 (used up by 1956). Under these aid programmes, the Soviets supplied the equipment and technical aid for a large number of industrial projects. The Soviet Union also played a major role in Chinese foreign policy, and it appears that China accepted Moscow's leadership in the international communist movement. Coordinating with the Soviets, Beijing supported revolutionary activity throughout Asia.

The First Five-Year Plan, 1953–57, was explicitly modelled on Soviet experience, and the Soviet Union provided both material aid and extensive technical advice on its planning and execution. The plan adopted Stalinist economic priorities. In a country where more than four-fifths of the population lived in rural areas, about four-fifths of all government investment was channelled into the urban economy. The vast majority of this investment went to heavy industry, leaving agriculture relatively starved of resources.

This transition was most obvious in the countryside. After land reform had been carried out, mutual aid teams allowed the communists to experiment with voluntary forms of agri-

cultural collectivization. A campaign was launched in late
1953 to organize small collectives, called lower-level agricultural producers' cooperatives, averaging 20 to 30 households.

Debate soon broke out within the CCP concerning how
quickly to move to higher stages of cooperative production in
the countryside. The debate was symptomatic of the larger
tensions within the party regarding urban and rural development. The strengths of Mao Zedong lay in agricultural policy,
social change, and foreign relations, and in the mid-1950s he
began to shift the national agenda more in the direction of his
own expertise.

In July 1955 Mao, against the wishes of most of his
colleagues in the CCP leadership, called for an acceleration
of the transition to lower-level, and then to higher-level,
agricultural producers' cooperatives in the countryside. The
key difference between these two forms concerned the middle
class of peasants and farmers able to live off their own land.
Wages were based on labour performed, not land contributed.
Middle-level peasants came to resent landless peasants, who
were being recruited into the new cooperatives.

Many middle-level peasants actively resisted these changes
and the measures for enforcing them—grain rationing, compulsory purchase quotas, and stricter regulations on savings
and wage rates. Nevertheless, Chinese agricultural organization in 1956 reached the approximate level of collectivization
achieved in the Soviet Union: a peasant owned his house, some
domestic animals, a garden plot, and his personal savings. By
the end of 1956, some seven-eighths of China's peasant households were organized into advanced cooperatives.

Mao combined this massive transformation of the agricultural sector with a call for the "socialist transformation" of
industry and commerce, in which the government would
become, in effect, the major partner. In Chinese communist

fashion, this change was not simply decreed from above. Extreme pressures were put on private merchants and capitalists in late 1955 to "volunteer" their enterprises for transformation into "joint state–private" firms. The results were sometimes extraordinary. All the capitalists in a given trade (such as textiles) would parade together to CCP headquarters to the beat of gongs and the sound of firecrackers. Once there, they would present a petition to the government, asking that the major interest in their firms be bought out at the rate that the government deemed appropriate. The government would graciously agree.

After the Five-Antis campaign, the government extended the reach of its trade unions into the larger capitalist enterprises, and the "joint labour–management" committees set up under government pressure in those firms usurped much of the power that the capitalists formerly had exercised. Thus, many Chinese capitalists saw the socialist transformation of 1955–56 as an almost welcome development, because it secured their position with the government while costing them little in money or power.

The socialist transformation of agriculture, industry, and commerce thus went relatively smoothly. Nevertheless, such changes could not take place without considerable tensions. Many peasants streamed into the cities in 1956–57 to escape the new cooperatives and to seek employment in the rapidly expanding state-run factories, where government policy kept wages rising rapidly. China's urban population mushroomed from 77 million in 1953 to 99.5 million by 1957.

Several problems also became increasingly pressing. First, CCP leaders found that the agricultural sector was not growing fast enough to provide additional capital for its own development and to feed the workers of the cities. Until then, agricultural policy had attempted to wring large production increases out of changes in organization and land ownership, with little capital investment. By 1956–57 that policy was shown to be inadequate. Second, Soviet assistance had been made available to China as loans, not grants. After 1956 China had to repay more each year than it borrowed. Third, the vastly expanded governmental responsibility for managing the country's urban firms and commerce required far more experts than before.

Thus far, the leadership's policies had been ambivalent toward the intelligentsia. It had required their services and prestige, but it had suspected also that many were untrustworthy, coming from urban and bourgeois backgrounds and often having close family and other personal ties with the KMT. After 1949 and particularly during the first part of the Korean War, the Central Committee launched a major campaign to re-educate teachers and scientists and to discredit Western-oriented scholarship.

In 1951 the emphasis shifted from general campaigns to self-reform; in 1955 it shifted once again to an intensive thought-reform movement, following the purge of Hu Feng, until then the party's leading spokesman on art and literature. This latter movement coincided with the denunciation of a scholarly study of the *Dream of the Red Chamber* (*Hongloumeng*), an eighteenth-century novel of tragic love and declining fortunes in a Chinese family. Literature without a clear class moral received blistering criticism, as did any hint that the party should not command art and literature.

In early 1956 party leaders publicly discussed the role of intellectuals in the new tasks of national construction and adopted the line "Let a hundred flowers blossom, a hundred schools of thought contend." The "hundred flowers" line explicitly encouraged "free-ranging" discussion and inquiry, with the explicit assumption that this would prove the superiority of Marxism-Leninism and speed the conversion of intellectuals to communism.

The response to the party's invitation for free discussion and criticism was gradual and cautious. Instead of embracing Marxism, moreover, many used the opportunity to translate and discuss Western works and ideas and blithely debated "reactionary" doctrines at the very moment Hungarian intellectuals were triggering a wave of anticommunist sentiment in Budapest.

Following this initial phase of the Hundred Flowers Campaign, Mao Zedong issued what was perhaps his most famous post-1949 speech "On the Correct Handling of Contradictions Among the People" (February 27, 1957). Its essential message was ambiguous. He stressed the importance of resolving "nonantagonistic contradictions" by methods of persuasion, but he stated that "democratic" methods of resolution would have to be consistent with centralism and discipline.

He left it unclear, however, when a contradiction might become an "antagonistic" struggle, but later concluded that the party would judge words and actions to be correct only if they united the populace, were beneficial to socialism, strengthened the state dictatorship, consolidated organizations (especially the party), and generally helped strengthen international communism.

In June, those who had thrown caution to the winds reaped the full fury of retaliation in an anti-rightist campaign. The intellectuals who had responded to Mao's call for open criticism were the first victims, but the movement quickly spread beyond that group to engulf many specialists in the government bureaucracy and state-run firms. By the fall, the fury of the campaign began to turn toward the countryside.

Between 1955 and 1957, changes in Soviet and US policies caused Chinese leaders to doubt the validity of a more cautious and conciliatory foreign policy. At the twentieth Congress of the Soviet Communist Party in 1956, First Secretary Nikita Khrushchev announced a de-Stalinization policy. This development angered Mao Zedong for two reasons: he thought, correctly, that it would undermine Soviet prestige, with potentially dangerous consequences in Eastern Europe, and he chafed at Khrushchev's warning to other communist parties not to let a wilful leader have his way unchecked.

Chinese leaders—Mao foremost among them—now began to question the wisdom of closely following the Soviet model. Economic difficulties provided a major set of reasons for moving away from that model. Increasing mutual distrust also exacerbated the situation. Nevertheless, at the end of 1957 the Soviet Union evidently agreed to provide China with the technical assistance needed to make an atomic bomb, and during 1958 the Soviet Union increased its level of aid to China. In the final analysis, however, the spiralling deterioration in Sino-Soviet relations proved impossible to reverse and China adopted a new, more militant foreign policy.

Mao personally felt increasingly uncomfortable with the alliance with the Soviet Union and with the social and political ramifications of the Soviet model of development. He disliked the Soviet system of centralized control by large government ministries, substantial social stratification, and strong urban bias. In addition, the Soviet model assumed that agricultural surplus need only be captured by the government and made to serve urban development. This was true for the Soviet Union in the late 1920s, when the model was developed, but the situation in China was different.

Mao therefore initiated a critique of China's slavish copying of Soviet military strategy culminating in the radical Great Leap Forward. The general line of socialist construction and the Great Leap Forward were first announced at the second session of the Eighth Party Congress in May 1958. The Congress called for a bold form of ideological leadership that could unleash a "leap forward" in technical innovation and economic output.

The basic idea was to convert the massive labour surplus in China's hinterlands into a huge production force through a radical reorganization of rural production. The search for the best organizational form to achieve this result led in August 1958 to popularization of the "people's commune", a huge rural unit that pooled the labour of tens of thousands of peasants from different villages in order to increase agricultural production, engage in local industrial production, enhance the availability of rural schooling, and organize a local militia force.

The Great Leap Forward

Under the commune system, agricultural and political decisions were decentralized, and ideological purity rather than expertise was emphasized. The peasants were organized into brigade teams, and communal kitchens were established so that women could be freed for work. Mao believed that through these radical organizational changes, combined with adequate political mobilization techniques, the Chinese countryside could be made to provide the resources both for its own development and for the continuing rapid development of the heavy industrial sector in the cities. Through this strategy of "walking on two legs", China could obtain the simultaneous development of industry and agriculture and, within the urban sector, of both large- and small-scale industry. If it worked, this would resolve the dilemma of an agricultural bottleneck that had seemed to loom large on the horizon as of 1957. It would, however, involve a major departure from the Soviet model, which would predictably lead to increased tensions between Beijing and Moscow.

Largely because of unusually good weather, 1958 was an exceptionally good year for agricultural output. However, by the end of that year, the top CCP leadership sensed that some major problems demanded immediate attention. The programme was implemented with such haste by overzealous cadres that implements were often melted to make steel in the backyard furnaces, many farm animals were slaughtered by discontented peasants, and great tracts of forested land were destroyed for fuel wood. These errors in implementation were made worse by a series of natural disasters and the withdrawal of Soviet technical personnel.

Initial optimism had led peasants in many areas to eat far more than they usually would have, and stocks of grain for the winter and spring months threatened to fall dangerously low. In addition, reports of sporadic peasant unrest cast some doubt on the rosy picture being presented to the leaders by their own statistical system. However, the fall harvest of 1958 had not been as large as expected. The inefficiency of the communes and the large-scale diversion of farm labour into small-scale industry disrupted China's agriculture so seriously that about 20 million people died of starvation between 1958 and 1962.

In February and March 1959 Mao Zedong began to call for appropriate adjustments to make policies more realistic without abandoning the Great Leap as a whole. Mao emerged as one of the most forceful advocates of scaling back the Great Leap in order to avert a potential disaster. He faced substantial resistance from provincial CCP leaders, whose powers had been greatly increased as part of the Great Leap strategy.

A meeting at Lushan in the summer of 1959 produced an unanticipated and ultimately highly destructive outcome. Defence Minister Peng Dehuai raised a range of criticisms of the Great Leap, based in large part on his own investigations. He summed these up in a letter that he sent to Mao during the conference. Mao waited eight days to respond to the letter and then attacked Peng for "right deviationism" and demanded the purge of Peng and all his followers.

The Lushan Conference resulted in several major decisions: Peng Dehuai was replaced as defence minister by Lin Biao (who would later be marked for succession to Mao's position of CCP chairman), the Great Leap Forward was scaled back, and a political campaign was launched to identify and remove all "rightist" elements. The third decision effectively cancelled the second, as party officials refused to scale back the Great Leap for fear of being labelled as "rightists". The net effect was to produce a "second leap", a new radical upsurge in policy that was not corrected until it produced results so disastrous that they called into question the very viability of the communist system.

The CCP celebrated the tenth anniversary of national victory in October 1959 in a state of near euphoria. The weather turned in 1959, however, and during the next two years China experienced a combination of floods and drought. By 1961 the rural disaster caught up with the cities, and urban industrial output plummeted by more than 25 per cent. As an emergency measure, nearly 30 million urban residents were sent back to the countryside because they could no longer be fed in the cities. The Great Leap Forward had run its course, and the system was in crisis.

By January 1962 Mao had, as he later put it, moved to the "second line" to concentrate "on dealing with questions of the direction, policy, and line of the party and the state". The "first line"—administrative and day-by-day direction of the state—had been given to Liu Shaoqi, who had assumed the chairmanship of the People's Republic of China in 1959 (although Mao retained his position of party chairman); additional responsibilities in the first line were given to Deng Xiaoping, another strong-minded organizer who, as general secretary, was the party's top administrator. By 1962 Mao had apparently begun to conclude that the techniques used by these comrades in the first line not only violated the basic thrust of the revolutionary tradition but also formed a pattern of error that mirrored what he viewed as the "modern revisionism" of the Soviet Union.

Under Liu and Deng, the CCP developed a series of documents in major policy areas to try to bring the country out of the rapidly growing crisis. In most instances, these documents were drafted with the assistance of experts who had been reviled during the Great Leap Forward. These documents marked a major retreat from recent radicalism. The communes were to be reduced so as to make them small enough to link peasants' efforts more clearly with their remuneration. Indeed, by 1962 in many areas of rural China, the collective system in agriculture had broken down completely, and individual farming was revived. Policy toward literature, art, and motion pictures permitted a "thaw" involving treatment of a far broader range of subjects and a revival of many older, pre-revolutionary artistic forms. The new programme in industry strengthened the hands of managers and made a worker's efforts more closely attuned to his rewards. Similar policies were adopted in other areas.

These policies raised basic questions about the future direction of the revolution. While almost all top CCP leaders had supported the launching of the Great Leap, there was disagreement over the lessons to be learned from the movement's dramatic failure. The Great Leap had been intended both as a means of accelerating economic development and as a vehicle for achieving a mass ideological transformation. All leaders agreed in its aftermath that a mobilization approach to economic development was no longer appropriate to China's conditions. Most also concluded that the age of mass political campaigns as an instrument to remould the thinking of the public was past.

Mao and a few of his supporters, however, still viewed class struggle as fundamental. Mao was in fact deeply troubled as he contemplated China's situation during 1961–65. He became convinced that China, like Russia after Stalin's death, was headed down the road toward revisionism. He used class struggle and ideological campaigns, as well as concrete policies in various areas, to try to prevent and reverse this slide into revolutionary purgatory. Mao's nightmare about revisionism played an increasing role in structuring politics in the mid-1960s.

Mao was not the only leader who harboured doubts. Others gathered around him and tried to use their closeness to Mao as a vehicle for enhancing their political power: Mao's political assistant of many years, Chen Boda, was an expert in the realm of ideology; Mao's wife, Jiang Qing, had strong policy views in the cultural sphere; Kang Sheng, whose strength lay both in his understanding of Soviet ideology and in his mastery of Soviet-style secret police techniques; and Lin Biao, who headed the military and tried to make it an ideal type of Maoist organization that combined effectiveness with ideological purity. Each of these people in turn had personal networks and resources to bring to a coalition. While their goals and interests did not entirely coincide, they all could unite on two efforts: enhancing Mao's power and upsetting Mao's relations with Liu Shaoqi (then the likely successor to Mao), Deng Xiaoping, and most of the remainder of the party leadership.

Mao undertook a number of initiatives in domestic and foreign policy during the period. The most important set of measures concerned the People's Liberation Army (PLA),

which he and Lin Biao tried to make into a model organization. Both men viewed the soldier-communist as the most
suitable candidate for the second- and third-generation leadership. Army uniformity and discipline, it was seen, could
transcend the divided classes, and all army men could be made
to comply with the rigorous political standards set by Mao's
leadership.

Lin Biao developed a simplified and dogmatized version of
Mao's thoughts—eventually published in the form of the
"Little Red Book", *Quotations from Chairman Mao*—to
popularize Maoist ideology among the relatively uneducated
military recruits. Mao then tried to expand the PLA's political
role. In 1963, he called on all Chinese to "learn from the PLA".
Then, starting in 1964, Mao insisted that political departments
modelled on those in the PLA be established in all major
government bureaucracies. In many cases, political workers
from the PLA itself staffed these new bodies, thus effectively
penetrating the civilian government apparatus. Other efforts,
such as a national propaganda campaign to learn from a
purported army hero, Lei Feng, also contributed to enhance-
ment of the PLA's prestige.

Mao's calls for "revolutionization" acquired a more nationalistic aspect, and the PLA assumed an even larger place in
Chinese political life. In late 1963 he called on intellectuals to
undertake a major reformulation of their academic disciplines
to support China's new international role. A drive began to
cultivate what one author called "newborn forces", and by
mid-1964 young urban intellectuals were embroiled in a major
effort by the Central Committee to promote those forces
within the party and league; meanwhile, their rural cousins
were buffeted by moves to keep the socialist education campaign under the party's organizational control through the use
of "work teams" and a cadre-rectification movement.

The Cultural Revolution

In the summer of 1964, Mao wrote a document titled "On Khrushchev's Phony Communism and Its Historical Lessons for the World", which summarized most of his doctrinal principles on class struggle, and political structure and operation. This summary provided the basis for the re-education ("revolutionization") of all youth hoping to succeed to the revolutionary cause. This high tide of revolutionization lasted until early August, when US air strikes on North Vietnam raised the spectre of war on China's southern border.

As the clash over issues became polarized in the autumn of 1965, the army initially provided the battleground. The issues concerned differences over policy directions and their implications for the organization of power and the qualifications of senior officials to lead. Much of the struggle went on behind the scenes; in public it took the form of personal vilification and ritualized exposés. In these critical months, the base of operations for Mao and Lin was the large eastern Chinese city of Shanghai, and newspapers published in that city, especially the *Liberation Army Daily*, carried public attacks on the targets selected.

The principal purpose of the Cultural Revolution was to revitalize revolutionary values for the successor generation of Chinese young people. The first target was the historian Wu Han, who doubled as the deputy mayor of Beijing. In a play Wu wrote, he had supposedly used allegorical devices to lampoon Mao and laud the deposed former minister of defence, Peng Dehuai. The denunciation of Wu and his play in November 1965 constituted the opening volley in an assault on cultural figures and their thoughts.

Mao formally launched the Cultural Revolution at the Eleventh Plenum of the Eighth Central Committee in August

1966. He shut down China's schools, and during the following months he encouraged Red Guards to attack all traditional values and "bourgeois" things and to test party officials by publicly criticizing them. Mao believed that this measure would be beneficial both for the young people and for the party cadres that they attacked.

The movement quickly escalated; many elderly people and intellectuals were not only verbally attacked but were physically abused, and many died. The Red Guards splintered into zealous rival factions, each purporting to be the true representative of Maoist thought. Mao's own personality cult, encouraged so as to provide momentum to the movement, assumed religious proportions. The resulting anarchy, terror, and paralysis completely disrupted the urban economy. Industrial production for 1968 dipped 12 per cent below that of 1966.

As the Cultural Revolution gained momentum, Mao turned for support to the youth as well as the army. In seeking to create a new system of education that would eliminate differences between town and country, workers and peasants, and mental and manual labour, Mao struck a responsive chord with the youth; it was their response that later provided him with his best shock troops. The attack against authors, scholars, and propagandists during the spring of 1966 emphasized the cultural dimension of the Cultural Revolution. Increasingly it was hinted that behind the visible targets lay a sinister "black gang" in the fields of education and propaganda and high up in party circles. Removal of Peng Zhen and Lu Dingyi and subsequently of Zhou Yang, then tsar of the arts and literature, indicated that this was to be a thorough purge. Clearly, a second purpose of the Cultural Revolution would be the elimination of leading cadres whom Mao held responsible for past ideological sins and alleged errors in judgment.

Gradual transference of the revolution to top echelons of the party was managed by a group centred on Mao Zedong, Lin Biao, Jiang Qing, Kang Sheng, and Chen Boda. In May 1966 Mao secretly assigned major responsibilities to the army in cultural and educational affairs.

Following the May instructions, the educational system received priority. "Big-character posters" or large wall newspapers (*dazibao*) spread from the principal campuses in Beijing throughout the land. University officials and professors were singled out for criticism, while their students, encouraged by the central authorities, held mass meetings and began to organize. In June the government dropped examinations for university admissions and called for a reform of entrance procedures and a delay in reopening the campuses. Party officials and their wives circulated among the campuses to gain favour and to obstruct their opponents. Intrigue and political manoeuvering dominated, although political lines were not at first sharply drawn or even well understood. The centres of this activity were Beijing's schools and the inner councils of the Central Committee; the students were the activists in a game they did not fully comprehend.

This phase of the Cultural Revolution ended in August 1966 with the convening of a plenary session of the Central Committee. Mao issued his own big-character poster as a call to "Bombard the headquarters," a call to denounce and remove senior officials, and a 16-point Central Committee decision was issued in which the broad outlines for the Cultural Revolution were laid down and supporters were rallied to the revolutionary banner. The immediate aim was to seize power from "bourgeois" authorities. The locus of the struggle would be their urban strongholds. Now more than ever, Mao's thoughts became the "compass for action".

Evidently fearing that China would develop along the lines of the Soviet revolution and concerned about his own place in history, Mao threw China's cities into turmoil in a gigantic effort to reverse the historic processes then under way. He ultimately failed in his quest, but his own efforts generated problems with which his successors would have to struggle for decades.

Mao adopted four goals for his Cultural Revolution: to replace his designated successors with leaders more faithful to his current thinking, to rectify the CCP, to provide China's youth with a revolutionary experience, and to achieve specific policy changes to make the educational, health care, and cultural systems less elitist. He initially pursued those goals through a massive mobilization of the country's urban youths—organized in groups called the Red Guards—while ordering the CCP and the PLA not to suppress the movement.

In February 1967 the chaos, combined with political outrages throughout the country, led many remaining top CCP leaders to call for a halt to the Cultural Revolution. During this attempt to beat back radicalism, more conservative forces clamped down on Red Guard activism in numerous cities. The movement, dubbed the "February adverse current", was quickly defeated and a new radical upsurge began. Indeed, by the summer of 1967, large armed clashes occurred throughout urban China, and even Chinese embassies abroad experienced takeovers by their own Red Guards.

During 1967 Mao called on the PLA under Lin Biao to step in on behalf of the Maoist Red Guards, but this politico-military task produced more division within the military than unified support for radical youths. Tensions surfaced in the summer, when Chen Zaidao, a military commander in the key city of Wuhan, arrested two key radical CCP leaders. Faced with possible widespread revolt among local military commanders, Mao tilted toward re-establishing some order.

This continued until 1968 when Mao decided to rebuild the CCP and bring things under greater control. The military dispatched officers and soldiers to take over schools, factories, and government agencies. The army simultaneously forced millions of urban Red Guards to move to the hinterlands to live, thereby removing the most disruptive force from the cities. Thus in 1968, society began to return to business, though not as usual. In October 1968 a plenary session of the Central Committee met to call for convening a party congress and rebuilding the CCP apparatus. From that point on, the issue of who would inherit political power as the Cultural Revolution wound down became a central question of Chinese politics.

By 1970 many of the stated goals of the Cultural Revolution had been translated into at least somewhat operational programmes termed the "three major differences"—those separating intellectual from manual labour, worker from peasant, and urban from rural. Many measures had been taken to make the educational system less elitist. The number of years at each level of schooling was shortened, and admission to a university became based on the recommendations of a student's work unit rather than on competitive examination. All youths were required to engage in at least several years of manual labour before attending a university.

Within schools, formal scholarship yielded in large measure to the study of politics and to vocational training. Examinations of the traditional type were abolished, and stress was placed on collective study. The authority of teachers in the classroom was seriously eroded. These trends reached their most extreme form when a student in the north-east was made a national hero by the radicals because he turned in a blank examination paper and criticized his teacher for having asked him the examination questions in the first place.

Many bureaucrats were forced to leave the relative comfort of their offices for a stint in "May 7 cadre schools", usually farms run by a major urban unit. People from the urban unit had to live on the farm, typically in quite primitive conditions, for varying periods of time. (For some, this amounted to a number of years, although by about 1973 the time periods in general had been held to about 6–12 months.) While on the farm the urban cadre would both engage in rigorous manual labour and undertake intensive, supervised study of ideology in order to reduce bureaucratic "airs".

Millions of Chinese youths were also sent to the countryside during these years. Initially, these were primarily Red Guard activists, but the programme soon achieved a more general character, and it became expected that most middle-school graduates would head to the countryside. While in the hinterlands, these young people were instructed to "learn from the poor and lower-middle peasants". Quite a few were merely sent to the counties immediately adjacent to the city from which they came. Others, however, were sent over long distances. Large groups from Shanghai, for instance, were made to settle in Heilongjiang, the northernmost province in the north-east, and Xinjiang in the far north-west.

The system of medical care was also revamped. Serious efforts were made to force urban-based medical staffs to devote more effort to serving the needs of the peasants. This involved both the reassignment of medical personnel to rural areas and, more important, a major attempt to provide short-term training to rural medical personnel called "barefoot doctors". This latter initiative placed at least a minimal level of medical competence in many Chinese villages; ideally, the referral of more serious matters was to be made to higher levels.

Another prong of the effort in the medical arena was to place relatively greater stress on the use of Chinese traditional medicine, which relied more heavily on locally available herbs and on such low-cost treatments as acupuncture. Western medicine was simply too expensive and specialized to be used effectively throughout China's vast hinterlands.

Mao's Twilight

As these programmatic aspects of the Cultural Revolution were being put in place and regularized, the political battle to determine who would inherit power at the top continued and intensified. Tensions first surfaced at a meeting of the Central Committee in the summer of 1970, when Chen Boda, Lin Biao, and their supporters made a series of remarks that angered Mao Zedong. Mao then purged Chen as a warning to Lin. At the end of 1970 Mao also initiated a criticism of Lin's top supporters in the military forces, calling them to task for their arrogance and unwillingness to listen to civilian authority. The situation intensified during the spring of 1971 until Lin Biao's son, Lin Liguo, evidently began to put together plans for a possible coup against Mao should this prove the only way to save his father's position.

During this period, Zhou Enlai engaged in extremely delicate and secret diplomatic exchanges with the USA, and Mao agreed to a secret visit to Beijing by the US national security adviser Henry Kissinger in July 1971. That visit was one of the more dramatic events of the Cold War era and laid the groundwork for US President Richard M. Nixon's trip to China the following February. At a time when the Vietnam War continued to blaze, China and the USA took major steps toward reducing their mutual antagonism in the face of the

Soviet threat. Lin Biao strongly opposed this opening to the USA—probably in part because it would strengthen the political hand of its key architect in China, Zhou Enlai—and the Kissinger visit thus amounted to a major defeat for Lin.

In September 1971 Lin died in a mysterious plane crash in Mongolia in what the Chinese claim was an attempt to flee to the Soviet Union. The Chinese high military command who had served under Lin was purged in the weeks following his death. Zhou Enlai was the major beneficiary of the death, and from late 1971 through mid-1973 he tried to nudge the system back toward stability. During 1972 Mao suffered a serious stroke, and Zhou learned that he had a fatal cancer. These developments highlighted the continued uncertainty over the succession. In early 1973 Zhou and Mao brought Deng Xiaoping back to power in the hope of grooming him as a successor. But Deng had been the second most important victim purged by the radicals during the Cultural Revolution, and his re-emergence made Jiang Qing, Mao's wife, and her followers desperate to return things to a more radical path.

From mid-1973, Chinese politics shifted back and forth between Jiang and her followers—later dubbed the Gang of Four—and the supporters of Zhou and Deng. The former group favoured political mobilization, class struggle, anti-intellectualism, egalitarianism, and xenophobia, while the latter promoted economic growth, stability, educational progress, and a pragmatic foreign policy. Mao tried unsuccessfully to maintain a balance among these different forces while continuing in vain to search for a suitable successor.

The balance tipped back and forth between the two groups. The radicals gained the upper hand from mid-1973 until mid-1974, during which time they whipped up a campaign that used criticism of Lin Biao and Confucius as an allegorical vehicle for attacking Zhou and his policies. By July 1974, however, economic decline and increasing chaos saw a shift back toward Zhou and Deng. With Zhou hospitalized, Deng assumed increasing power from the summer of 1974 through the late fall of 1975. During this time Deng sought (with Zhou's full support) to put the Four Modernizations (of agriculture, industry, science and technology, and defence) at the top of the country's agenda. To further this effort, Deng continued to rehabilitate victims of the Cultural Revolution, and he commissioned the drafting of an important group of documents much like those developed in 1960–62. They laid out the basic principles for work in the party, industry, and science and technology. Their core elements were anathema to the radicals, who used their power in the mass media and the propaganda apparatus to attack Deng's efforts.

The radicals finally convinced Mao that Deng's policies would lead eventually to a repudiation of the Cultural Revolution and even of Mao himself. Mao therefore sanctioned criticism of these policies in the wall posters that were a favourite propaganda tool of the radicals. Zhou died in January 1976, and Deng delivered his eulogy. Deng then disappeared from public view and was formally purged (with Mao's backing) in April. The immediate reason for Deng's downfall was a group of massive demonstrations in Beijing and other cities that took advantage of the traditional Qingming festival to pay homage to Zhou's memory and thereby challenge the radicals.

In the immediate wake of Deng's purge, many of his followers also fell from power, and a political campaign was launched to "criticize Deng Xiaoping and his right-deviationist attempt to reverse correct verdicts [on people during the Cultural Revolution]". Only Mao's death in September and the purge of the Gang of Four by a coalition of political, police, and military leaders in October 1976 brought this effort to vilify Deng to a close. Although it was officially ended by the eleventh Party Congress in August 1977, the Cultural Revolution had in fact concluded with Mao's death and the purge of the Gang of Four.

After Mao

Mao's death left Hua Guofeng, a compromise candidate elevated to the premiership by Mao following the purge of Deng Xiaoping, as the chairman of the CCP and thus the official leader of China. Hua tried to consolidate his position by stressing his ties to Mao and his fidelity to Mao's basic ideas, but many others in the top leadership wanted to move away from these issues, and Hua's position eroded over the remainder of the decade. Despite some uncertainty, Deng was rehabilitated and formally brought back into his previous offices in the summer of 1977.

Lacking detailed information on the economy, the leaders adopted an overly ambitious 10-year plan in early 1978 and used the government's resources to the limit throughout that year to increase investment and achieve rapid economic growth. Much of that growth consisted of reactivating capacity that had lain idle because of political disruption. Future growth would be harder to achieve, and long-term trends in matters such as capital-output ratios made it increasingly clear that the old strategies would be less effective.

One of the major changes of 1978 was China's sharp turn toward participation in the international economy. While in the 1970s there had been a resumption of the foreign trade that had been largely halted in the late 1960s, along with far more active and Western-oriented diplomatic initiatives, the changes during and after 1978 were fundamental. China's leaders became convinced that large amounts of capital could be

acquired from abroad to speed up the country's modernization, a change in attitude that elicited an almost frenetic
response from foreign bankers and entrepreneurs. These several strands came together in late 1978 at a major meeting of
the CCP leadership, when China formally agreed to establish
full diplomatic relations with the USA.

China's leaders also formally adopted the Four Modernizations as the country's highest priority, with all other tasks to
be subordinated to that of economic development. This set of
priorities differed so fundamentally from those pursued during
the Cultural Revolution that the implications for future policy
and for the interests of various sectors of the population were
profound.

The opening of China's economy to the outside world
proceeded apace. In the late 1970s the country adopted a
joint-venture law, and it subsequently enacted numerous other
laws (such as one governing patents) to create an attractive
environment for foreign capital. An initial experiment with
"special economic zones" along the southern coast in the late
1970s led in 1984 to a decision to open 14 cities to more
intense engagement with the international economy. The idea
was to move toward opening ever larger sections of the
country to foreign trade and investment.

Within the domestic economy, numerous experiments were
undertaken in finance, banking, planning, urban economic
management, and rural policy. Of these, by far the most
important were the series of measures taken toward the
roughly four-fifths of the population that lived in the countryside at the time. Prices paid for farm products were sharply
increased in 1979, thus pumping significant additional resources into the agricultural sector. The collective farming
system was gradually dismantled in favour of a return to
family farming. At first, families were allowed to contract

for the use of collective land for a limited period of time. Subsequently, the period of those contracts was extended, and subcontracting (essentially, allowing one family to accumulate large amounts of land) was permitted.

Peasants were also allowed far greater choice in what crops to plant, and many abandoned farming altogether in favour of establishing small-scale industries or transport companies and other services. Thus, rural patterns of work, land leasing, and wealth changed markedly after 1978. Exceptionally good weather during the early 1980s contributed to record harvests.

The reforms in the urban economy had more mixed results, largely because the economic system in the cities was so much more complex. Those reforms sought to provide material incentives for greater efficiency and to increase the use of market forces in allocating resources. Problems arose because of the relatively irrational price system, continuing managerial timidity, and the unwillingness of government officials to give up their power over economic decisions, among other difficulties. In the urban as well as the rural economy, the reformers tackled some of the fundamental building blocks of the Soviet system that had been imported during the 1950s.

Reforms have continued in the rural and urban areas. Rural producers have been given more freedom to decide how to use their earnings, whether for agricultural or other economic activities. Private entrepreneurship in the cities and the rationalization, privatization and, in some cases, dismantling of state-owned enterprises have gained speed. At the same time, the central government has moderated the pace of change—primarily to avoid increases in social unrest resulting from rising unemployment—and constructed a social safety net for those who lose their jobs.

The reformers led by Deng Xiaoping tried after 1978 to reduce the level of political coercion in Chinese society. Millions of victims of past political campaigns were released from labour camps, and bad "class labels" were removed from those stigmatized by them. This dramatically improved the career and social opportunities of millions of former political pariahs. To a considerable extent, moreover, the range of things considered political was narrowed, so that mundane elements such as style of dress and grooming and preferences in music and hobbies were no longer considered politically significant. More importantly, criticizing policy no longer triggered political retaliation against the critics. Overall, the role of the Public Security (police) forces was cut back substantially.

The reformers also tried to make preparations for their own political succession. Deng proved masterful at maintaining a viable coalition among the diverse forces at the top. By the end of 1981 he had succeeded in nudging Hua Guofeng and others of the more-rigid Maoists out of high-level positions. Although he refused to take the top positions for himself, Deng saw his supporters become premier (Zhao Ziyang and then Li Peng) and general secretary of the CCP (Hu Yaobang, Zhao, and Jiang Zemin), and he worked hard to try to consolidate and maintain their hold on power.

In early 1982 the CCP leadership made a concerted attempt to restructure the leading bodies in both the government and the party, and much was reorganized, with the appointment of many new officials. This general effort continued, with the focus increasingly on the bloated military establishment, but progess slowed considerably after the initial burst of organizational reformism.

Throughout 1982–85 the CCP carried out a "rectification" campaign designed to restore morals to its membership and weed out those who did not support reform. This campaign highlighted the increasing difficulties inherent in maintaining discipline and limiting corruption at a time of rapid change, when materialistic values were being officially propagated.

By the mid-1980s, China was in transition, with core elements of the previous system called into question while the ultimate balance that would be struck remained unclear even to the top participants. The reform movement began to sour in 1985. Financial decentralization and the two-price system combined with other factors to produce inflation and encourage corruption. China's population, increasingly exposed to foreign ideas and standards of living, put pressure on the government to speed the rate of change within the country.

These forces produced open unrest within the country in late 1986 and again on a much larger scale in the spring of 1989. By 1989 popular disaffection with the CCP and the government had become widespread. Students—eventually joined by many others—took to the streets in dozens of cities from April to June to demand greater freedom and other changes. Government leaders, after initial hesitation, used the army to suppress this unrest in early June (most visibly in Tiananmen Square), with substantial loss of life. China's elderly revolutionaries then reverted to more conservative economic, political, and cultural policies in an attempt to re-establish firm control. In 1992, however, Deng Xiaoping publicly criticized what he called the country's continuing "leftism" and sought to renew efforts at economic reform. Economic growth had been especially remarkable in southern China, which had developed the highest concentration of private-sector enterprise. Since the mid-1990s the CCP has worked to drastically accelerate market reforms in banking, taxes, trade, and investments. These reforms have continued apace, and the party has attempted to increase public support by conducting energetic anti-corruption campaigns that rely in part on high-profile prosecutions and occasional executions of high-level officials accused of corruption.

Jiang proved to be a capable successor to Deng. He replaced Zhao Ziyang as general secretary in 1989 after the Tiananmen incident and was also named chair of the Central Military Commission (1989) and president of the National People's Congress (1993). He combined a pragmatic, reform-minded economic policy with an insistence that the party maintain strong control over the government. Jiang consolidated his power after Deng's death in 1997 to become China's paramount ruler, but gradually relinquished his posts to Hu Jintao in 2002–04.

In education, the reformers gave top priority to training technical, scientific, and scholarly talent to world-class standards. This involved recreating a highly selective and elitist system of higher education, with admission based on competitive academic examination. Graduate study programmes were introduced, and thousands of Chinese were sent abroad for advanced study. Large numbers of foreign scholars were also used to help upgrade the educational system. Somewhat ironically, the value the reformers attached to making money had the unintended consequence of encouraging many brilliant people to forgo intellectual careers in favour of more lucrative undertakings. The range of cultural fare available was broadened greatly, and new limits were constantly tested. Few groups had suffered so bitterly as China's writers and artists, and policies since the 1980s have reflected the ongoing battle between cultural liberals and more orthodox officials.

True re-integration of the People's Republic of China into the international community can be said to date to 1971, when it replaced Taiwan (Republic of China; ROC) as China's representative to the United Nations. With that event, many countries that had formerly recognized the ROC established relations with the People's Republic. The normalization of diplomatic ties with the USA, which began in 1973, culminated in 1979.

China's foreign policy since the mid-1970s generally has reflected the country's preoccupation with domestic economic development and its desire to promote a peaceful and stable environment in which to achieve these domestic goals. Except for its disagreement with Vietnam over that country's invasion of Cambodia in 1978, China has by and large avoided disputes and encouraged the peaceful evolution of events in Asia. China adopted a policy of "one country, two systems" in order to provide a framework for the successful negotiation with Great Britain for the return of Hong Kong and adjacent territories in 1997 and with Portugal for the return of Macau in 1999; both were given special administrative status. Furthermore, China became an advocate of arms control and assumed a more constructive, less combative stance in many international organizations.

The suppression of the demonstrations in 1989 set back China's foreign relations. The USA, the European Community (European Union since 1993), and Japan imposed sanctions, though by 1992 China had largely regained its international standing with all but the USA. But by the mid-1990s both sides had taken steps toward improved relations, and China retained its most-favoured-nation status in US trade—subject to annual review by the US Congress until 2000, when Congress made the status permanent.

China gains Hong Kong

At midnight on June 30/July 1, 1997, the crown colony of Hong Kong officially reverted to Chinese sovereignty, ending 156 years of British rule. After a formal handover ceremony on

July 1, the colony became the Hong Kong Special Administrative Region (HKSAR) of the People's Republic of China.
The ceremony culminated a 13-year transition that had been
initiated by the Sino-British Joint Declaration on the Question
of Hong Kong, signed by the heads of the two governments in
December 1984.

The agreement stipulated that under Chinese rule the
HKSAR would enjoy a high degree of autonomy, except in
matters of foreign relations and defence, and that the social
and economic systems as well as the lifestyle in Hong Kong
would remain unchanged for 50 years after 1997. Many
observers, however, expressed considerable scepticism about
China's pledge to abide by the "one country, two systems"
plan outlined in the agreement. They feared that China would
drastically curtail the rights and freedoms of Hong Kong
residents.

Great Britain had acquired Hong Kong Island from China in
1842, when the Treaty of Nanjing was signed at the end of the
first Opium War (1839–42). Unsatisfied with incomplete
control of the harbour, the British forced China to cede
Kowloon Peninsula south of what is now Boundary Street
and Stonecutters Island less than 20 years later, after the
second Opium War (1856–60). By the Convention of 1898,
the New Territories together with 235 islands were leased to
Britain for 99 years from July 1, 1898. After the communists
took power in China in 1949, Hong Kong became a sanctuary
for hundreds of thousands of refugees fleeing communist rule.
In the following decades the Chinese government insisted that
the treaties giving Britain sovereignty over Hong Kong were
invalid.

Although in 1984 Britain and China agreed on the terms of
the handover of Hong Kong, Sino-British cooperation during
the transition period deteriorated after the appointment in

1992 of Chris Patten as Hong Kong's last colonial governor. Breaking with past practice, Patten initiated a series of political reforms designed to give the people of Hong Kong a greater voice in government via democratic elections to the Legislative Council (LegCo). China's crackdown on the student-led democracy movement in 1989 fed anxiety in Hong Kong regarding the handover and led to the political awakening of a previously quiescent population.

Beijing made efforts to stonewall Patten's reforms, which it condemned as a betrayal of London's earlier promises to manage the transition as an exercise in which Hong Kong had no voice of its own. When Hong Kong's Democratic Party, led by barrister Martin Lee, routed pro-Beijing politicians in the 1995 LegCo elections, Beijing denounced Patten and began a series of strong measures aimed at re-establishing its influence. On March 24, 1996, China's 150-member Preparatory Committee, which had been created to oversee the handover, voted to dissolve LegCo and install a provisional legislature after Hong Kong returned to Chinese sovereignty.

In December 1996 a China-backed special election committee selected the 60 members of the provisional body, just days after it had overwhelmingly elected 59-year-old shipping magnate Tung Chee-hwa the first chief executive of the HKSAR. Tung, whose tottering corporate empire had been salvaged by a large infusion of government-supplied capital in the 1980s, soon signalled his intention to roll back Patten's reforms, announcing in April 1997 proposals to restrict political groups and public protests after the handover. In essence, what Lee called the "Singaporization" of Hong Kong, i.e. the imposition of authoritarian control, had begun even before the Union Jack was lowered in the colony for the last time.

Pomp and pageantry marked the formal handover ceremony. In attendance were numerous dignitaries from around the world, including President Jiang Zemin and Premier Li Peng of China, British Prime Minister Tony Blair, Prince Charles, and US Secretary of State Madeleine Albright. Prince Charles, who gave a short speech in which he congratulated the colony on its political, economic, and social successes, told the people of Hong Kong, "We shall not forget you, and we shall watch with the closest interest as you embark on this new era of your remarkable history."

President Jiang, the first mainland Chinese head of state to visit Hong Kong since 1842, reassured residents that China would carry out the "one country, two systems" plan of local autonomy, which had been contrived principally by Chinese paramount leader Deng Xiaoping. Deng had passed away on February 19, just four and a half months before the handover he had hoped to witness. President Jiang hailed the "return of Hong Kong to the motherland" as a great historical event that presaged Taiwan's eventual reunification with mainland China.

On the morning of the handover, several thousand specially trained troops of the Chinese People's Liberation Army were deployed in Hong Kong as garrison forces symbolizing the reassertion of China's sovereignty. Chinese authorities did not attempt to suppress several rallies outside the LegCo building on June 30–July 1, even when Lee addressed thousands of demonstrators from a balcony after LegCo had officially been dissolved. The protests proceeded peacefully.

The USA, rather than Great Britain, was the principal Western power interested in holding China to its pledge of respecting Hong Kong's political and economic autonomy. Both US President Bill Clinton and Secretary of State Madeleine Albright informed Beijing that its behaviour with respect to Hong Kong would be considered a touchstone in Sino-American relations, and US congressional leaders reinforced this message. Chinese leaders, meanwhile, severely restricted the access of their own citizens to Hong Kong, whose per capita gross domestic product of more than US$24,000 was roughly 40 times that of China and whose habits of free expression and political participation were not ones that Beijing wished its own citizens to emulate.

China in the Twenty First Century

On October 1, 1999, President Jiang Zemin and leaders of the Communist Party of China (CCP) celebrated the 50th anniversary of communist rule in China with a massive military parade through downtown Beijing. Deng Xiaoping, who ruled China between 1977 and the late 1990s, had rescued the CPC by repudiating Maoism and initiating a period of rapid economic growth, social transformation, and relative political stability. Jiang, a lesser figure than Mao or Deng, saw himself as third in the line of communist dynasts. By 1999 the country over which he presided was vastly more wealthy and powerful than the China of 50 years before, but it still faced a daunting set of problems.

The run-up to the tenth anniversary of the June 4, 1989, Tiananmen Square incident revived memories of the student-led pro-democracy movement that preceded it. The authorities pre-empted any commemoration of the incident by closing Tiananmen Square for renovation, and the anniversary passed quietly inside China. In Hong Kong, a crowd of 70,000 gathered to mark the anniversary.

The turn of the new millennium was marked by stability. The triumvirate of President Jiang, National People's Congress Chairman Li Peng, and Premier Zhu Rongji remained in control. Waiting in the wings for Jiang's scheduled retirement in 2002 as CCP general secretary was the man Jiang had apparently tapped as his successor, Hu Jintao, a 56-year-old member of the Standing Committee of the Political Bureau who ranked fifth in China's power hierarchy. After graduating with a degree in engineering from Qinghua University, Beijing, in 1965, Hu had followed the career trajectory of a typical successful party apparatchik. He had served as provincial party secretary in Guizhou and then Tibet in the late 1980s. He became a member of the CCP Central Committee in 1982 and of the Political Bureau Standing Committee 10 years later.

China, nonetheless, was encumbered with a nineteenth-century ideology and a mid-twentieth-century industrial plant but was determined to become one of the world's leading powers in the twenty first century. There was good reason to suppose that such an ambitious goal lay within reach. By 2000, however, the Chinese government found itself struggling with a number of long-standing problems. Among them were managing the increasingly complex economy, curbing corruption, maintaining domestic order, keeping pressure on Taiwan, and preventing further deterioration in relations with the USA.

Political and religious intolerance continued. For years one locus of unrest had been Xinjiang province, where a militant minority among the 9 million Uigurs, a Turkic-speaking Muslim people, had resorted to force in their campaign to overturn Chinese rule. With sporadic violence continuing in Xinjiang, Beijing initiated a massive effort in 2000 to accelerate the economic development of China's vast western region, including not only Xinjiang but also Tibet, Sichuan province, and several other economically depressed provinces. The western development project shifted state investment priorities away from the prosperous coastal provinces to the lagging interior, where poverty remained a major problem.

Meanwhile, restrictions on Tibetan Buddhism and Tibetan culture were tightened. The Dalai Lama charged that Beijing was pursuing a policy of cultural genocide. In 2000, Beijing suffered a major humiliation with the spectacular flight to India of the young Karmapa Lama, who was received by the Dalai Lama and allowed to remain in India despite Chinese protests. Beijing had counted on the previously docile Karmapa Lama to help it implement its Tibetan policy.

Beijing's crackdown on Falun Gong, a spiritual movement that blended elements of Buddhism and Taoism with meditation and exercise, continued. Braving certain arrest, groups of Falun Gong followers periodically practised their faith in Beijing's Tiananmen Square and were quickly taken into custody. Human rights groups estimate that a few thousand Falun Gong members died in prison. The government also proscribed the activities of similar groups, including Zhong Gong, whose charismatic leader, Zhang Hongbao, sought political asylum in the American territory of Guam, from which Beijing sought unsuccessfully to extradite him on criminal charges.

Evangelical Christians and Roman Catholics loyal to the Vatican were other targets of repression. Beijing, reacting sourly to the Vatican's intention to canonize 130 Chinese Catholics martyred between 1648 and 1930, charged that most of them had been imperialist agents and deserved to die.

In sum, a rising tide of religious faith lapped at the foundations of communist rule as a significant portion of the population looked to a variety of homegrown and domesticated foreign religions for spiritual fulfilment.

Chinese authorities wrestled too with the question of how to control traffic on the information highway as the number of Internet users in China surged (from about 60 million in 2002, to more than 150 million at the beginning of 2007).

As China's population—growing by 10 million annually—surpassed the 1.3 billion mark, authorities reaffirmed the one-child policy, which, they claimed, had prevented at least 250 million births over the past 20 years. Widespread evasion of this policy persisted in rural areas, although not in the cities. The difficulty of policing the vast rural reaches of China was underscored by a campaign to stop the selling of rural women and girls into prostitution. Tens of thousands of such unfortunates were kidnapped annually or hoodwinked with false promises of urban factory employment. Thousands of boys were likewise kidnapped and coerced into becoming pickpockets under the harsh control of professional criminals.

According to its own experts, China had been slow to address the growing problem of AIDS and sexually transmitted diseases, which had been increasing at an annual rate of 30 per cent for a few years. Sex education was still very limited, and few resources had been invested in promoting safe sexual practices. Lax procedures for collecting and processing blood donations had contributed to the spread of AIDS, as had widespread addiction to opiates and needle-sharing among drug addicts.

The environment, long taken for granted, also became a critical issue in the new millennium. Both an immediate and a long-term threat to China's prosperity was the country's growing water crisis. China was endowed with only one-quarter of the world's per capita average of water resources, and the demands that agriculture, industry, and a growing urban population put on water supplies had already led to severe depletion of groundwater levels, conflicts between upstream and downstream consumers, and theft of water by desperate farmers. Perhaps a fifth or more of the country's water supply was wasted through inefficient irrigation systems, antiquated delivery systems, and the lack of realistic pricing systems for water resources.

China made some progress in curbing emissions of carbon dioxide, carbon monoxide, and nitrous oxide, even as it added new coal-burning power plants and other facilities at an unprecedented rate. The switchover from coal to natural gas and the ongoing conversion of Beijing's bus and taxi fleet from diesel fuel and gasoline to liquefied petroleum gas contributed to the amelioration of the air in the capital city. Beijing announced plans to address the severe water shortage affecting all of northern China by encouraging less water-intensive agricultural practices, shutting factories that polluted groundwater and surface water, and constructing new sewage-treatment plants.

The determination of national and municipal officials to improve Beijing's environment was motivated in part by the desire to show the city's best face to the world. An opportunity to do so arrived when the International Olympic Committee awarded the 2008 Summer Olympics to Beijing. Upon receiving the news, jubilant Communist Party and government leaders, as well as ordinary citizens, joined in a rare spontaneous mass celebration in Tiananmen Square. In this connection Beijing unveiled plans to invest US$34 billion in new stadiums, parks, transportation systems, housing, and pollution-abatement measures.

A new era in Chinese politics and economic development began in 2003. At the tenth National People's Congress in March, former Communist Party of China (CCP) general secretary Jiang Zemin passed the post of state presidency to CCP General Secretary Hu Jintao but retained the top military post until 2004, when Hu finally consolidated his power.

One of the key issues of Hu's presidency was the economy and in particular China's relationship with the USA and the World Trade Organization (WTO). Hu and US President George W. Bush met at international events in France and Thailand, and they exchanged views on north-eastern Asian security, the war on terrorism, bilateral trade, and the Taiwan issue. Much to the satisfaction of China, during both meetings in 2003 Bush upheld the "one-China" policy of the US government, although he also reiterated the US commitment to defend Taiwan. Amid Taiwan's call for a "defensive referendum" against the mainland's display of missiles, Prime Minister Wen's visit to the USA in December 2003 reconfirmed Bush's support of mainland China's position. Both governments seemed satisfied that bilateral political relations were as good as they had been in 30 years.

China–US trade relations were not so rosy, however. China received a frontal attack from the USA on its rigid foreign currency exchange rates, which the USA considered unfair terms of trade. Washington initially insisted that Beijing float its exchange rates but later softened its demands, its position weakened by the fact that China was now among the leading creditors from whom the US Treasury and banks were heavily borrowing. There were some indications that not all American businesses supported an inflexible US trade policy toward China. In accordance with WTO regulations, China removed barriers against American cars and car parts; imports of 15,000 cars and trucks as well as more than US$1 billion in parts from Big-Three American automakers were to be allowed.

China's entry into the world market had powerful effects. A quarter-century of economic reform since Deng's Four Modernizations had produced a sizable middle class. A 2004 report of the Chinese Academy of Social Sciences estimated that 19 per cent of the population had entered the middle-level income stratum, with family income between 150,000 and 300,000 yuan (about US$18,000 to US$36,000). This group had steadily increased by 1 per cent annually in recent years. Those who first entered the stratum included business people in science and technology-oriented sectors; professionals in legal, financial, security, insurance, and accounting services; managers and executives in multinational corporations; and successful private businessmen. The Ministry of Labour and Social Security launched a new plan to train 500,000 "blue-collar high-tech experts" in order to meet the rising demand for labour in the manufacturing and service sectors. This group would also join the middle class in the near future.

Nonetheless, the labour market continued to face challenges from unemployment and the withering of the state economic sector. Reforms in the state sector continued to create surplus workers. The registered unemployment rate increased from 3.1 per cent in 1998 to 4.2 per cent in 2003. Among the 27.8 million workers laid off during this period, only 18.5 million had found new jobs. Under WTO regulations, the import of cheaper agricultural products would further reduce farmers' income and job opportunities in rural areas. It was estimated that there were 150 million rural workers who did not have full-time jobs, and these people continued to migrate to the cities and the south, where the economy was better.

In 2006 another reshuffling of leadership in China saw Chen Liangyu removed from the office of Shanghai party secretary and from the Politburo for corruption. Other high-ranking officials lost their jobs as a result and the vacancies were filled by former functionaries of President Hu Jintao. The subsequent policy debate in Beijing evolved from a year-long critique of various reform programmes into a rethinking of the reform directions and finally, at the National People's Congress in March, into an ideological debate over socialism and capitalism.

One group pointed to the social problems that the reforms had brought, such as social injustice, official corruption, income disparity, and social unrest, and argued that the reforms had exhausted public resources without achieving sustainable development. For example, 60 per cent of recent land deals were illegal, according to one government report. The other group argued that such problems would phase out as the reforms continued. Such debate derailed the passage of what would have been a landmark bill protecting private-property rights, although leaders expressed their commitment to the reforms.

Two political ideas started to emerge: intra-party democratization and increasing independence of the judicial system. For the first time in history, three scholars were appointed to high posts in the Supreme People's Procuratorate. Party scholars and advisers started to entertain certain democratic ideas, which included competitive elections for party positions and nomination privileges to be expanded to the People's Congress and the People's Political Consultative Conference. As a pilot project, competitive elections of party secretaries had already been held at the village and township levels. Sichuan province dispatched six senior officials to the USA to job-shadow their American counterparts for eight months.

Changes also took place in other areas. After an explosion at a chemical plant in north-eastern China in 2005 that spilled toxic matter into the Songhua River and contaminated the drinking water of millions of people, the government earmarked US$3.3 billion to improve water quality by 2010. China's State Environmental Protection Administration revealed that the state was to spend US$175 billion in environmental protection from 2006 to 2010. This was the first serious response to environmental problems resulting from rapid industrialization such as deforestation, land degradation, and pollution.

China introduced 17 new laws and regulations concerning trademarks, copyrights, patents, and customs. In the first half of 2006, the National Bureau of Customs handled 1,076 cases of intellectual property rights violations. In Chinese courts the international brands LVMH Moët Hennessy – Louis Vuitton, Chanel, Burberry, Gucci, Prada, and Adidas won trademark-infringement lawsuits. Luxury goods company LVMH won a lawsuit against its fellow French business Carrefour in a Beijing court over counterfeiting. When the government tightened regulations on karaoke bars, however, many questioned whether what was being protected was intellectual property rights or monopoly.

The year 2006 also saw the completion of the construction of the Three Gorges Dam, the defeat of a bill that would have punished selective abortion based on the foetus's sex, establishment of trade unions in Wal-Mart stores in China when the retail giant planned to hire 150,000 additional staff, and the announcement that China had already exceeded UNICEF's goal for 2015 for improvement of children's health.

China's financial reform had brought in significant international investment. In 2005 alone the China Banking Regulatory Commission approved 19 foreign investments, in stakes as high as 20 per cent of 16 Chinese local banks. The Bank of China gave up control of 16.85 per cent of its stocks to four foreign banks for US$3 billion, in addition to US$11.2 billion worth of stocks sold on the Hong Kong market. Australia and New Zealand Banking Group invested US$110 million in Tianjin City Commercial Bank as a way to get access to the Chinese financial market. British petroleum company BP paid US$44 million in exchange for a 20 per cent stake in China's main jet-fuel importer, China Aviation Oil. SEB of France acquired 61 per cent of Zhejiang Supor Cookware, the biggest Chinese producer of kitchen appliances. South Korea's Telecom bought US$1 billion in bonds, a 6.7 per cent stake, in China Unicom to tap the world's largest wireless market.

The target of Morgan Stanley and Goldman Sachs Group in 2006 was to double their spending on China's hot real estate to

US$7 billion, and in June Citigroup said it wanted to increase its investment in real estate in China to US$800 million over three years. International Hotel Group opened four new hotels in a month, increasing its ownership to 57 hotels in China. It planned to build 125 hotels by the 2008 Beijing Olympics.

Such unprecedented openness of the financial sector received widespread criticism in China as a part of the debate between socialism and capitalism, and arguments sometimes took on a nationalist tinge. The trend worried many Chinese—especially after Goldman Sachs bought a 60.72 per cent stake in a major Chinese company—because foreigners seemed to be buying Chinese assets on the cheap, profiting at the expense of domestic labour and lessening government control of strategic national resources. The Chinese regulatory agency defended its handling of foreign investments by pointing to its stringent rules of entry and lower costs of financial sector restructuring. Another US$350 million quota was granted to Morgan Stanley and Goldman Sachs.

Yet there were also consequences. Because China was by 2006 now consuming 8 per cent of the world's energy, the security of energy resources for economic production continued to be a focal point of Beijing's diplomacy. After his US visit that year, President Hu made stops in Saudi Arabia, Morocco, Nigeria, and Kenya. Premier Wen Jiabao later travelled to seven other African countries, including Angola, the continent's second largest oil producer. The China National Offshore Oil Corporation took a 45 per cent stake in the Nigerian Oil Mining License (OML) 130 oil field near the Niger Delta in Nigeria.

Hu signed an agreement with visiting Russian President Vladimir Putin to build gas pipelines from Russia to China, and China National Petroleum Corporation, the largest Chinese oil company, bought a US$500 million stake in the newly listed Russian petroleum giant Rosneft. Russian oil exports to China in 2006 nearly doubled from the previous year.

China also expressed interest in Iran's oil and Australia's uranium and had started building a 900-km (560-mile) oil pipeline through Myanmar (Burma). As China and India, the world's two most populous countries, continued their rapid development, a new word, *Chindia*, drew the world's attention to their strategic economic partnership.

Since the Deng era, the Chinese leadership and ordinary people alike had been proclaiming that their nation was destined to be a major power, one whose economic and political reach would extend into every corner of the world. In the early years of the twenty first century, that hope seemed to be very well founded, and China's influence continues to grow in unexpected quarters, from the deserts of northern Africa to the boardrooms of London and New York.

PART 3

THE NATION TODAY

4

GOVERNMENT AND SOCIETY

The Chinese Government Today

Despite its size, the People's Republic of China is organized along unitary rather than federal principles. Both the government and the CCP operate "from the top down", arrogating to the "Centre" all powers that are not explicitly delegated to lower levels. To run the country, the government and the CCP have established roughly parallel national bureaucracies extending from Beijing down to local levels.

These bureaucracies are assisted by various "mass organizations" (e.g. trade unions, a youth league, women's associations, and writers' and other professional associations) that encompass key sectors of the population. These organizations, with their extremely large memberships, have generally served as transmission lines for communicating and uniformly implementing policies affecting their members. No voluntary associations are permitted to function that are wholly independent of the CCP and government leadership.

The CCP and government bureaucracies themselves are organized along territorial and functional lines. The territorial organization is based on a number of administrative divisions, with both a CCP committee and a "people's government" in charge of each. These territorial divisions include the national level in Beijing (the Centre), 33 provincial-level units (four directly administered cities, five autonomous regions, the Hong Kong and Macau Special Administrative Regions, and 22 provinces, excluding Taiwan), some 330 prefectural bodies, more than 2,850 county-level entities, and numerous cities, towns, and townships. Some larger cities are themselves divided into urban wards and counties. This territorial basis of organization is intended to coordinate and lend coherence to the myriad policies from the Centre that may affect any given locale.

The functionally-based political organization is led on the government side by ministries and commissions under the State Council and on the CCP side by Central Committee departments. These central-level functional bodies sit atop hierarchies of subordinate units that have responsibility for the sector or issue area under concern. Subordinate functional units typically are attached to each of the territorial bodies.

This complex structure is designed to coordinate national policy (such as that toward the metallurgical industry), assure some coordination of policy on a territorial basis, and enable the CCP to keep control over the government at all levels of the national hierarchy. One unintended result of this organizational approach is that China employs more than 10 million officials, more than the population of many of the world's countries.

There are tensions among these different goals, and thus a great deal of shifting has occurred since 1949. During the early and mid-1950s the government's functional ministries and commissions at the Centre were especially powerful. The Great

Leap Forward, starting in 1958, shifted authority toward the provincial- and lower-level territorial CCP bodies. During the Cultural Revolution, starting in 1966, much of the political system became so disrupted that the People's Liberation Army (PLA) was called in and assumed control. When the PLA fell under a political cloud, the situation became remarkably fluid and confused for much of the 1970s.

Since then the general thrust has been toward less detailed CCP supervision of the government and greater decentralization of government authority where possible. But the division of authority between CCP and government and between territorial and functional bodies has remained in a state of flux, as demonstrated by a trend again toward centralization at the end of the 1980s and subsequent efforts toward decentralization since the late 1990s. The Chinese communist political system still has not become institutionalized enough for the distribution of power among important bodies to be fixed and predictable.

Constitutional Framework

The fourth constitution of the People's Republic of China was adopted in 1982. It vests all national legislative power in the hands of the National People's Congress and its Standing Committee. The State Council and its Standing Committee, by contrast, are made responsible for executing rather than enacting the laws. This basic division of power is also specified for each of the territorial divisions (province, county, etc.), with the proviso in each instance that the latitude available to authorities is limited to that specified by law.

All citizens 18 years of age and older who have not been deprived of their political rights are permitted to vote, and direct popular suffrage is used to choose People's Congress members up to the county level. Above the counties, delegates at each level elect those who will serve at the People's Congress of the next higher level. Were this constitution an accurate reflection of the real workings of the system, the People's Congresses and their various committees would be critical organs in the Chinese political system. In reality, though, they are not.

Actual decision-making authority in China resides in the state's executive organs and in the CCP. At the national level the top government executive organ is the State Council, led by the premier. The constitution permits the appointment of vice-premiers, a secretary-general, and an unspecified number of councillors of state and heads of ministries and commissions. The premier, vice-premiers, state councillors, and secretary-general meet regularly as the Standing Committee, in which the premier has the final decision-making power. This Standing Committee of the State Council exercises major day-to-day decision-making authority, and its decisions de facto have the force of law.

While it is not so stipulated in the constitution, each vice-premier and councillor assumes responsibility for the work of one or more given sectors or issues, such as education, energy policy, or foreign affairs. The leader concerned then remains in contact with the ministries and the commissions of the State Council that implement policy in that area. This division of responsibility permits a relatively small body such as the Standing Committee of the State Council (consisting of fewer than 20 people) to monitor and guide the work of a vast array of major bureaucratic entities. When necessary, of course, the Standing Committee may call directly on additional expertise in its deliberations. The National People's Congress meets roughly annually and does little more than ratify the decisions already made by the State Council.

Parallel to the State Council system is the central leadership of the CCP. The distribution of power among the various organs at the top of the CCP—the Standing Committee of the Political Bureau (Politburo), the Political Bureau itself, and the Secretariat—has varied a great deal, and from 1966 until the late 1970s the Secretariat did not function at all. There is in any case a partial overlap of membership among these organs and between these top CCP bodies and the Standing Committee of the State Council. In addition, formally retired elder members of the party have often exercised decisive influence on CCP decision-making.

Role of the CCP

According to the CCP constitution of 1982, the National Party Congress is the highest decision-making body. Because the Party Congress typically convenes only once in five years, the Central Committee is empowered to act when the Congress is not in session. Further, the Political Bureau can act in the name of the Central Committee when the latter is not in session, and the Standing Committee of the Political Bureau guides the work of the Political Bureau. The Secretariat is charged with the daily work of the Central Committee and the Political Bureau. The general secretary of the party presides over the Secretariat and also is responsible for convening the meetings of the Political Bureau and its Standing Committee. The Secretariat works when necessary through several departments (the department for organization, for example, or the department for propaganda) under the Central Committee.

Until 1982 the CCP had a chairmanship that was unique among ruling communist parties. Mao Zedong held this office until his death in 1976, and Hua Guofeng was chairman until his removal from office in 1981. Hu Yaobang then served as party chairman until the post was abolished in 1982. The decision to redefine the position was part of the effort to reduce the chances of any one leader again rising to a position above the party, as Mao had done. China's government still has a chairmanship, but the office has only limited power and is largely ceremonial.

The division of power among the leading CCP organs and between them and the State Council is constantly shifting. The Standing Committee of the Political Bureau and the Political Bureau as a whole have the authority to decide on any issue they wish to take up. The Secretariat has also at times played an extremely powerful and active role, meeting more frequently than either the Political Bureau or its Standing Committee and making many important decisions on its own authority. Similarly, the State Council has made many important decisions, but its power is always exercised at the pleasure of the CCP leadership.

Since the late 1970s China has taken a number of initiatives to move toward a more institutionalized system in which the office basically determines the power of its incumbent rather than vice versa, as has often been the case. Thus, for example, the CCP and state constitutions adopted in 1982 (and subsequently amended somewhat) for the first time stipulated a number of positions that confer membership status on the Standing Committee of the Political Bureau. These positions are the head of the Party Military Affairs Commission, the general secretary of the CCP, the head of the Central Advisory Committee, and the head of the Central Discipline Commission. In addition, for the first time under the stipulations of the constitution, limits of two consecutive terms were placed on the government offices of premier, vice-premier, and state councillor. There were no similar constitutional restrictions on the tenure of incumbents to top CCP positions.

In theory, the CCP sets major policy directions and broadly supervises the implementation of policy to ensure that its will is not thwarted by the state and military bureaucracies. The CCP also assumes major responsibility for instilling proper values in the populace. The government, according to the theory, is responsible for carrying out CCP policy, making the necessary decisions as matters arise. Of course, this clear division of labour quickly becomes blurred for a number of reasons. For example, only since the late 1970s has a concerted effort been made to appoint different people to the key executive positions in the CCP and the government. Prior to that time, the same individual would head both the CCP committee and the government body in charge of any given area. At the highest levels the premier of the government and the chairman of the party continue to sit on the CCP Political Bureau.

More fundamentally, it is often impossible to clearly separate policy formation and implementation in a huge, complex set of organizations charged with a multiplicity of tasks. The tendency has been for CCP cadres to become increasingly involved in day-to-day operations of the government, until some major initiative was taken by the top national leadership to reverse the trend. While the distinction between the CCP and the government is of considerable significance, therefore, the ruling structure in China can also be viewed from the functional point of view mentioned above. The careers of individual officials may shift among posts in both the CCP and the government, but for most officials all posts are held within one area of concern, such as economics, organization or personnel, security, propaganda, or culture.

Administration

A hierarchy of organization and personnel has been embedded in virtually all CCP and government bodies. Even on the government side, all officials in these personnel departments are members of the CCP, and they follow rules and regulations that are not subject to control by the particular bodies of which they are formally a part. This system has been used to assure higher-level CCP control over the appointments to all key positions in the CCP, government, and other major organizations (enterprises, universities, etc.).

For much of the period between 1958 and 1978, these personnel departments applied primarily political criteria in making appointments. They systematically discriminated against intellectuals, specialists, and those with any ties or prior experience abroad. From 1978 to 1989, however, official policy was largely the reverse, with ties abroad being valued because of China's stress on "opening the door" to the international community. A good education became an important asset in promoting careers, while a history of political activism counted for less or could even hinder upward mobility. A partial reversion to pre-1978 criteria was decreed in 1989, followed by periods of shifting between the two policies.

Two important initiatives have been taken to reduce the scope of the personnel bureaucracies. First, during 1984 the leaders of various CCP and government bodies acquired far greater power to appoint their own staffs and to promote from among their staffs on their own initiative. The leaders themselves still must be appointed via the personnel system, but most others are no longer fully subject to those dictates. Second, a free labour market has been encouraged for intellectuals and individuals with specialized skills, a policy that could further reduce the power of the personnel bodies.

The legal apparatus that existed before the changes made during the Cultural Revolution was resurrected in 1980. The State Council again has a Ministry of Justice, and procuratorial organs and a court system were re-established. The legal framework for this system was provided through the adoption of various laws and legal codes. One significant difference was that for the first time the law provided that there should be no discrimination among defendants based on their class origin. China also re-established a system of lawyers.

The actual functioning of this legal apparatus, however, has continued to be adversely affected by a shortage of qualified personnel and by deeply ingrained perspectives that do not accord the law priority over the desires of political leaders. Thus, for example, when the top CCP leadership ordered a severe crackdown on criminal activity in 1983, thousands were arrested and executed without fully meeting the requirements of the newly passed law on criminal procedures. That law was subsequently amended to conform more closely with the actual practices adopted during the crackdown. Subsequently, similar campaigns have been mounted against criminal activity.

The People's Liberation Army (PLA) is the unified organization of all Chinese land, sea, and air forces. The history of the PLA is officially traced to the Nanchang Uprising of August 1, 1927, which is celebrated annually as PLA Day. The PLA is the world's largest military force, with an estimated 2.25 million members. Military service is compulsory for all men at the age of 18; women may register for duty in the medical, veterinary, and other technical services. Demobilized servicemen are carried in a ready reserve, which is reinforced by a standby reserve of veterans and by the militia.

The PLA is formally under the command of the Central Military Commission of the CCP; there is also an identical commission in the government, but it has no clear independent functions. The CCP commission is far more powerful than the Ministry of National Defence, which operates under the State Council, and it assures continuing CCP control over the armed forces. The political leadership has made a concerted effort to create a professional military force restricted to national defence and to the provision of assistance in domestic economic construction and emergency relief. This conception of the role of the PLA requires the promotion of specialized officers who can understand modern weaponry and handle combined arms operations. Troops around the country are stationed in seven military regions and more than 20 military districts. Despite the drive to modernize the PLA, limited military budgets and other constraints have caused the sophistication of conventional military armaments and of logistics and command-and-control systems to lag behind that of other major military powers.

The role of the Public Security forces of China began to change in the late 1970s. The definition and designation of what poses a threat to security, for example, were narrowed, and there was a decline in the scope of activities of the security forces. The practice of political suppression, the victims of which once numbered in the tens of millions, was reduced, and in the late 1970s a large (but unknown) number of people were released from labour or other camps run by the Public Security forces. Also, during the 1980s the "open door" policy toward the outside world led to the adoption of a more relaxed attitude by the Public Security forces regarding their efforts to control and restrict the activities of foreigners in China. From 1990, however, the trend was generally toward a stricter policy and tighter controls.

Specific organizational and policy initiatives have also affected the role of the Public Security forces. The trend toward creating a body of codified law and toward establishing a legal system that operates according to that law has in itself reduced the arbitrary power once exercised by the Public Security system. (By the 1970s that system had effectively acquired the power to arrest, convict, sentence, and detain any individual without interference from any other "outside" body.) The Public Security Ministry also has relinquished administrative control over counter-espionage and economic crimes, which was transferred to a Ministry of State Security.

Society in Transformation

China is arguably the oldest civilization on Earth, and its people are keenly aware of ancestral customs and rituals, honouring Confucian ideals of respect for one's ancestors and of obligations to others—and to the State. Even so, sweeping transformations have marked the nation since the end of the Mao Zedong era. In the three decades since, China has witnessed a dramatic growth in its population, rapid urbanization, the transition from planning to market, and integration into the global economy. Former premier Deng Xiaoping ushered in great confusion even as he ushered in a market revolution by proclaiming that socialism and capitalism need not be antagonistic or mutually exclusive: "Whether a cat is black or white makes no difference," he famously said. "As long as it catches mice, it is a good cat." To those raised on Maoist orthodoxy, such a statement was a source of great dissonance; to this day, some have resisted becoming part of the new, quasi-capitalist China, even if home-grown entrepreneurs and the nouveau riche have adopted it wholeheartedly.

The new China is much different from the old. Many of its cities, notably Shanghai and Beijing, are centres of tremendous wealth and all that comes with it, from luxury automobiles to fashion and expensive, exclusive residential developments. Those cities are vastly wealthier than the countryside, which has been overlooked in many development schemes; one result is that the cities are increasingly flooded with country people, millions of whom have left farms and villages in search of non-agricultural work. In a supposedly classless society, the gulf between rich and poor constantly widens, just as other markers of social discontinuity are increasingly common.

One measure, for instance, is the surprising arrival of obesity on the Chinese scene. Obesity was once rare in China, a consequence of factors such as food shortages, hard work, regular exercise, and the general absence of private automobiles; in the first years of the twenty first century, however, a fifth of the world's billion overweight or obese people were Chinese: data from a nationwide health survey undertaken in 2002 showed that 14.7% of Chinese were overweight and another 2.6% were obese, and that associated health problems such as high blood pressure, heart disease, and diabetes were on the rise. Of particular concern was the prevalence of weight problems among children aged 7–18; the number of overweight children increased twenty-eight times and obesity increased four times between 1985 and 2000. Another mark of this curious trend is the emergence of "fat farms" that cater to children, as well as the increasing presence of books and products related to dieting.

Some of this transformation can be attributed to a slow decline in physical fitness activities, once a hallmark of daily life in China. Some can be attributed to dietary changes; as the economy improves and wealth grows, prepared foods high in fats and salt have become more available and more popular, while more meat and dairy products and fewer vegetables are consumed. Some can even be attributed to the so-called little emperor phenomenon, a result of the Chinese government's declaration in 1979 of the "one child policy". Meant to curb a rapidly growing population, the policy has had an unintended consequence: a single child is now cared for, typically, by parents and grandparents, becoming the centre of a small constellation that seems at odds with the communitarian, anti-individualistic, and self-sacrificing ideals of the Mao era.

In modern China, as family members increasingly disperse to distant cities and towns to find work, the nuclear family more and more resembles the Western one of parents and perhaps a grandparent or two, with other relatives seen every year or so. The Chinese nuclear family may not even include both parents, because the incidence of divorce has soared since the strict state laws regulating marriage were relaxed in 1978. (The divorce rate, for example, jumped by nearly 300,000 between 2003 and 2004, when 1.6 million Chinese couples divorced.) The government reports that irreconcilable personality differences, extramarital affairs, and financial problems are the most frequent causes of divorce, with 70 per cent of divorce suits initiated by women. The divorce rate is highest in large cities such as Shanghai and Guangzhou, although it is also high in the relatively rural provinces of Xinjiang and Liaoning.

The coming years will prove to be challenging for China's people and rulers as still more transformations occur, the result of global and local changes wrought by climate change, resource scarcity, the evolving economy, an aging population, and other factors.

5

THE ECONOMY

General Considerations

Despite China's size, the wealth of its resources, and the fact that about one-fifth of the world's population lives within its borders, its role in the world economy until late in the twentieth century was relatively small. However, since the late 1970s China has dramatically increased its interaction with the international economy, and has become a dominant figure in world trade. Both China's foreign trade and its gross national product (GNP) have experienced sustained and rapid growth, especially since foreign-owned firms began using China as an export platform for goods manufactured there.

The Chinese economy thus has been in a state of transition since the late 1970s as the country has moved away from a Soviet-type economic system. Agriculture has been decollectivized, the non-agricultural private sector has grown rapidly, and government priorities have shifted toward high-tech and light, rather than heavy, industries. Nevertheless, key bottlenecks have continued to constrain growth. Available energy has not been sufficient to run all of the country's installed industrial capacity, the transport system has remained inadequate to move sufficient quantities of such critical commodities as coal, and the communications system has not been able to meet the needs of a centrally planned economy of China's size and complexity.

China's underdeveloped transport system—combined with important differences in the availability of natural and human resources and in industrial infrastructure—has produced significant variations in the regional economies of China. The three wealthiest regions are along the south-east coast, centred on the Pearl (Zhu) River delta; along the east coast, centred on the lower Yangtze River; and near the Bo Hai (Gulf of Zhili), in the Beijing-Tianjin-Liaoning region. It is the rapid development of these areas that is having the most significant effect on the Asian regional economy as a whole, and Chinese government policy is designed to remove the obstacles to accelerated growth in these wealthier regions. At the same time, a major priority of the government is the economic development of the interior of the country to help it catch up with the more prosperous coastal regions.

China is the world's largest producer of rice and is among the principal sources of wheat, corn (maize), tobacco, soybeans, peanuts (groundnuts), and cotton. The country is one of the world's largest producers of a number of industrial and mineral products (including cotton cloth, tungsten, and antimony), and is an important producer of cotton yarn, coal, crude oil, and a number of other products. Its mineral resources are probably among the richest in the world but are only partially developed. China has acquired some highly sophisticated production facilities through foreign investment and joint ventures with foreign partners. The technological level and quality standards of many of its industries have improved rapidly in recent times.

The labour force and the pricing system are still areas of concern. Underemployment is common in both urban and rural areas, and there is a strong fear of the disruptive effects that widespread unemployment could cause. The prices of some key commodities, especially of industrial raw materials and major industrial products, are still determined by the state, although the proportion of these commodities under state control continues to decline. A major exception is energy, which the government continues to regulate.

China's increasing contact with the international economy and its growing use of market forces to govern the domestic allocation of goods have exacerbated this problem. Over the years, large subsidies were built into the price structure, and these subsidies grew substantially from the late 1970s to the early 1990s, when subsidies began to be eliminated. A significant factor was China's acceptance into the WTO in 2001, which carried with it stipulations about further economic liberalization and government deregulation.

China has been a socialist country since 1949 and, for nearly all of that time, the government has played a major role in the economy. In the industrial sector, for example, the state long owned outright nearly all of the firms producing China's manufacturing output. The proportion of overall industrial capacity controlled by the government has gradually declined, although heavy industries have remained largely state-owned. In the urban sector the government has set the prices for key commodities, determined the level and general distribution of investment funds, prescribed output targets for major enterprises and branches, allocated energy resources, set wage levels and employment targets, run the wholesale and retail networks, and controlled financial policy and the banking system. The foreign trade system became a government monopoly in the early 1950s. In the countryside from the mid-1950s, the government prescribed cropping patterns, set the level of prices, and fixed output targets for all major crops.

By the early twenty first century, however, much of this system was in the process of changing, as the role of the central government in managing the economy was reduced and the role of both private initiative and market forces increased. Nevertheless, the government continues to play a dominant role in the urban economy, and its policies on such issues as agricultural procurement still exert a major influence on performance in the rural sector.

The effective exercise of control over the economy requires an army of bureaucrats and a highly complicated chain of command, stretching from the top down to the level of individual enterprise. The CCP reserves the right to make broad decisions on economic priorities and policies, but the government apparatus headed by the State Council assumes the major burden of running the economy. The State Planning Commission and the Ministry of Finance are also concerned with the functioning of virtually the entire economy.

The entire planning process involves considerable consultation and negotiation. The main advantage of including a project in an annual plan is that the raw materials, labour, financial resources, and markets are guaranteed by directives that have the force of law. In fact, however, a great deal of economic activity goes on outside the scope of the detailed plan, and the tendency has been for the plan to become narrower rather than broader in scope.

There are three types of economic activity in China: those stipulated by mandatory planning, those done according to indicative planning (in which central planning of economic outcomes is indirectly implemented), and those governed by market forces. The second and third categories have grown at the expense of the first, but goods of national importance and almost all large-scale construction have remained under the mandatory planning system. The market economy generally involves small-scale or highly perishable items that circulate within local market areas only. Almost every year brings additional changes in the lists of goods that fall under each of the three categories.

Operational supervision over economic projects has devolved primarily to provincial, municipal, and county governments. In addition, enterprises themselves are gaining increased independence in a range of activities. Overall, therefore, the Chinese industrial system contains a complex mixture of relationships. In general, the State Council exercises relatively tight control over resources deemed to be of core importance for the performance of the entire economy. Less important aspects of the system are devolved to lower levels for detailed decisions and management. In all spheres, moreover, the need to coordinate units that are in different bureaucratic hierarchies produces a great deal of informal bargaining and consensus building.

Although the state controlled agriculture in the 1950s and 1960s, rapid changes were made in the system from the late 1970s. The major vehicles for dictating state priorities—the people's communes and their subordinate teams and brigades—have been either abolished or vastly weakened. Peasant incentives have been raised both by price increases for state-purchased agricultural products and by permission to sell excess production on a free market. Greater freedom is permitted in the choice of what crops to grow, and peasants are allowed to contract for land that they will work, rather than simply working most of the land collectively. The system of procurement quotas (fixed in the form of contracts) is being phased out, although the state can still buy farm products and control surpluses in order to affect market conditions.

Economic Policies since the 1950s

The First Five-Year Plan (1953–57) emphasized rapid industrial development, partly at the expense of other sectors of the economy. The bulk of the state's investment was channelled into the industrial sector, while agriculture, which occupied more than four-fifths of the economically active population, was forced to rely on its own meagre capital resources for a substantial part of its fund requirements. Within industry, iron and steel, electric power, coal, heavy engineering, building materials, and basic chemicals were given first priority; in accordance with Soviet practice, the aim was to construct large, sophisticated, and highly capital-intensive plants. A great many of the new plants were built with Soviet technical and financial assistance, and heavy industry grew rapidly.

As the Second Five-Year Plan—which resembled its predecessor—got under way in 1958, the policy of the Great Leap Forward was announced. In agriculture this involved forming communes, abolishing private plots, and increasing output through greater cooperation and greater physical effort. In industry the construction of large plants was to continue, but it was to be supplemented by a huge drive to develop small industry, making use of a large number of small, simple, locally built and locally run plants. A spectacular drop in agricultural production ensued. Meanwhile, the indiscriminate backyard production drive failed to achieve the desired effects and yielded large quantities of expensively produced substandard goods. These difficulties were aggravated when Soviet aid and technicians were withdrawn. By late 1960 the country faced an economic crisis of the first order.

The authorities responded with a complete about-turn in policy. Private plots were restored, the size of the communes was reduced, and greater independence was given to the production team. There was also a mass transfer of unemployed industrial workers to the countryside, and industrial investment was temporarily slashed in order to free up resources for farm production. The agricultural situation improved immediately, and by 1963 some resources were being redirected to the capital goods industry.

The Great Proletarian Cultural Revolution began in 1966 but, unlike the Great Leap, it did not have an explicit economic philosophy. Nevertheless, industrial production was badly affected by the ensuing decade of confusion and strife, which also left some difficult legacies for the Chinese economy. In industry, wages were frozen and bonuses cancelled. Combined with the policies of employing more workers than necessary to soak up unemployment and of never firing workers once hired, this action essentially eliminated incentives to work hard. In addition, technicians and many managers lost their authority and could not play an effective role in production in the wake of the movement. Overall output continued to grow, but capital-to-output ratios declined. In agriculture, per capita output in 1977 was no higher than in 1957.

Rural economic reform initiated after Mao Zedong's death began with major price increases for agricultural products in 1979. By 1981 the emphasis had shifted to breaking up collectively tilled fields into land that was contracted out to private families to work. During that time the size of private plots (land actually owned by individuals) was increased, and most restrictions on selling agricultural products in free markets were lifted.

In 1984 much longer-term contracts for land were encouraged (generally 15 years or more), and the concentration of land through subleasing of parcels was made legal. In 1985 the government announced that it would dismantle the system of planned procurements with state-allocated production quotas in agriculture. Peasants who had stopped working the land were encouraged to find private employment in the countryside or in small towns. They did not obtain permission to move to major cities, however.

The basic thrusts of urban economic reform were toward integrating China more fully with the international economy; making enterprises responsible for their profits and losses; reducing the state's role in directing, as opposed to guiding, the allocation of resources; shifting investment away from the metallurgical and machine-building industries and toward light and high-technology industries, while retaining an emphasis on resolving the energy, transportation, and communications bottlenecks; creating material incentives for individual effort and a consumer ethos to spur people to work harder; rationalizing the pricing structure; and putting individuals into jobs for which they have specialized training, skills, or talents. At the same time, the state has permitted a private sector to develop and has allowed it to compete with state firms in a number of service areas and, increasingly, in such larger-scale operations as construction.

A number of related measures were established to enhance the incentives for enterprise managers to increase the efficiency of their firms. Replacement of the profit-remission system with tax and contracting systems was designed to reward managers by permitting firms to retain a significant portion of increases in production. Managerial authority within firms was strengthened, and bonuses were restored and allowed to grow to substantial proportions. Managers were also given enhanced authority to hire, fire, and promote workers.

Reductions in central government planning were accompanied by permission for enterprises to buy and sell surplus goods on essentially a free-market basis, and the prices thus obtained often were far higher than for goods produced to meet plan quotas. The state plan was also used to redirect some resources into the light industrial sector. The state, for example, has given priority in energy consumption to some light industrial enterprises that produce high-quality goods.

The reduction in the scope of mandatory planning is based on the assumption that market forces can more efficiently allocate many resources. This assumption in turn requires a rational pricing system that takes into account any and all extant technologies and scarcities. Because extensive subsidies were built into the economic system, however, price reform became an extremely sensitive issue. The fear of inflation also served as a constraint on price reform. Nevertheless, the fact that products produced in excess of amounts targeted in the plan can be sold, in most cases, at essentially free-market prices has created a two-tiered price system that is designed to wean the economy from the administratively fixed prices of an earlier era.

Efforts to create a freer labour market are also part of the overall emphasis on achieving greater efficiency. As with price reform, tampering with a system that keeps many citizens living more comfortably and securely than would an economically more rational system risks serious repercussions in relations with the public. Changes have proceeded slowly in this sensitive area.

A decision was made in 1978 to permit direct foreign investment in several small "special economic zones" along the coast. These zones were later increased to 14 coastal cities and three coastal regions. All these places provided favoured tax treatment and other advantages for the foreign investor.

Laws on contracts, patents, and other matters of concern to foreign businesses were also passed in an effort to attract international capital to aid China's development. The largely bureaucratic nature of China's economy, however, has posed inherent problems for foreign firms that want to operate in the Chinese environment, and China gradually has had to add more incentives to attract foreign capital.

The changes in China's economic thinking and strategy since 1978 have been so great—with the potential repercussions for important vested interests so strong—that actual practice inevitably has lagged considerably behind declared policy. Notable during this period have been the swings in economic policy between an emphasis on market-oriented reforms and a return to at least partial reliance on centralized planning.

Agriculture

As a result of topographic and climatic features, the area suitable for cultivation is small: only about 10 per cent of China's total land area. Of this, slightly more than half is unirrigated, and the remainder is divided roughly equally between paddy fields and irrigated areas; good progress has been made in improving water conservancy. In addition, the quality of the soil in cultivated regions varies around the country, and environmental problems such as floods, drought, and erosion pose serious threats in many areas.

Nevertheless, about two-thirds of the population lives in the countryside, and until the 1980s a large proportion of them made their living directly from farming. Since then many have been encouraged to leave the fields and pursue other activities, such as handicrafts, commerce, factory work, and transport;

and by the mid-1980s farming had dropped to less than half of the value of rural output. Although the use of farm machinery has been increasing, for the most part the Chinese peasant depends on simple, non-mechanized farming implements.

Western China, comprising Tibet, Xinjiang, and Qinghai, has little agricultural significance except for areas of oasis farming and cattle raising. Rice, China's most important crop, is dominant in the southern provinces, many of which yield two harvests per year. In North China wheat is of the greatest importance, while in the central provinces wheat and rice vie with each other for the top place. Millet and kaoliang (a variety of grain sorghum) are grown mainly in the north-east and some central provinces, which—together with some northern areas—also produce considerable quantities of barley. Most of the soybean crop is derived from the north and the north-east, and corn (maize) is grown in the centre and the north. Tea comes mainly from the hilly areas of the south-east. Cotton is grown extensively in the central provinces, but it is also found to a lesser extent in the south-east and in the north. Tobacco comes from the centre and parts of the south. Other important crops are potatoes, sugar beet, and oilseeds.

Animal husbandry constitutes the second most important component of agricultural production. China is the world's leading producer of pigs, chickens, and eggs, and it also has sizable herds of sheep and cattle. Since the mid-1970s, greater emphasis has been placed on increasing the livestock output.

Wholesale destruction of China's accessible forests over a long period of time gave way to an energetic reforestation programme that has proved to be inadequate; forest resources are still fairly meagre. The principal forests are found in the Qin (Tsinling) Mountains and the central mountain ranges and in the uplands of Sichuan and Yunnan. Because they are inaccessible, the Qin forests are not worked extensively, and much of the country's timber comes from Heilongjiang, Jilin, Sichuan, and Yunnan.

Resources and Power

China is well endowed with mineral resources, and more than three dozen minerals have proven economically important reserves. The country has rich overall energy potential, but most of it remains to be developed. In addition, the geographical distribution of energy places most of these resources far from their major industrial users. Basically, the north-east is rich in coal and petroleum, the central part of North China has abundant coal, and the south-west has great hydroelectric potential. However, the industrialized regions around Guangzhou (Canton) and the lower Yangtze region around Shanghai have too little energy, while there is little industry located near major energy resource areas other than in the southern part of the north-east. Thus, although energy production has expanded rapidly, it has continued to fall short of demand, and China has been purchasing increasing quantities of foreign petroleum and natural gas.

China's most important mineral resources are hydrocarbons, of which coal is the most abundant. Although deposits are widely scattered (some coal is found in every province), most of the total is located in the northern part of the country. The province of Shanxi is thought to contain about half of the total; other important coal-bearing provinces include Heilongjiang, Liaoning, Jilin, Hebei, and Shandong. Apart from these northern provinces, significant quantities of coal are present in Sichuan, and there are some deposits of importance in Guangdong, Guangxi, Yunnan, and Guizhou. A large part of the country's reserves consists of good bituminous coal, but there are also large deposits of lignite. Anthracite is present in several places (especially Liaoning, Guizhou, and Henan), but overall it is not significant.

China's energy production has grown rapidly since 1980, but it has continued to fall considerably short of demand. This is partly because energy prices were long held so low that industries had few incentives to conserve. Increasingly, however, demand has outstripped supply. In addition, it has often been necessary to transport fuels (notably coal) great distances from points of production to consumption. Coal provides about two-thirds of China's energy consumption, although its proportion is slowly declining. Petroleum production, which grew rapidly from an extremely low base in the early 1960s, has increased much more gradually from 1980. Natural gas production still constitutes only a small (though increasing) fraction of overall energy production, but gas is supplanting coal as a domestic fuel in the major cities.

China's electricity-generating capacity has expanded dramatically since 1980, and the proportion allocated to domestic consumption also has grown considerably. Some four-fifths of all power generated is at thermal plants, with nearly all the rest at hydroelectric installations; only a tiny proportion is from nuclear energy, from plants located near Shanghai and Guangzhou.

This energy expansion comes at a great cost, however, as does China's modernization overall. Chinese factories and power plants release nearly 600 tons of mercury into the atmosphere every year, along with 22.5 million tons of sulphur and an estimated 3.4 billion tons of carbon dioxide. By these measures, China is now the largest polluter in the world, contributing substantially to the layer of particulates, gases, and smoke that shrouds the planet. It is this layer, made up mostly of industrial and automotive emissions, along with quantities of naturally occurring dust and ash, which many see as driving global warming.

Paradoxically, the presence of so much sulphur in that layer was first marked by a few years of slightly colder temperatures, because the tiny airborne particles actually deflect the sun's rays and send its heat back into space. However, the cooling effect soon passes to a cumulative warming one. With the addition of constant stores of pollutants to the atmosphere, increased global warming is the inevitable result, for when terrestrial heat is trapped under that shroud rather than escaping into space, as it normally does, then the well-observed "greenhouse effect" ensues, with markedly rising temperatures and side effects ranging from increased desertification to the melting of ice caps and glaciers to rising sea levels to mass extinctions of plant and animal species. China has long experience with hunger, another result, and is already feeling the greenhouse effect—as indeed is the rest of the world.

The reasons are easily deduced. China has 16 of the world's 20 most polluted cities, according to the World Bank. Temperatures in the nation have been rising regionally (as they have globally), affecting weather systems and reducing the amount of rainfall—and, visibly, the annual flow of the nation's major river systems. At the same time, glaciers in China's high mountains are melting rapidly, causing increased erosion and flash flooding in the environmentally-sensitive uplands.

Just as alarming is the rise in pollution-related mortality. By 2010, as many as 600,000 Chinese will die each year of respiratory illnesses. Asthma, the chronic inflammation of the airway, was once fairly rare in China; it now afflicts millions of people, just as rates of asthma have risen elsewhere in the industrialized world, and it accounts for tens of thousands of deaths annually, especially on hot days, as heat exacerbates the condition. There is some evidence to suggest that changing climatic conditions are conducive to new epidemic diseases such as SARS and avian flu, and untold numbers of deaths, birth defects, and the like may be attributed to the high levels of mercury and other toxins in the environment.

Finance and Trade

China's financial institutions are owned by the state. The principal instruments of fiscal and financial control are the People's Bank of China and the Ministry of Finance, both subject to the authority of the State Council. The People's Bank, which replaced the Central Bank of China in 1950 and gradually took over private banks, fulfils many of the functions of Western central and commercial banks. It issues the renminbi (yuan; the national currency), controls circulation, and plays an important role in disbursing budgetary expenditures. Furthermore, it handles the accounts, payments, and receipts of government organizations and other bodies, which enables it to exercise detailed supervision over their financial and general performance in the light of the state's economic plans.

The People's Bank is also responsible for foreign trade and other overseas transactions (including remittances by overseas Chinese), but these functions are exercised through the Bank of China, which maintains branch offices in a number of European and Asian countries.

Other important financial institutions include the People's Construction Bank of China, responsible for capitalizing a portion of overall investment and for providing capital funds for certain industrial and construction enterprises; the Industrial and Commercial Bank of China, which conducts ordinary commercial transactions and acts as a savings bank for the public; the Agricultural Bank of China, which serves the agricultural sector; and the China Investment Bank, which handles foreign investment. Many foreign banks maintain offices in China's larger cities and the special economic zones.

China's economic reforms greatly increased the economic role of the banking system. Whereas virtually all investment capital was previously provided on a grant basis in the state plan, policy has shifted to a loan basis through the various state financial institutions. More generally, increasing amounts of funds are made available through the banks for economic purposes. Enterprises and individuals can go to the banks to obtain loans outside the state plan, and this has proved to be a major source of financing both for new firms and for the expansion and modernization of older enterprises.

Foreign sources of capital have also become increasingly important. China has received loans from the World Bank and several United Nations programmes, as well as from several countries (particularly Japan) and from commercial banks. Hong Kong and Taiwan have become major conduits for—as well as sources of—this investment. Stock exchanges have been operating at Shanghai and Shenzen since 1990, and the government began allowing the first foreign firms to trade in the market in 2003.

Trade has become an increasingly important part of China's overall economy, and it has been a significant tool used for economic modernization. The direction of China's foreign trade has undergone marked changes since the early 1950s. In 1950 some three-quarters of the total was accounted for by trade with non-communist countries, but by 1954—one year after the end of hostilities during the Korean War—the situation was completely reversed, and communist countries accounted for about three-quarters. During the next few years, the communist world lost some of its former importance, but it was only after the Sino-Soviet breach of 1960—which resulted in the cancellation of Soviet credits and the withdrawal of Soviet technicians—that the non-communist world began to see a rapid improvement in its position. In 1965 China's trade with other socialist countries made up only about one-third of the total.

A significant part of China's trade with the developing countries has been financed through credits, grants, and other forms of assistance. At first, from 1953 to 1955, aid went mainly to North Korea and North Vietnam and some other communist states; but from the mid-1950s large amounts— mainly grants and long-term interest-free loans—were promised to politically uncommitted developing countries. The principal efforts were made in Asia—especially to Indonesia, Myanmar (Burma), Pakistan, and Ceylon (Sri Lanka)—but large loans were also granted in Africa (Ghana, Algeria, Tanzania) and in the Middle East (Egypt). After Mao Zedong's death in 1976, however, the Chinese scaled back such efforts.

During the 1980s and 1990s, China's foreign trade came full circle. Trade with all communist countries diminished to insignificance, especially with the demise of most socialist states. By contrast, trade with non-communist developed and developing countries became predominant. In general, China has had a positive balance of trade with its trading partners since 1990. Hong Kong became one of China's major partners prior to its reincorporation into the country; it remains prominent in domestic trade, notably in its reliance on the mainland for agricultural products. Taiwan has also become an important trading partner, and Taiwan investors have become prominent in many sectors of the Chinese economy, particularly in the manufacturing industries centred in the southern coastal region. Owing to this level of development, as of 2005, more than 800,000 business people from Taiwan were resident on the mainland, while some 35 per cent of Taiwan's direct foreign investment went to China. As wages on the mainland increase . . . however, that investment is likely to fall somewhat as foreign investors move on to countries with less expensive labour markets, such as Vietnam.

Most of China's imports consist of machinery and apparatus (including semiconductors, computers, and office machines), chemicals, and fuels. The main import sources are Japan, Taiwan, South Korea, the countries of the European Union (EU), and the USA. Regionally, almost half of China's imports come from East and Southeast Asia, and some one-quarter of its exports go to the same countries.

The great bulk of China's exports consists of manufactured goods, of which electrical and electronic machinery and equipment and clothing, textiles, and footwear are by far the most important. Agricultural products, chemicals, and fuels are also significant exports. The USA, Japan, EU countries, and South Korea are the principal export destinations. In the first years of the twenty first century, China was an important presence in the economies of all those nations, particularly the USA.

Transportation and Telecommunications

Great emphasis has been placed on developing the country's transport infrastructure because it is so closely related to developing the national economy, consolidating the national defence system, and strengthening national unification. Nevertheless, China's domestic transport system continues to constitute a major constraint on economic growth and the efficient movement of goods and people. Railroads, some still employing steam locomotives, provide the major means for freight haulage, but their capacity cannot meet demand for the shipment of coal and other goods. In addition, roads and waterways are providing an increasing proportion of China's overall transport.

Since 1949 China's transport and communications policies, influenced by political, military, and economic considerations, have experienced changes of emphasis in different periods. Thus, just after 1949 the primary concern was to repair existing lines of communication, to give priority to military transport needs, and to strengthen political control. During most of the 1950s, new lines were built, while at the same time old lines were improved. During the Great Leap Forward much of the improvement of regional transportation became the responsibility of the general population, and many small railways were constructed. After 1963, emphasis was placed on developing transportation in rural, mountainous, and especially forested areas, in order to help promote agricultural production; simultaneously the development of international communications was energetically pursued, and the scope of ocean transport was broadened considerably.

Initially, as China's railways and highways were mostly concentrated in the coastal regions, access to the interior was difficult. This situation has been improved considerably, as railways and highways have been built in the remote border areas of the northwest and southwest. All parts of China, except certain remote areas of Tibet, are accessible by rail, road, water, or air. Indeed, in 2006, the Qinghai–Tibet rail line, the world's highest, was completed, making the highlands accessible to visitors and, increasingly, to Chinese settlers.

Post and telecommunications were re-established rapidly in the 1950s and 1960s. By 1952 the principal post and telecommunications network centred on Beijing, and links to all large cities had been established. Great progress was made in improving the postal service under the First Five-Year Plan. Postal service was also developed in the rural areas. Besides extending rural postal routes, the problem of delivering mail to places below the county level was solved by enlisting the aid of the population. From 1954 onward a system of mail delivery by rural postal workers was tried in agricultural cooperatives, and in 1956 this system was extended throughout the country. By 1959 the national postal network was complete.

When the People's Republic was established in 1949, China had only a rudimentary telecommunications system, limited largely to the eastern coastal cities, the Nanjing region, and a few interior cities. Work quickly got under way to repair and expand the system, and from 1956 telecommunications routes were extended more rapidly. The same lines were used for both telegraphic and telephone service to increase the efficiency of the communication system, and Teletype and television broadcast services were also added. By 1963 telephone wire linked Beijing to the large cities and the capitals of all provinces and autonomous regions, and capitals in turn were connected to the administrative seats of the counties, smaller municipalities, and larger market towns.

By the 1970s, radio telecommunications equipment was beginning to replace wire lines, and microwave and satellite transmissions were soon introduced; China launched its first television broadcast satellite in 1986. The pace of telecommunications growth and technology upgrading increased even more rapidly after 1990, especially as fibre-optics systems and digital technology were installed. China's telecommunications services were further enhanced from 1997, when Hong Kong's highly advanced systems were acquired. In the late 1990s, foreign companies were allowed to invest in the country's telecommunications sector, further encouraging growth. Notable has been the tremendous increase in cellular phone use; China became the world leader in the early twenty first century, in terms of number of subscribers.

Despite these advances, China's telecommunications infrastructure has not been able to keep up with demand. A large proportion of the country's population still has little or no access even to basic telephone service. The number of cellular phones has grown enormously, surpassing that for standard (i.e. landline) telephones in 2003. Internet use has also increased dramatically although the government exercises firm control, particularly over Chinese-language material on the Internet, with many terms (such as the name of Hu Jintao's reported mistress) blocked and many web sites also blocked. Apart from the BBC (whose web site is blocked), there is less censorship of English-language web sites.

The Internet

The Internet has become pervasive throughout all developed areas of China, with modern Internet cafes offering high-speed access enjoying particular popularity. New buildings increasingly offer high-speed wireless access as an amenity. The backbone of the system is a mix of terrestrial and satellite links; a 2005 project called the ChinaNet Next Carrying Network (CN2) brought a major upgrade to the Internet infrastructure across the country. As in the developed world, the Internet is a major vehicle of economic development and of opening communications channels between China and its trading partners and other nations.

The Chinese government has been careful throughout this period of development to keep tight controls over what its citizens may and may not read and see, however. Using sophisticated filters, government censors routinely block access to any web pages that address the sovereignty of Taiwan, human rights abuses in Tibet, and the like. So pervasive are these controls that the view of the world that the Internet brings proves highly favourable to the government. As Chinese seeking to create blogs have discovered, words such as "democracy", "freedom", and "human rights" are forbidden, bringing up the corrective message that such terms are "prohibited language". The Beijing government insists that it is within its rights to do so, and it shows no signs of relaxing its hold on expression.

The Press

Dozens of daily newspapers are published in China, nearly all of the major ones in Beijing. The principal national paper is *Renmin Ribao* ("People's Daily"), the organ of the CCP; other papers with large circulations include *Guangming Ribao* ("Brightness Daily") and *Gongren Ribao* ("Workers' Daily"). *China Daily* is the leading English-language paper. The chief news service is the government-run New China News Agency (Xinhuashe). Beijing remains the centre of China's publishing industry.

The New China News Agency was founded in 1931 as the press outlet of the CCP. It was first set up in the Red Army-controlled area in Jiangxi province and in the mid-1930s was moved to Yan'an. The agency is now headquartered in Beijing and has offices around the world. NCNA has domestic and international services for Chinese and non-Chinese media. Like most of the news media in China, it operates under governmental control, and its releases reflect official policies and promote state programmes. These strictures were greatly tightened in the 1960s during the Cultural Revolution, when many Chinese journalists were jailed for deviating from its standards, but were substantially relaxed after the fall from power of the Gang of Four a decade later.

Renmin Ribao carries serious, politically oriented articles and numerous speeches and reports by government or party leaders. News about these leaders is always carried on the front page. The newspaper's contents reflect official policy, and it is read throughout China by many times its circulation, which by the end of the twentieth century was about 3 million. Before the 1980s, copies of the paper were posted for public view in display cases at street intersections, and articles were frequently read at local party meetings, reprinted in local newspapers, or quoted in Radio Beijing programs. Village schools often placed quotations from the paper on bulletin boards.

Renmin Ribao editorials deal with such subjects as politics and culture, communist theory and philosophy, and Marxist economics. In the days of the Cultural Revolution, they reflected the anti-intellectual climate of that period; after Mao Zedong's death, the editorials exposed the activities of the Gang of Four and pointed the way to the pragmatic policies of Mao's successors. More social and economic news has appeared in the paper since that time. Regional editions carrying some local news have been available since the 1990s. An overseas edition has been published since 1985, and in 1997 an Internet version of the paper was created, with translations in Russian, French, English, and Arabic.

PART 4

CULTURE

6

RELIGION

China is one of the great centres of world religious thought and practices. It is known especially as the birthplace of the religio-philosophical schools of Confucianism and Taoism (Daoism), belief systems that formed the basis of Chinese society and governance for centuries. Buddhism came to China perhaps as early as the third century BCE and was a recognized presence there by the first century CE. The country became an incubator for many of the great present-day Buddhist sects, including Zen (Chan) and Pure Land and, by its extension into Tibet, the source of Tibetan Buddhism. In addition, hundreds of animist, folk, and syncretic religious practices developed in China, including the movement that spawned the Taiping Rebellion of the mid-nineteenth century.

The political and social upheavals in China during the first half of the twentieth century had a disintegrating effect on Confucianism, Daoism, and (outside Tibet) Buddhism, and traditional observances of these were greatly weakened. From 1949 the country became officially atheist, although state-monitored religious practices continued to be allowed. However, some religions were persecuted, notably Tibetan Buddhism after China assumed military control of Tibet in 1959. The Chinese government has gradually relaxed many of its earlier restrictions on religious institutions and practices, but it still curtails those it considers threats to the social and political order, including the spiritual exercise discipline called Falun Gong, or Falun Dafa.

Today, about two-fifths of China's people claim they are non-religious or atheist. Adherents to various indigenous folk religions, collectively more than one-quarter of the total population, comprise the largest group of those professing a belief. Members of non-Han minorities constitute the bulk of those following Buddhism and Islam. Christians are a small but significant and growing minority, many of them recent converts to Evangelical Protestant denominations.

Confucianism

Propagated by Confucius in the sixth–fifth century BCE and followed by the Chinese people for more than two millennia, Confucianism has traditionally been the substance of learning, the source of values, and the social code of the Chinese.

Confucianism, a Western term that has no counterpart in Chinese, is a world view, a social ethic, a political ideology, a scholarly tradition, and a way of life. Sometimes viewed as a philosophy and sometimes as a religion, Confucianism may be understood as an all-encompassing humanism that neither denies nor slights Heaven. East Asians may profess themselves to be Taoists, Buddhists, or Christians but, by announcing their religious affiliations, seldom do they cease to be Confucians.

Both the theory and practice of Confucianism have indelibly marked the patterns of government, society, education, and family in China. Although it is an exaggeration to characterize traditional Chinese life and culture as Confucian, Confucian ethical values have for well over 2,000 years served as the source of inspiration as well as the court of appeal for human interaction between individuals, communities, and nations in the Chinese world.

The story of Confucianism does not begin with Confucius. Nor was Confucius the founder of Confucianism in the sense that Buddha was the founder of Buddhism and Christ the founder of Christianity. Rather, Confucius considered himself a transmitter who consciously tried to reanimate the old in order to improve the new. He proposed retrieving the meaning of the past by breathing vitality into seemingly outmoded rituals. Confucius' love of antiquity was motivated by his strong desire to understand why certain rituals, such as the ancestral cult, reverence for Heaven, and mourning ceremonies, had survived for centuries. His journey into the past was a search for roots, which he perceived as grounded in humanity's deepest needs for belonging and communicating. He had faith in the cumulative power of culture. The fact that traditional ways had lost vitality did not, for him, diminish their potential for regeneration in the future. In fact, Confucius' sense of history was so strong that he saw himself as a conservationist responsible for the continuity of the cultural values and the social norms that had worked so well for the civilization of the Zhou dynasty.

The scholarly tradition envisioned by Confucius can be traced to the sage-kings of antiquity. Although the earliest dynasty confirmed by archaeology is the Shang dynasty (seventeenth–eleventh century BCE), the historical period that Confucius claimed as relevant was much earlier. Confucius may have initiated a cultural process known in the West as Confucianism, but he and those who followed him considered themselves part of a tradition, later identified by Chinese historians as the *rujia* ("scholarly tradition") that had its origins two millennia previously, when the legendary Yao and Shun created a civilized world through moral persuasion.

Confucius' hero was Zhou Gong, or the Duke of Zhou (d. 1094 BCE), who was said to have helped consolidate and refine the "feudal" ritual system. This system was based on blood ties, marriage alliances, and old covenants as well as on newly negotiated contracts and was an elaborate system of mutual dependence. The appeal to cultural values and social norms for the maintenance of interstate as well as domestic order was predicated on a shared political vision, namely, that authority lies in universal kingship, heavily invested with ethical and religious power by the mandate of Heaven, and that social solidarity is achieved not by legal constraint but by ritual observance. Its implementation enabled the Zhou dynasty to survive in relative peace and prosperity for more than five centuries.

Inspired by the statesmanship of Zhou Gong, Confucius harboured a lifelong dream to be in a position to emulate the duke by putting into practice the political ideas he had learned from the ancient sages and worthies. Although Confucius never realized his political dream, his conception of politics as moral persuasion became more and more influential.

The idea of Heaven, unique in Zhou cosmology, was compatible with the concept of the Lord-on-High in the Shang dynasty. The Lord-on-High may have referred to the progenitor of the Shang royal lineage so that the Shang kings could claim their position as divine descendants, as the emperors of Japan later did, but Heaven to the Zhou kings was a much more generalized anthropomorphic God. They believed that the mandate of Heaven (the functional equivalent of the will of the Lord-on-High) was not constant and that there was no guarantee that the descendants of the Zhou royal house would be entrusted with kingship, for "Heaven sees as the people see and Heaven hears as the people hear"; thus the virtues of the kings were essential for the maintenance of their power and authority. This emphasis on benevolent rulership, expressed in numerous bronze inscriptions, was both a reaction to the collapse of the Shang dynasty and an affirmation of a deep-rooted world view.

Partly because of the vitality of the feudal ritual system and partly because of the strength of the royal household itself, the Zhou kings were able to control their kingdom for several centuries. In 771 BCE, however, they were forced to move their capital eastward to present-day Luoyang to avoid barbarian attacks from Central Asia. Real power thereafter passed into the hands of feudal lords. Since the surviving line of the Zhou kings continued to be recognized in name, they still managed to exercise some measure of symbolic control. By Confucius' time, however, the feudal ritual system had been so fundamentally undermined that the political crises also precipitated a profound sense of moral decline: the centre of symbolic control could no longer hold the kingdom from total disintegration.

Confucius' response was to address himself to the issue of learning to be human. In so doing he attempted to redefine and revitalize the institutions that for centuries had been vital to political stability and social order: the family, the school, the local community, the state, and the kingdom. Confucius did not accept the status quo, which held that wealth and power spoke the loudest. He felt that virtue, both as a personal quality and as a requirement for leadership, was essential for individual dignity, communal solidarity, and political order.

The *Lunyu* (*Analects*), the most revered sacred scripture in the Confucian tradition, was probably compiled by the second generation of Confucius' disciples. Based primarily on the Master's sayings, preserved in both oral and written transmissions, it captures the Confucian spirit in form and content in the same way that the Platonic dialogues embody Socratic pedagogy.

The *Analects* has often been viewed by the critical modern reader as a collection of unrelated conversations randomly put together. This impression may have resulted from the mistaken conception of Confucius as a mere common-sense moralizer who gave practical advice to students in everyday situations. If a person approaches the *Analects* as a communal memory, a literary device on the part of those who considered themselves beneficiaries of the Confucian Way to continue the Master's memory and to transmit his form of life as a living tradition, he comes close to what it has been revered for in China for centuries. Dialogues are used to show Confucius in thought and action, not as an isolated individual but as the centre of relationships. Actually, the sayings of the *Analects* reveal Confucius' personality—his ambitions, his fears, his joys, his commitments, and above all his self-knowledge.

The purpose, then, in compiling these distilled statements centring on Confucius seems not to have been to present an argument or to record an event but to offer an invitation to readers to take part in an ongoing conversation. Through the *Analects* Confucians for centuries learned to re-enact the awe-inspiring ritual of participating in a conversation with Confucius.

One of Confucius' most significant personal descriptions is the short autobiographical account of his spiritual development found in the *Analects*: "At 15 I set my heart on learning; at 30 I firmly took my stand; at 40 I had no delusions; at 50 I knew the Mandate of Heaven; at 60 my ear was attuned; at 70 I followed my heart's desire without overstepping the boundaries of right" (2:4).

Confucius' life as a student and teacher exemplified his idea that education was a ceaseless process of self-realization.

When one of his students reportedly had difficulty describing him, Confucius came to his aid: "Why did you not simply say something to this effect: he is the sort of man who forgets to eat when he engages himself in vigorous pursuit of learning, who is so full of joy that he forgets his worries, and who does not notice that old age is coming on?" (7:18).

Confucius was deeply concerned that the culture (*wen*) he cherished was not being transmitted and that the learning (*xue*) he propounded was not being taught. His strong sense of mission, however, never interfered with his ability to remember what had been imparted to him, to learn without flagging, and to teach without growing weary. What he demanded of himself was strenuous: "It is these things that cause me concern: failure to cultivate virtue, failure to go deeply into what I have learned, inability to move up to what I have heard to be right, and inability to reform myself when I have defects" (7:3).

What he demanded of his students was the willingness to learn: "I do not enlighten anyone who is not eager to learn, nor encourage anyone who is not anxious to put his ideas into words" (7:8).

The community that Confucius created was a scholarly fellowship of like-minded men of different ages and different backgrounds from different states. They were attracted to Confucius because they shared his vision and to varying degrees took part in his mission to bring moral order to an increasingly fragmented polity. This mission was difficult and even dangerous. Confucius himself suffered from joblessness, homelessness, starvation, and occasionally life-threatening violence. Yet his faith in the survivability of the culture that he cherished and the workability of the approach to teaching that he propounded was so steadfast that he convinced his followers as well as himself that Heaven was on their side. When Confucius' life was threatened in Kuang, he said: "Since the death of King Wen [founder of the Zhou dynasty] does not the mission of culture (*wen*) rest here in me? If Heaven intends this culture to be destroyed, those who come after me will not be able to have any part of it. If Heaven does not intend this culture to be destroyed, then what can the men of Kuang do to me?" (9:5).

This expression of self-confidence informed by a powerful sense of mission may give the impression that there was presumptuousness in Confucius' self-image. Confucius, however, made it explicit that he was far from attaining sagehood and that all he really excelled in was "love of learning" (5:27). To him, learning not only broadened his knowledge and deepened his self-awareness but also defined who he was. He frankly admitted that he was not born endowed with knowledge, nor did he belong to the class of men who could transform society without knowledge. Rather, he reported that he used his ears widely and followed what was good in what he had heard and used his eyes widely and retained in his mind what he had seen. His learning constituted "a lower level of knowledge" (7:27), a level that was presumably accessible to the majority of human beings. In this sense Confucius was neither a prophet with privileged access to the divine nor a philosopher who had already seen the truth but a teacher of humanity who was also an advanced fellow traveller on the way to self-realization.

As a teacher of humanity Confucius stated his ambition in terms of concern for human beings: "To bring comfort to the old, to have trust in friends, and to cherish the young" (5:25). Confucius' vision of the way to develop a moral community began with a holistic reflection on the human condition. Instead of dwelling on abstract speculations such as man's condition in the state of nature, Confucius sought to understand the actual situation of a given time and to use that as his point of departure. His aim was to restore trust in government and to transform society into a moral community by cultivating a sense of humanity in politics and society. To achieve that aim, the creation of a scholarly community, the fellowship of *junzi* (noblemen or, as commonly translated "superior men"), was essential. In the words of Confucius' disciple Zengzi, the true nobleman "must be broad-minded and resolute, for his burden is heavy and his road is long. He takes humanity as his burden. Is that not heavy? Only with death does his road come to an end. Is that not long?" (8:7).

The fellowship of *junzi* as moral vanguards of society, however, did not seek to establish a radically different order. Its mission was to redefine and revitalize those institutions that for centuries were believed to have maintained social solidarity and enabled people to live in harmony and prosperity. An obvious example of such an institution was the family.

It is related in the *Analects* that Confucius, when asked why he did not take part in government, responded by citing a passage from an ancient classic, the *Shujing* ("Classic of History"), "Simply by being a good son and friendly to his brothers a man can exert an influence upon government!" to show that what a person does in the confines of his home is politically significant (2:21). This maxim is based on the Confucian conviction that cultivation of the self is the root of social order and that social order is the basis for political stability and universal peace.

The assertion that family ethics is politically efficacious must be seen in the context of the Confucian conception of politics as "rectification" (*zheng*). Rulers should begin by rectifying their own conduct; that is, they are to be examples who govern by moral leadership and exemplary teaching rather than by force. Government's responsibility is not only to provide food and security but also to educate the people. Law and punishment are the minimum requirements for order; the higher goal of social harmony, however, can only be attained by virtue expressed through ritual performance. To perform rituals, then, is to take part in a communal act to promote mutual understanding.

One of the fundamental Confucian values that ensures the integrity of ritual performance is *xiao* (filial piety). Indeed, Confucius saw filial piety as the first step toward moral excellence, which he believed lay in the attainment of the cardinal virtue, *ren* (humanity). To learn to embody the family in the mind and heart is to become able to move beyond self-centredness or, to borrow from modern psychology, to transform the enclosed private ego into an open self. Filial piety, however, does not demand unconditional submissiveness to parental authority but recognition of and reverence for the source of life. The purpose of filial piety, as the ancient Greeks expressed it, is to enable both parent and child to flourish. Confucians see it as an essential way of learning to be human.

Confucians, moreover, are fond of applying the family metaphor to the community, the country, and the universe. They prefer to address the emperor as the son of Heaven, the king as ruler-father, and the magistrate as the "father-mother official" because to them the family-centred nomenclature implies a political vision. When Confucius said that taking care of family affairs is itself active participation in politics, he had already made it clear that family ethics is not merely a private concern; the public good is realized by and through it.

Confucius defined the process of becoming human as being able to "conquer yourself and return to ritual" (12:1). The dual focus on the transformation of the self (Confucius is said to have freed himself from four things: "opinionatedness, dogmatism, obstinacy, and egoism" [9:4]) and on social participation enabled Confucius to be loyal (*zhong*) to himself and considerate (*shu*) of others (4:15). It is easy to understand why the Confucian "golden rule" is "Do not do unto others what you would not want others to do unto you!" (15:23). Confucius' legacy, laden with profound ethical implications, is captured by his "plain and real" appreciation that learning to be human is a communal enterprise: "A man of humanity, wishing to establish himself, also establishes others, and wishing to enlarge himself, also enlarges others. The ability to take as analogy of what is near at hand can be called the method of humanity" (6:30).

The Confucianization of Chinese society reached its apex during the Qing dynasty (1644–1911/12) when China was again ruled by a conquest (Manchu) dynasty. The Qing emperors outshone their counterparts in the Ming in presenting themselves as exemplars of Confucian kingship. They transformed Confucian teaching into a political ideology, indeed a mechanism of control. Jealously guarding their Imperial prerogatives as the ultimate interpreters of Confucian truth, they undermined the freedom of scholars to transmit the Confucian Way by imposing harsh measures, such as literary inquisition.

At the time of the first Opium War (1839–42) East Asian societies had been Confucianized for centuries. The continuous growth of Mahayana Buddhism throughout Asia and the presence of Taoism in China, shamanism in Korea, and Shintoism in Japan did not undermine the power of Confucianism in government, education, family rituals, and social ethics. In fact, Buddhist monks were often messengers of Confucian values, and the coexistence of Confucianism with Taoism, shamanism, and Shintoism actually characterized the syncretic East Asian religious life. The impact of the West, however, so fundamentally undermined the Confucian roots in East Asia that it has come to be widely debated whether or not Confucianism can remain a viable tradition in modern times.

Beginning in the nineteenth century, Chinese intellectuals' faith in the ability of Confucian culture to withstand the impact of the West became gradually eroded. This loss of faith may be perceived in Lin Zexu's (1785–1850) moral indignation against the British, followed by Zeng Guofan's (1811–72) pragmatic acceptance of the superiority of Western technology, Kang Youwei's (1858–1927) sweeping recommendation for political reform, and Zhang Zhidong's (1837–1909) desperate, eclectic attempt to save the essence of Confucian learning, which, however, eventually led to the anti-Confucian iconoclasm of the so-called May Fourth Movement in 1919. The triumph of Marxism–Leninism as the official ideology of the People's Republic of China in 1949 relegated Confucian rhetoric to the background. The modern Chinese intelligentsia, however, maintained unacknowledged, sometimes unconscious, continuities with the Confucian tradition at every level of life—behaviour, attitude, belief, and commitment. Indeed, Confucianism remains an integral part of the psycho-cultural construct of the contemporary Chinese intellectual as well as of the Chinese peasant.

The emergence of Japan and other newly industrialized Asian countries and regions (e.g. South Korea, Singapore, and Taiwan) as the most dynamic region of economic development since World War II has raised questions about how the typical East Asian institutions, still suffused with Confucian values—such as a paternalistic government, an educational system based on competitive examinations, the family with emphasis on loyalty and cooperation, and local organizations informed by consensus—have adapted themselves to the imperatives of modernization.

Some of the most creative and influential intellectuals in contemporary China have continued to think from Confucian roots. Xiong Shili's ontological reflection, Liang Shuming's cultural analysis, Feng Youlan's reconstruction of the learning of the principle, He Lin's new interpretation of the learning of the mind, Tang Junyi's philosophy of culture, Xu Fuguan's social criticism, and Mou Zongsan's moral metaphysics are noteworthy examples. Although some of the most articulate intellectuals in the People's Republic of China criticize their Confucian heritage as the embodiment of authoritarianism, bureaucratism, nepotism, conservatism, and male chauvinism, others in mainland China, Taiwan, Singapore, and North America have imaginatively established the relevance of Confucian humanism to China's modernization. The revival of Confucian studies in South Korea, Taiwan, Hong Kong, and Singapore has been under way for more than a generation, though Confucian scholarship in Japan remains unrivalled. Confucian thinkers in the West, inspired by religious pluralism and liberal democratic ideas, have begun to explore the possibility of a third epoch of Confucian humanism. They uphold that its modern transformation, as a creative response to the challenge of the West, is a continuation of its classical formulation and its medieval elaboration. Scholars in mainland China have also begun to explore the possibility of a fruitful interaction between Confucian humanism and democratic liberalism in a socialist context.

Taoism

Taoism, also spelled Daoism, has shaped Chinese life for more than 2,000 years. In the broadest sense, a Taoist attitude toward life can be seen in the accepting and yielding, the joyful and carefree sides of the Chinese character, an attitude that offsets and complements the moral and duty-conscious, austere and purposeful character ascribed to Confucianism.

Taoism is also characterized by a positive, active attitude toward the occult and the metaphysical (theories on the nature of reality), whereas the agnostic, pragmatic Confucian tradition considers these issues of only marginal importance.

Taoist thought permeates Chinese culture, including many aspects not usually considered Taoist. In Chinese religion, the Taoist tradition—often serving as a link between the Confucian tradition and folk tradition—has generally been more popular and spontaneous than the official (Confucian) state cult and less diffuse and shapeless than folk religion.

Taoist philosophy and religion found their way into all Asian cultures influenced by China, especially those of Vietnam, Japan, and Korea.

Behind all forms of Taoism stands the figure of Laozi (Laotzu), traditionally regarded as the author of the classic text known as the *Laozi*, or the *Daodejing* (*Tao-te Ching*, "Classic of the Way of Power"). The first mention of Laozi is found in another early classic of Taoist speculation, the *Zhuangzi* (fourth–third century BCE), so called after its author. In this work Laozi is described as being one of Zhuangzi's own teachers, and the same book contains many of the Master's (Laozi's) discourses, generally introduced by the questions of a disciple. The *Zhuangzi* also presents seven versions of a meeting of Laozi and Confucius. Laozi is portrayed as the elder and his Taoist teachings confound his celebrated interlocutor. The *Zhuangzi* also gives the only account of Laozi's death. Thus, in this early source, Laozi appears as a senior contemporary of Confucius (sixth–fifth century BCE) and a renowned Taoist master, a curator of the archives at the court of the Zhou dynasty (*c.* 1066–221 BCE) and, finally, a mere mortal.

The first consistent biographical account of Laozi is found in the "Historical Records" (*Shiji*)—China's first universal history (second century BCE)—of Sima Qian. This concise résumé has served as the classical source on the philosopher's life. Laozi's family name was Li, his given name Er; and he occupied the post of archivist at the Zhou court. He is said to have instructed Confucius on points of ceremony. Observing the decline of the Zhou dynasty, Laozi left the court and headed west. At the request of Yin Xi, the guardian of the frontier pass, he wrote his treatise on the Tao in two scrolls. He then left China behind, and what became of him is not known. The historian quotes variant accounts, including one that attributed to Laozi an exceptional longevity; the narrative terminates with the genealogy of eight generations of Laozi's supposed descendants. With passing references in other early texts, this constitutes the body of information on the life of the sage as of the second century BCE; it is presumably legendary.

Modern scholarship has little to add to the *Shiji* account, and the *Daodejing*, regarded by many scholars as a compilation that reached its final form only in the third century BCE, rather than the work of a single author, stands alone, with all its attractions and enigmas, as the fundamental text of both philosophical and religious Taoism.

The work's 81 brief sections contain only about 5,000 characters in all, from which fact derives still another of its titles, Laozi's Five Thousand Words. The text itself appears in equal measure to express a profound quietism and determined views on government. It is consequently between the extremes of meditative introspection and political application that its many and widely divergent interpreters have veered.

The *Daodejing* was meant as a handbook for the ruler. He should be a sage whose actions pass so unnoticed that his very existence remains unknown. He imposes no restrictions or prohibitions on his subjects; "so long as I love quietude, the people will of themselves go straight. So long as I act only by inactivity, the people will of themselves become prosperous."

He does not teach them discrimination, virtue, or ambition because "when intellect emerges, the great artifices begin. When discord is rife in families, 'dutiful sons' appear. When the State falls into anarchy, 'loyal subjects' appear." Thus, it is better to banish wisdom, righteousness, and ingenuity, and the people will benefit a hundred-fold.

Therefore the Holy Man rules by emptying hearts (minds) and filling bellies, weakening wills and strengthening bones, ever striving to make the people knowledgeless and desireless. War is condemned but not entirely excluded: "Arms are ill-omened instruments", and the sage uses them only when he cannot do otherwise. He does not glory in victory; "he that has conquered in battle is received with rites of mourning."

The book shares certain constants of classical Chinese thought but clothes them in an imagery of its own. The sacred aura surrounding kingship is here rationalized and expressed as "inaction" (*wuwei*), demanding of the sovereign no more than right cosmological orientation at the centre of an obedient universe. Survivals of archaic notions concerning the compelling effect of renunciation—which the Confucians sanctified as ritual "deference" (*rang*)—are echoed in the recommendation to "hold to the role of the female", with an eye to the ultimate mastery that comes of passivity.

It is more particularly in the function attributed to the Tao, or Way, that this little tract stands apart. The term Tao was employed by all schools of thought. The universe has its Tao; there is a Tao of the sovereign, his royal mode of being, while the Tao of man comprises continuity through procreation. Each of the schools, too, had its own Tao, its way or doctrine. But in the *Daodejing*, the ultimate unity of the universal Tao itself is being proposed as a social ideal. It is this idealistic peculiarity that seems to justify later historians and bibliographers in their assignment of the term Taoist to the *Daodejing* and its successors.

From a literary point of view, the *Daodejing* is distinguished for its highly compressed style. Unlike the dialectic or anecdotal composition of other contemporary treatises, it articulates its cryptic subject matter in short, concise statements. More than half of these are in rhyme, and close parallelism recurs throughout the text. No proper names occur anywhere. Although its historical enigmas are apparently insoluble, there is abundant testimony to the vast influence exercised by the book since the earliest times and in surprisingly varied social contexts. Among the classics of speculative Taoism, it alone holds the distinction of having become a scripture of the esoteric Taoist movements, which developed their own interpretations of its ambiguities and transmitted it as a sacred text.

Knowledge of the sage Zhuangzi is even less well defined than that of Laozi. Most of Sima Qian's brief portrait of the man is transparently drawn from anecdotes in the *Zhuangzi* itself and as such has no necessary basis in fact. The *Zhuangzi*, however, is valuable as a monument of Chinese literature and because it contains considerable documentary material, describing numerous speculative trends and spiritual practices of the Warring States period (475–221 BCE).

Whereas the *Daodejing* is addressed to the sage-king, the *Zhuangzi* is the earliest surviving Chinese text to present a philosophy for private life, a wisdom for the individual. Zhuangzi is said to have preferred the doctrine of Laozi over all others; many of his writings strike the reader as metaphorical illustrations of the terse sayings of the "Old Master".

Whereas Laozi in his book as well as in his life (in legend) was concerned with Taoist rule, Zhuangzi, some generations later, rejected all participation in society. He compared the servant of state to the well-fed decorated ox being led to

sacrifice in the temple and himself to the untended piglet
blissfully frolicking in the mire.

Here there is none of the *Daodejing*'s studied density. The
rambling *Zhuangzi* opens with a sprightly fable, illustrating
the incomprehension of small wildfowl of the majestic splendour of a gigantic bird. There is a colloquy between the Lord of
the Yellow River and the God of the Eastern Ocean, in which
the complacent self-satisfaction of the lesser spirit is shaken by
his unexpected meeting with inconceivable vastness. Humble
artisans are depicted, who, through the perfect mastery of their
craft, exemplify for their social superiors the art of mastering
life. Life and death are equated, and the dying are seen to
welcome their approaching transformation as a fusion with
the Tao. Its concluding chapter is a systematic account of the
pre-eminent thinkers of the time, and the note of mock despair
on which it closes typifies the *Zhuangzi*'s position regarding
the more formal, strait-laced ideologies that it parodies.

Among the strange figures that people the pages of *Zhuangzi* are a very special class of spiritualized being. Dwelling far
apart from the turbulent world of men, dining on air and
sipping the dew, they share none of the anxieties of ordinary
folk and have the smooth, untroubled faces of children. These
"supreme men", or "perfect men", are immune to the effects of
the elements, untouched by heat and cold. They possess the
power of flight and are described as mounting upward with a
fluttering (*xian*) motion. Their effortless existence was the
ultimate in autonomy, the natural spontaneity that *Zhuangzi*
ceaselessly applauds. These striking portraits may have been
intended to be allegorical, but whatever their original meaning, these Immortals (*xian*), as they came to be called, were to
become the centre of great interest. Purely literary descriptions
of their freedom, their breathtaking mobility, and their age-
lessness were construed as practical objectives by later gen-

erations. By a variety of practices, men attempted to attain these qualities in their own persons, and in time *Zhuangzi*'s unfettered paragons of liberty were to see themselves classified according to kind and degree in a hierarchy of the heavenly hosts.

What Laozi calls the "permanent Tao" in reality is nameless. The name (*ming*) in ancient Chinese thought implied an evaluation assigning an object its place in a hierarchical universe. The Tao is outside these categories. "It is something formlessly fashioned, that existed before Heaven and Earth; . . . Its name (*ming*) we do not know; Tao is the byname that we give it. Were I forced to say to what class of things it belongs I should call it Immense."

Tao is the "imperceptible, indiscernible", about which nothing can be predicated but that latently contains the forms, entities, and forces of all particular phenomena: "It was from the Nameless that Heaven and Earth sprang; the Named is the mother that rears the Ten Thousand Beings, each after its kind." The Nameless (*wuming*) and the Named (*you ming*), Not-Being (*wu*) and Being (*you*), are interdependent and "grow out of one another".

The conception of the universe common to all Chinese philosophy is as a hierarchically organized mechanism in which every part reproduces the whole. Humankind is a microcosm (small universe) corresponding rigorously to this macrocosm (large universe); his body reproduces the plan of the cosmos. Between man and universe there exists a system of correspondences and participations that the ritualists, philosophers, alchemists, and physicians have described but certainly not invented. This originally magical feeling of the integral unity of mankind and the natural order has always characterized the Chinese mentality, and the Taoists especially have elaborated upon it. The five organs of the body and its orifices and the dispositions, features, and passions of man correspond to the five directions, the five holy mountains, the sections of the sky, the seasons, and the elements (*wuxing*), which in China are not material but more like five fundamental phases of any process in space-time. Whoever understands man thus understands the structure of the universe. In religious Taoism the interior of the body is inhabited by the same gods as those of the macrocosm.

The law of the Tao as natural order refers to the continuous reversion of everything to its starting point. Anything that develops extreme qualities will invariably revert to the opposite qualities: "Reversion is the movement of the Tao" (*Laozi*). All being issues from the Tao and ineluctably returns to it.

For society, any reform means a type of return to the remote past; civilization is considered a degradation of the natural order, and the ideal is the return to an original purity. For the individual, wisdom is to conform to the rhythm of the universe. The Taoist mystic, however, not only adapts himself ritually and physiologically to the alternations of nature but creates a void inside himself that permits him to return to nature's origin. Laozi, in trance, "wandered freely in the origin of all beings". Thus, in ecstasy he escaped the rhythm of life and death by contemplating the universal return. "Having attained perfect emptiness, holding fast to stillness, I can watch the return of the ever active Ten Thousand Beings." The number 10,000 symbolizes totality.

All parts of the universe are attuned in a rhythmical pulsation. Nothing is static; all beings are subjected to periodical mutations and transformations that represent the Chinese view of creation. Instead of being opposed with a static ideal, change itself is systematized and made intelligible, as in the theory of the five phases (*wuxing*) and in the 64 hexagrams of the *Yijing* (*Classic of Changes*), which are basic recurrent constellations in the general flux. An unchanging unity (the permanent Tao) was seen as underlying the kaleidoscopic plurality.

Zhuangzi's image for creation was that of the activity of the potter and the bronze caster "to shape and to transform" (*zaohua*). These are two phases of the same process: the imperceptible Tao shapes the universe continuously out of primordial chaos; the perpetual transformation of the universe by the alternations of Yin and Yang, or complementary energies (seen as night and day or as winter and summer), is nothing but the external aspect of the same Tao. The shaping of the Ten Thousand Beings by the Supreme Unity and their transformation by Yin and Yang are both simultaneous and perpetual. Thus, the saint's ecstatic union is a "moving together with the Tao; dispersing and concentrating, his appearance has no consistency." United with the permanent Tao, the saint's outer aspect becomes one of ungraspable change. Because the gods can become perceptible only by adapting to the mode of this changing world, their apparitions are "transformations" (*bianhua*); and the magician (*huaren*) is believed to be one who transforms rather than one who conjures out of nothing.

The power acquired by the Taoist is *de*, the efficacy of the Tao in the realm of Being, which is translated as "virtue". Laozi viewed it, however, as different from Confucian virtue: "The man of superior virtue is not virtuous, and that is why he has virtue. The man of inferior [Confucian] virtue never strays from virtue, and that is why he has no virtue."

The "superior virtue" of Taoism is a latent power that never lays claim to its achievements; it is the "mysterious power" (*xuande*) of Tao present in the heart of the sage—"the man of superior virtue never acts (*wuwei*), and yet there is nothing he leaves undone."

Wuwei is not an ideal of absolute inaction nor a mere "not overdoing". It is an action so well in accordance with thing that its author leaves no trace of himself in his work. The sage who practices wuwei lives out of his original nature before it was tampered with by knowledge and restricted by morality; he has reverted to infancy (that is, the undiminished vitality of the newborn state); he has "returned to the state of the Uncarved Block (*pu*)". *Pu* is uncut, unpainted wood, simplicity. Society carves this wood into specific shapes for its own use and thus robs the individual piece of its original totality. Any wilful human intervention is believed to be able to ruin the harmony of the natural transformation process.

In the ideal society there are no books; the *Laozi* (*Daodejing*) itself would not have been written but for the entreaty of the guardian of the pass Yin Xi, who asked the "Old Master" to write down his thoughts. In the Golden Age, past or future, knotted cords are the only form of records. The people of this age are "dull and unwitting, they have no desire; this is called uncarved simplicity. In uncarved simplicity the people attain their true nature."

In the Taoist view, all beings and everything are fundamentally one; opposing opinions arise only when people lose sight of the Whole and regard their partial truths as absolute. They are then like the frog at the bottom of the well who takes the bit of brightness he sees for the whole sky.

Thus, Zhuangzi's holy man fully recognizes the relativity of notions like good and evil and true and false. He is neutral and open to the extent that he offers no active resistance to any would-be opponent, whether it be a person or an idea. "When you argue, there are some things you are failing to see. In the gr___ st Tao nothing is named; in the greatest disputation, ___ is said." The person who wants to know the Tao is ___n't meditate, don't cogitate . . . Follow no school, ___ ay, and then you will attain the Tao"; discard ___ rget distinctions, reach no-knowledge. The mystic does not speak because declaring unity, by creating the duality of the speaker and the affirmation, destroys it. Those who speak about the Tao (like Zhuangzi himself) are "wholly wrong. For he who knows does not speak; he who speaks does not know."

Zhuangzi's descriptions of the indescribable Tao, as well as of those who have attained union with the Tao, are invariably poetic. Taoists prefer to convey their ecstatic insights in images and parables. The Tao is low and receiving as a valley, soft and life-giving as water, and it is the "mysterious female", the source of all life, the Mother of the Ten Thousand Beings. Man should become weak and yielding as water that overcomes the hard and the strong and always takes the low ground; he should develop his male and female sides but "prefer femininity", "feed on the mother", and find within himself the well that never runs dry. Tao is also the axis, the ridgepole, the pivot, and the empty centre of the hub.

Much ancient Chinese mythology has been preserved by the Taoists, who drew on it to illustrate their views. A chaos (*hundun*) myth is recorded as a metaphor for the undifferentiated primal unity; the mythical emperors (Huangdi and others) are extolled for wise Taoist rule or blamed for introducing harmful civilization. Dreams of mythical paradises and journeys on clouds and flying dragons are metaphors for the wanderings of the soul, the attainment of the Tao, and the identity of dream and reality.

Taoists have transformed and adapted some ancient myths to their beliefs. Thus, the Queen Mother of the West (Xiwangmu), who was a mountain spirit, pestilence goddess, and tigress, became a high deity—the Fairy Queen of all immortals.

Taoism has made many contributions to Chinese culture, in particular to the practice of medicine and to the arts. The earliest surviving medical book, the *Huangdi Neijing*, or "The Yellow Emperor's Esoteric Classic" (third century BCE), presents itself as the teachings of a legendary Celestial Master addressed to the Yellow Emperor. Experiments with minerals, plants, and animal substances, inspired to some extent by Taoist dietetics and by the search for the elixir of life, resulted in the 52 chapters of pharmacopoeia called *Bencao gangmu*, or "Great Pharmacopoeia" (sixteenth century).

This interest in science is considered a reflection of the Taoist emphasis on direct observation and experience of the nature of things, as opposed to Confucian reliance on the authority of tradition. The Taoist secret of efficacy is to follow the nature of things; this does not imply scientific experimentation but rather a sensitivity and skill obtained by "minute concentration on the Tao running through natural objects of all kinds". This knowledge and skill cannot be handed down but is that which the men of old took with them when they died (*Zhuangzi*). The image for it is the skill of the artisan admired by the Taoists in their numerous parables on wheelwrights, meatcutters, sword makers, carvers, animal tamers, and musicians.

Though extolling the intuitive comprehension and skilful handling of matter, the Taoists did not observe nature in the Western sense and rejected technology out of their aversion to the artificial. Any new idea or discovery in China was phrased as "what the old masters really meant". This ideology of rediscovery makes it hard to study the evolution of scientific thought. Some progress over the ages (for example, in alchemy) can be seen, but the Taoist contribution to Chinese science might be smaller than it has been assumed.

Taoist literature manifests such richness and variety that scholars tend naturally to seek the symbolic modes of expression that served as points of unity within its historical diversity. No image is more fundamental to all phases of Taoism than that of the child. *Daodejing* praises the infant's closeness to the Tao in its freedom from outside impressions, and *Zhuangzi* describes the spiritual beings nurtured on primal substances, air and dew, as having the faces of children. Thus many of the spirits, both indwelling and celestial, in the esoteric system are described as resembling newborn babes, while the Immortals who appear in visions, though hundreds of years old, are at most adolescent in appearance.

Other persistent images are those of mountain and cavern. Present in the older texts, they are carried over, with particular connotations, into the later works. The mountain as a meeting place of Heaven and Earth, gods and men, and master and disciple (as already in *Zhuangzi*), takes on a vast downward extension. Beneath the mountains are the great "Cavern-heavens" (*dongtian*) of esoteric Taoism, staffed by a numerous immortal hierarchy. Thus, for example, while Mao Shan is only some 400 metres (1,300 feet) high to the gaze of the profane, the initiate knows that its luminous grottoes plunge thousands of metres into the earth. And *light* is everywhere in Taoist revelation: spirits and paradises alike gleam with brilliance unknown in the world of men.

Already during the Warring States period and the early Han, Taoism had made its appearance in the works of the other schools. Both direct quotations and patent imitations were frequent, and citations from *Daodejing* and *Zhuangzi* abound throughout later Chinese literature, as do reminiscences of both their style and their content. Esoteric Taoist writings, too, held great fascination for men of letters. Their response might vary from a mere mention of the most celebrated Immortals to whole works inspired directly by specific Taoist texts and practices. Many a poet recorded his search, real or metaphorical, for Immortals or transcendent herbs or described his attempts at compounding an elixir. A certain number of technical terms became touchstones of poetic diction. The revealed literature of Mao Shan came to have the greatest effect on secular writings.

As works of great literary refinement, the *Lives of the Perfected* directly inspired a very famous tale, the *Intimate Life of Emperor Wu of Han* (*Hanwudi neizhuan*; late sixth century), which in highly polished terms describes the visit to the emperor of a goddess, the Queen Mother of the West. This work, in turn, made a decisive contribution to the development of Tang romantic fiction.

Literary accounts of fantastic marvels also drew heavily on the wonders of Mao Shan hagiography and topography. The Mao Shan influence on Tang poetry was no less important. Precise references to the literature of the sect abound in the poems of the time, while many of the greatest poets, such as Li Bai, were formally initiated into the Mao Shan organization. As awareness of these influences increases, scholars are faced with the intriguing question of the possible religious origins of whole genres of Chinese literature.

A number of early Chinese books of spiritual interest claim to have been inspired by pictures seen on the walls of local temples. A similar tradition attaches to the *Lives of the Immortals,* said to derive from a pictorial work called *Portraits of the Immortals*. As has been noted, the Immortals were depicted on Han mirrors. Other illustrative materials were in close relation to the earliest esoteric Taoist literature. Graphic guides existed from early times to aid in the identification of sacred minerals and plants, particularly mushrooms. A later specimen of such a work is to be found in the Taoist Canon.

This practical aspect of Taoist influence resulted in the exceptionally high technical level of botanical and mineralogical drawing that China soon attained. In calligraphy, too,

Taoists soon set the highest standard. One of the greatest of all calligraphers, Wang Xizhi (303–361), was an adherent of the Way of the Celestial Master, and one of his most renowned works was a transcription of the *Book of the Yellow Court*. The efficacy of talismans, in particular, depended on the precision of the strokes from which they were created.

Figure painting was another field in which Taoists excelled. China's celebrated painter Gu Kaizhi, a practising Taoist, left an essay containing directions for painting a scene in the life of the first Celestial Master, Zhang Daoling. Many works on Taoist themes, famous in their time but now lost, have been attributed to other great early masters. Of these, some may have been painted for use in ritual, and religious paintings of the Taoist pantheon are still produced today. The Taoist scriptures, with their instructions for visualization of the spiritual hierarchy, including details of apparel and accoutrements, are ready-made painter's manuals.

Finally, the language of speculative Taoism was pressed into service as the basic vocabulary of Chinese aesthetics. Consequently, many secular artists attempted to express their own conceptions of the "natural spontaneity" of *Zhuangzi* and *Laozi*'s "spirit of the valley". Here Taoism found still wider imaginative extension, and the efforts of these painters are embodied in those magnificent landscapes that have come to be thought of as most characteristically Chinese.

The principal refuge of Taoism today is on Taiwan. Its establishment on the island is doubtless contemporary with the great emigration from the opposite mainland province of Fujian in the seventeenth and eighteenth centuries. The religion, however, has received new impetus since the 63rd celestial master, Zhang Enbu, took refuge there in 1949. On Taiwan, Taoism may still be observed in its traditional setting, distinct from the manifestations of popular religion that surround it. Hereditary Taoist priests (Taiwanese *sai-kong*), called "blackheads" (*wutou*) from their headgear, are clearly set off from the exorcists (*fashi*) or "redheads" (*hong-tou*) of the ecstatic cults.

Their lengthy rites are still held, now known under the term *jiao* ("offering"), rather than the medieval *zhai* ("retreat"). The liturgy chanted, in expanded Song form, still embodies elements that can be traced back to Zhang Daoling's sect. The religion has enjoyed a renaissance since the 1960s, with great activity being carried on in temple building and restoration.

The most significant event in the past several centuries of Taoist history, however, is probably the ordination (in 1964) in Taiwan of a Dutch scholar, K.M. Schipper, as a Taoist priest. His systematic, first-hand researches into Taoist practices may very well revolutionize scholarly knowledge of the religion, which will thus acquire an unforeseen historical extension, in the West and into the future.

Buddhism

The first mention of Buddhism in China (65 CE) occurs in a Taoist context, at the court of a member of the Imperial family known for his devotion to the doctrines of Huang-Lao. The Indian religion was at first regarded as a foreign variety of Taoism; the particular Buddhist texts chosen to be translated during the Han period reveal the Taoist preoccupation of the earliest converts with rules of conduct and techniques of meditation. Early translators employed Taoist expressions as equivalents for Buddhist technical terms.

Thus, the Buddha, in achieving enlightenment (*bodhi*), was described as having "obtained the Tao"; the Buddhist saints (*arhat*) become perfected immortals (*zhenren*); and "nonaction" (*wuwei*) was used to render nirvana (the Buddhist state of bliss). A joint sacrifice to Laozi and the Buddha was performed by the Han emperor in 166 CE. During this period occurred the first reference to the notion that Laozi, after vanishing into the west, became the Buddha. This theory enjoyed a long and varied history. It claimed that Buddhism was a debased form of Taoism, designed by Laozi as a curb on the violent natures and vicious habits of the "western barbarians", and as such was entirely unsuitable for Chinese consumption.

A variant theory even suggested that, by imposing celibacy on Buddhist monks, Laozi intended the foreigners' extinction. In approximately 300 CE, the Taoist scholar Wang Fou composed a "Classic of the Conversion of the Barbarians" (*Hua-hujing*), which was altered and expanded in subsequent centuries to encompass new developments in the continuing debate. Although there is no evidence that the earliest Taoist organization, literature, or ceremonies were in any way indebted to Buddhism, by the fourth century there was a distinct Buddhist influence upon the literary form of Taoist scriptures and the philosophical expression of the most eminent Taoist masters.

Buddhism developed from the teachings of the Buddha (Sanskrit: "awakened one"), a teacher who lived in northern India between the mid-sixth and the mid-fourth centuries BCE. Spreading from India to Central and Southeast Asia, China, Korea, and Japan, Buddhism has played a central role in the spiritual, cultural, and social life of Asia.

There is disagreement among scholars about the dates of the Buddha's birth and death. Many modern scholars believe that the historical Buddha lived from about 563 to about 483 BCE. Many others believe that he lived about 100 years later (from about 448 to 368 BCE). At this time in India, there was much discontent with Brahmanic (Hindu high-caste) sacrifice and ritual. In northwestern India there were ascetics who tried to create a more personal and spiritual religious experience than that found in the Vedas (Hindu sacred scriptures). In the literature that grew out of this movement, the Upanishads, a new emphasis on renunciation and transcendental knowledge can be found. Religiously, this was a time of doubt, turmoil, and experimentation.

Buddhism, like many of the sects that developed in northeastern India at the time, was constituted by the presence of a charismatic teacher, by the teachings this leader promulgated, and by a community of adherents that was often made up of renunciant members and lay supporters. In the case of Buddhism, this pattern is reflected in the Triratna, i.e. the "Three Jewels" of Buddha (the teacher), *dharma* (the teaching), and *sangha* (the community).

The historical figure referred to as the Buddha (whose life is known largely through legend) was born on the northern edge of the Ganges River basin, an area on the periphery of the ancient civilization of North India, in what is today southern Nepal. He is said to have lived for 80 years. His family name was Gautama (in Sanskrit) or Gotama (in Pali), and his given name was Siddhartha (Sanskrit: "he who achieves his aim") or Siddhatta (in Pali). He is frequently called Shakyamuni, "the sage of the Shakya clan". In Buddhist texts he is most commonly addressed as Bhagavat (often translated as "Lord"), and he refers to himself as the Tathagata, which can mean both "one who has thus come" and "one who has thus gone".

Traditional sources on the date of his death—or, in the language of the tradition, his "passage into nirvana"—range from 2420 to 290 BCE. Scholarship in the twentieth century limited this range considerably, with opinion generally divided between those who believed he lived from about 563 to 483 BCE and those who believed he lived about a century later.

In the centuries following the founder's death, Buddhism developed in two directions represented by two different groups. One was called the Hinayana (Sanskrit: "Lesser Vehicle"), a term given to it by its Buddhist opponents. This more conservative group, which included what is now called the Theravada (Pali: "Way of the Elders") community, compiled versions of the Buddha's teachings that had been preserved in collections called the *Sutta Pitaka* and the *Vinaya Pitaka* and retained them as normative.

The other major group, which calls itself the Mahayana (Sanskrit: "Greater Vehicle"), recognized the authority of other teachings that, from the group's point of view, made salvation available to a greater number of people. These supposedly more advanced teachings were expressed in sutras that the Buddha purportedly made available only to his more advanced disciples. As Buddhism spread, it encountered new currents of thought and religion.

The teaching attributed to the Buddha was transmitted orally by his disciples, prefaced by the phrase "evam me sutam" ("thus have I heard"); therefore, it is difficult to say whether or to what extent his discourses have been preserved as they were spoken. They usually allude to the place and time they were preached and to the audience to which they were addressed. Buddhist councils in the first centuries after the Buddha's death attempted to specify which teachings attributed to the Buddha could be considered authentic.

In the centuries following the Buddha's death, the story of his life was remembered and embellished, his teachings were preserved and developed, and the community that he had established became a significant religious force. Many of the wandering ascetics who followed the Buddha settled in permanent monastic establishments and developed monastic rules. At the same time, the Buddhist laity came to include important members of the economic and political elite.

During its first century of existence, Buddhism spread from its place of origin in Magadha and Kosala throughout much of northern India, including the areas of Mathura and Ujjayani in the west. By the middle of the third century BCE, Buddhism had gained the favour of a Mauryan king, Asoka, who had established an empire that extended from the Himalayas in the north to almost as far as Sri Lanka in the south.

Although there are reports of Buddhists in China as early as the third century BCE, Buddhism was not actively propagated there until the early centuries of the Common Era. According to tradition, Buddhism was introduced into China after the Han emperor Mingdi (reigned 57/58–75/76 CE) dreamed of a flying golden deity in what was interpreted as a vision of the Buddha. The emperor dispatched emissaries to India who returned to China with the *Sutra in Forty-two Sections*, which was deposited in a temple outside the capital of Louyang. However this may be, Buddhism most likely entered China gradually, first primarily through Central Asia and later by way of the trade routes around and through Southeast Asia.

Chinese pilgrims began to visit India between 400 and 700 CE. Among these pilgrims was Faxian, who left China in 399, crossed the Gobi Desert, visited various holy places in India, and returned to China with numerous Buddhist scriptures and statues.

The most famous of the Chinese travellers, however, was the seventh-century monk Xuanzang. When he arrived in north-western India, he found "millions of monasteries". In the north-east Xuanzang visited various holy places and studied Yogacara philosophy at Nalanda. After visiting Assam and southern India, he returned to China, carrying with him copies of more than 600 sutras.

Buddhism in China during the Han dynasty was deeply coloured with magical practices, which made it compatible with popular Chinese Taoism, an integral component of contemporary folk religion. Instead of the doctrine of no-self, early Chinese Buddhists seem to have taught the indestructibility of the soul. Nirvana became a kind of immortality. They also taught the theory of karma, the values of charity and compassion, and the need to suppress the passions.

Until the end of the Han dynasty, there was a virtual symbiosis between Taoism and Buddhism, and both religions advocated similar ascetic practices as a means of attaining immortality. It was widely believed that Laozi, the founder of Taoism, had been reborn in India as the Buddha. Many Chinese emperors worshipped Laozi and the Buddha on the same altar. The first translations of Buddhist sutras into Chinese—namely, those dealing with topics such as breath control and mystical concentration—utilized a Taoist vocabulary to make them intelligible to the Chinese.

After the Han period, Buddhist monks were often used by non-Chinese emperors in the north of China for their political–military counsel and their skill in magic. At the same time, in the south Buddhism penetrated the philosophical and literary circles of the gentry. One of the most important contributions to the growth of Buddhism in China during this period was the work of translation. The greatest of the early translators was the learned monk Kumarajiva, who had studied the Hindu Vedas, the occult sciences, and astronomy, as well as the Hinayana and Mahayana sutras before he was taken to the Chinese court in 401 CE.

During the 5th and 6th centuries CE, Buddhist schools from India were established in China, and new, specifically Chinese schools were formed. Buddhism was a powerful intellectual force in China; monastic establishments proliferated; and Buddhism became established among the peasantry. Thus, it is not surprising that, when the Sui dynasty (581–618) established its rule over a reunified China, Buddhism flourished as a state religion.

The golden age of Buddhism in China occurred during the Tang dynasty (618–907 CE). Although the Tang emperors were usually Taoists themselves, they favoured Buddhism, which had become extremely popular. Under the Tang the government extended its control over the monasteries and the ordination and legal status of monks. From this time forward, the Chinese monk styled himself simply *zhen* ("subject").

During this period several Chinese schools developed their own distinctive approaches and systematized the vast body of Buddhist texts and teachings. There was a great expansion in the number of Buddhist monasteries and the amount of land they owned. It was also during this period that many scholars made pilgrimages to India and returned with texts and spiritual and intellectual inspiration that greatly enriched Buddhism in China.

Buddhism was never able to replace Taoism and Confucianism, however, and in 845 the emperor Wuzong began a major persecution. According to records, 4,600 Buddhist temples and 40,000 shrines were destroyed, and 260,500 monks and nuns were forced to return to lay life.

Buddhism in China never recovered completely from the great persecution of 845. It did maintain much of its heritage, however, and it continued to play a significant role in the religious life of China. On one hand, Buddhism retained its identity as Buddhism and generated new forms of expression. These included texts such as the *yulu* ("recorded sayings") of famous teachers, which were oriented primarily toward monks, as well as more literary creations such as the *Journey to the West* (written in the sixteenth century) and *Dream of the Red Chamber* (eighteenth century). On the other hand, Buddhism coalesced with the Confucian, Neo-Confucian, and

Taoist traditions to form a complex multireligious ethos within which all three traditions were more or less comfortably encompassed.

The various schools that retained the greatest vitality in China were the Chan school (better known in the West by its Japanese name, Zen), noted for its emphasis on meditation, and the Pure Land tradition, which emphasized Buddhist devotion. The former school was most influential among the cultured elite, especially through the arts. Chan artists during the Song dynasty (960–1279) had a decisive impact on Chinese landscape painting. Artists used images of flowers, rivers, and trees, executed with sudden, deft strokes, to evoke an insight into the flux and emptiness of all reality.

The Pure Land tradition was most influential among the population as a whole and was sometimes associated with secret societies and peasant uprisings. But the two seemingly disparate traditions were often very closely linked. In addition, they were mixed with other Buddhist elements such as the so-called "masses for the dead" that had originally been popularized by the practitioners of Esoteric Buddhism.

A reform movement aimed at revitalizing the Chinese Buddhist tradition and adapting its teachings and institutions to modern conditions took shape during the early twentieth century. However, the disruptions caused by the Sino-Japanese War (1937–45) and the subsequent establishment of a communist government in China (1949) were not helpful to the Buddhist cause. During the Cultural Revolution (especially 1966–69), Buddhist temples and monasteries suffered massive destruction, and the Buddhist community was the victim of severe repression. After 1976 the Chinese government pursued a more tolerant policy, and Buddhism began to show new life. The extent and depth of continuing Buddhist vitality, however, is difficult to determine.

* * *

The main text of the Pure Land schools is the *Sukhavativyuha-sutra* ("Pure Land Sutra"). Written in northwestern India probably before the beginning of the second century CE, the *Sukhavativyuha* exists in two original versions, a longer one that emphasizes good works and a shorter version that emphasizes faith and devotion alone. This sutra tells of a monk, Dharmakara, who heard the preaching of Lokeshvararaja Buddha aeons ago and asked to become a buddha. After millions of years of study, Dharmakara vowed, among other things, to establish a Pure or Happy Land (Chinese: Qingtu), also known as the Western Paradise, if he achieved Buddhahood.

In this Pure Land no evil would exist, the people would be long-lived, they would receive whatever they desired, and from there they might attain nirvana. Dharmakara then revealed in a series of 48 vows the means by which this Pure Land can be reached. Several vows emphasize meditation and good works on earth as a prerequisite, but the 18th one (a famous vow in the later development of Pure Land schools) states that, if one merely calls the name of the Buddha at the moment of death, then one will be reborn in the Pure Land.

By the third century CE, the Amitabhist doctrine had spread from India to China, where a school based on it gradually became the most popular form of Buddhism. The basic doctrines of the Pure Land schools emphasize the importance of devotion. Pure Land leaders teach that a person reaches salvation not by individual effort or the accumulation of merit but through faith in the grace of the buddha Amitabha. The main practice of those who follow the Pure Land teachings is not the study of the texts or meditation on the Buddha but rather the constant invocation of the name Amitabha. Furthermore, in Pure Land Buddhism the attainment of nirvana is not the most prominent goal; it is rather to become reborn in the Pure Land of Amitabha.

The Chan or Zen school of Buddhism emphasizes medi-
tation as the way to awareness of ultimate reality. Despite
Indian influences, Chan is generally considered a specifically
Chinese product, a view reinforced by the fact that fourth–
fifth-century Chinese Buddhist monks, such as Huiyuan and
Sengzhao, taught beliefs and practices similar to those of the
Chan school before the traditional date of its arrival in China.

Most Chinese texts name a South Indian monk, Bodhidharma, who arrived in China about 520 CE, as the founder
of the Chan school. Bodhidharma is regarded as the first Chan
patriarch and the 28th patriarch of the Indian meditation school.
The Indian school began with the monk Kashyapa, who received
Buddha Shakyamuni's supreme teaching, which is found in the
Lankavatara-sutra ("Descent to the Island of Lanka").

The sutra teaches that all beings possess a buddha nature,
often equated with *shunya* (Sanskrit: "the void") in Chan, and
that realization of this fact is enlightenment (Chinese: wu;
Japanese: satori). The truly enlightened one cannot explain
this ultimate truth or reality, nor can books, words, concepts,
or teachers, for it is beyond the ordinary duality of subject and
object and must be realized in direct personal experience.

The emphasis on spontaneity and naturalness stimulated the
development of a Chan aesthetic that profoundly influenced
later Chinese painting and writing. The relative success of the
Chan tradition in subsequent Chinese history is demonstrated
by the fact that virtually all Chinese monks eventually came to
belong to one of the two Chan lineages.

Tibetan Buddhism

Buddhism, according to Tibetan tradition, was introduced into
Tibet during the reign of King Srong-brtsan-sgam-po (*c.* 627–
c. 650). His two queens were early patrons of the religion and

were later regarded in popular tradition as incarnations of the Buddhist saviouress Tara. The religion received active encouragement from Khri-srong-lde-btsan, in whose reign (*c.* 755–797) the first Buddhist monastery in Tibet was built at Bsam-yas (Samye), the first seven monks were ordained, and the celebrated Tantric master Padmasambhava was invited to come from India.

Many legends surround Padmasambhava, who was a *mahasiddha* ("master of miraculous powers"); he is credited with subduing the Bon spirits and demons (the spirits and demons associated with the indigenous religion of Tibet) and with subjugating them to the service of Buddhism. At the time, Chinese Buddhist influences were strong, but it is recorded that a council held at the Bsam-yas monastery (792–794) decided that the Indian tradition should prevail.

Among the Vajrayana schools of Tibet and neighbouring regions, the Rnying-ma-pa claims to preserve most purely the teachings of Padmasambhava. The Rnying-ma-pa makes fuller use than any other school of the "discovered" texts of Padmasambhava. These texts are believed to have been hidden since the early ninth century, when persecution began in Tibet, and their discovery began in the eleventh century and continued until the late twentieth century. Their importance to this school is reinforced by the Rnying-ma-pa notion that "hidden treasure" has strong spiritual and historical overtones.

The Rnying-ma-pa order divides Buddhist teaching into nine progressively superior groups and subdivides the tantras in a manner different from that of other Vajrayana schools. The six groups of tantras are: Kriya, or ritual; Upayoga, which involves the convergence of the two truths and meditation on the pentad of buddhas; Yoga, which involves the evocation of the god, the identification of the self with the god, and meditation on the mandala; Mahayoga, which involves meditation on the factors of human consciousness (*skandhas*) as divine forms; Anuyoga, which involves secret initiation into the presence of the god and his consort and meditation on "voidness" in order to destroy the illusory nature of things; and Atiyoga, which involves meditation on the union of the god and his consort, leading to the experience of bliss. Members of the order believe that those initiated into the Kriya can attain Buddhahood after seven lives, the Upayoga after five lives, the Yoga after three lives, the Mahayoga in the next existence, the Anuyoga at death, and the Atiyoga in the present existence.

Following a period of suppression that lasted almost two centuries (from the early 800s to the early 1000s), Buddhism in Tibet enjoyed a revival. During the eleventh and twelfth centuries, many Tibetans travelled to India to acquire and translate Buddhist texts and to receive training in Buddhist belief and practice. With the assistance of the renowned Indian master Atisa, who arrived in Tibet in 1042, Buddhism was established as the dominant religion. From this point forward Buddhism penetrated deeply into all aspects of Tibetan life, and it became the primary culture of the elite and a powerful force in affairs of state.

One of the great achievements of the Buddhist community in Tibet was the translation into Tibetan of a vast corpus of Buddhist literature, including the *Bka'-'gyur* ("Translation of the Buddha Word") and *Bstan-'gyur* ("Translation of Teachings") collections. The *Bka'-'gyur* contains six sections: (1) Tantra, (2) Prajnaparamita, (3) Ratnakuta, a collection of small Mahayana texts, (4) Avatamsaka, (5) Sutras (mostly Mahayana sutras, but some Hinayana texts are included), and (6) Vinaya. The *Bstan-'gyur* contains 224 volumes with 3,626 texts, divided into three major groups: (1) stotras (hymns of praise) in one volume, including 64 texts, (2) commentaries on

tantras in 86 volumes, including 3,055 texts, and (3) commentaries on sutras in 137 volumes, including 567 texts.

A major development in the history of Tibetan Buddhism
occurred in the late fourteenth or early fifteenth century, when
a great Buddhist reformer named Tsong-kha-pa established the
Dge-lugs-pa school, known more popularly as the Yellow Hats.
In 1578 representatives of this school converted the Mongol
Altan Khan, and under the Khan's sponsorship their leader (the
so-called third Dalai Lama) gained considerable monastic power.

In the middle of the seventeenth century, the Mongol over-
lords established the fifth Dalai Lama as the theocratic ruler of
Tibet. The succeeding Dalai Lamas, who were regarded as
successive incarnations of the bodhisattva Avalokitesvara,
held this position during much of the remainder of the pre-
modern period, ruling from the capital, Lhasa.

The fifth Dalai Lama instituted the high office of Panchen
Lama for the abbot of the Tashilhunpo monastery, located to
the west of Lhasa. The Panchen Lamas were regarded as
successive incarnations of the buddha Amitabha. Unlike the
Dalai Lama, the Panchen Lama has usually been recognized
only as a spiritual ruler.

Throughout much of Tibetan history, many of the great
monasteries were controlled by aristocratic abbots who were
able to marry and pass along their monastic possessions to
their sons. Monks were often warriors, and monasteries
became armed fortresses. The Manchus in the eighteenth
century and subsequently the British, the nationalist Chinese,
and the Chinese communists have all tried to exploit the
division of power between the Panchen and the Dalai lamas.

In October 1950 the Chinese army entered eastern Tibet,
overwhelming the poorly equipped Tibetan troops. An appeal
by the Dalai Lama to the United Nations was denied, and
support from India and Britain was not forthcoming. A

Tibetan delegation summoned to China in 1951 signed a treaty dictated by the Chinese. It professed to guarantee Tibetan autonomy and religion but also allowed the establishment at Lhasa of Chinese civil and military headquarters. In 1959, the Dalai Lama fled to India.

Since then, Tibetan refugees have set up a major centre in Dharmsala in northern India and have been dispersed to many different places. These exiles have made great efforts to preserve their Buddhist tradition and to spread Tibetan Buddhist teachings in the lands where they have settled, while the Dalai Lama has become an internationally recognized public figure and, in the eyes of the Chinese government, a gadfly.

In Tibet, Buddhists have suffered periods of destructive attacks and severe persecution, especially but not exclusively during the Cultural Revolution. In the late twentieth century, this lessened somewhat, and a sense of normalcy was restored. Nevertheless, many Tibetan Buddhists remained strongly nationalistic, and their relationship with China continued to be very tense.

Falun Gong

The Chinese "practice of the Wheel of Dharma" is the controversial Chinese spiritual movement founded by Li Hongzhi in 1992; its adherents exercise ritually to obtain mental and spiritual renewal. The teachings of Falun Gong draw from the Asian religious traditions of Buddhism, Taoism, Confucianism, and Chinese folklore as well as those of Western New Age movements. The movement's sudden emergence in the 1990s was a great concern to the Chinese government, which viewed Falun Gong as a cult. The origins of the movement are found both in long-standing Chinese practices and in recent events.

Qigong (Chinese: "Energy Working"), the use of meditation techniques and physical exercise to achieve both good health and peace of mind, has a long history in Chinese culture and religion; however, practitioners in modern China present these techniques as purely secular in an effort to escape official restrictions against independent religious activity. Nevertheless, in the late twentieth century new masters appeared who taught forms of *Qigong* more clearly rooted in religion.

The most influential of these, Li Hongzhi, worked in law enforcement and corporate security before becoming the full-time spiritual leader of Falun Gong in 1992.

Li was born into an intellectual family on July 7, 1952, (or in 1951, according to followers) in Jilin province, China. He studied under masters from the Buddhist and Taoist faiths. With the surge in China in the late 1980s of *Qigong*-related activities, Li decided to synthesize his techniques in order to establish a synergy between the mind and nature. He compiled many of his lectures into a book entitled *Zhuan falun*, which served as the main text for his methodology. In it, he called for spiritual enlightenment through meditation and the striving toward a high moral standard of living.

While in traditional Chinese Buddhism *falun* means the "wheel of law" or "wheel of dharma", Li uses the word to indicate the centre of spiritual energy, which he locates in the lower abdomen and believes can be awakened through a set of exercises called *Xiulian* ("Cultivating and Practising"). Unlike other *Qigong* groups, Falun Gong insists that its founder is the only authoritative source for determining the correct exercises and that a spiritual discipline, the "cultivation of the *Xinxing*" ("Mind–Nature"), is essential to the success of the exercises.

On a more esoteric level, Li also teaches that demonic space aliens seek to destroy humanity and, since their arrival in 1900, have manipulated scientists and world leaders. Critics of the movement not only ridicule such claims but regard its reliance on *Xiulian* as an alternative to official medicine as hazardous to the members' health. Indeed, the Chinese government claims that 1,400 Falun Gong devotees have died as a result of this alleged rejection of modern medicine.

After gathering a large following in China (100 million, according to Falun Gong, or between 2 and 3 million, according to the Chinese government), Li took his movement abroad in the mid-1990s, settling permanently in New York City in 1998. The next year, a massive campaign was launched by the medical establishment (including both practitioners and academics) and the Chinese government to denounce Falun Gong as a *xiejiao* ("teaching of falsehood", or "cult"). Unlike other Chinese organizations, Falun Gong responded strongly, staging an unauthorized demonstration of more than 10,000 followers in Beijing on April 25, 1999, which prompted an even greater government response.

Li, allegedly unaware of the ensuing events, left China just one day before the protest, travelling to Australia for a presentation. He did not return. Three months later, Chinese President Jiang Zemin declared the practitioners of Falun Gong a threat to the government and issued a warrant for Li's arrest while detaining thousands of his followers, some of whom were officials for the Chinese Communist regime. Millions of Li's books and cassette tapes were destroyed in the crackdown.

The party's attempt to kindle a Maoist-style campaign against Falun Gong during an era of political disillusionment failed to make much headway. Its parallel efforts to revive its own ideology through a campaign of promoting the study of Marxism-Leninism-Maoism was equally unsuccessful. The government's actions may drive Falun Gong and other sects underground, but their beliefs and practices will probably survive in a variety of forms.

THE CHINESE DYNASTIES
BY FRANCES WOOD

The Bronze Age: The Shang (1600–1066 BCE) and Zhou (1066–221 BCE)

The first historical dynasty, the Shang, ruled in north China from c. 1600 to 1066 BCE. Burials and inscriptions tell us something of the Shang belief in heaven and the afterlife. They recognized a supreme God in heaven who ruled in parallel with the Shang ruler on earth and they also sacrificed to the spirits of ancestors, both distant and near. Consciousness of family relations, which include ancestors, has remained a constant feature of Chinese life, sanctified by Confucius in the sixth–fifth century BCE. It also seems clear that there was a view of the afterlife in which the spirit lived very much the same life as before death, requiring food and drink (provided in the tomb) and servants and chariots.

The Shang rulers were eventually overthrown by the Zhou, a group who came from the west (Shaanxi province) of the Shang kingdom. The Zhou continued many of the Shang practices like the ritual use of bronze and jade, and the same sort of burials.

Qin Shi huang di: The "First Unifier"

After the central rule of Zhou broke down, the country was divided into seven warring states. The young ruler of the state of Qin led campaigns against the other states and finally succeeded in establishing the short-lived dynasty of the Qin, 221–206 BCE. The name "unifier" comes not only from his unifying the separate states into one but also from his imposition of the Qin weights and measures, coinage and rather antiquated writing system over all others.

To Westerners, the Qin Emperor is best known for his lavish tomb outside the modern city Xi'an, near his capital city.

To the Chinese, however, the Qin Emperor is known as the "burner of the books" because of his determination to eradicate intellectual opposition, particularly from Confucianists. He followed the legalist philosophy which held that morality was not enough to govern society (a shocking view to the Confucianists, for whom morality is all). The ideal legalist state was government on the basis of self-interest with a system of rewards and punishments and a complex legal system underpinning them.

Revolts broke out against the Qin and there was a struggle for power, most notably between Xiang Yu, commander of the northern army of the rebel state of Chu, who attempted to destroy the Emperor's mausoleum, and a commander, Liu Bang, bandit turned general of the southern Chu army, who eventually succeeded in establishing the Han dynasty.

Han Dynasty: 206 BCE–220 CE

The Han establishment of a centralized bureaucratic government was based on the Confucian ideology of paternalistic rule by superior, educated and moral men. An imperial university was set up in 124 BCE which within a hundred years had 3,000 students, and the curriculum consisted entirely of the Confucian classics with forms of examination being held at court to select "men of talent" to govern.

When the Han fell in AD 220 CE, a period of disunion
(220–581 CE) followed with separate states taking
control of different parts of China.

The Sui Dynasty: 581–618 CE

Just as the first Qin emperor united the separate states in
221 BCE into a short-lived empire characterized in folklore
as ruthless and tyrannical, the first Emperor of the Sui (581–
618 CE) reunited the country and gained his own position in
Chinese folklore as a brutal tyrant. In both cases it is partly
the "golden age" which followed their necessarily rigorous
regimes that colours the traditional view.

Apart from paving the way for the Tang rulers by
reuniting China, another of the great contributions of
the Sui was the linking of an existing canal system,
bringing grain to the capital, which was to lead to the
final construction of the Grand Canal joining Hangzhou
and Kaifeng.

The first Sui Emperor was succeeded in 604 BCE by his
son.

The Tang Dynasty: 618–907 CE

The Tang dynasty, once established, is still viewed as
the "golden age"; for nearly three centuries there was
peace at home and a solid economic base for the
prosperity of the country. The government required a
vast revenue to support the growing bureaucracy, for
the Tang restored the old Han system and refined it
into an enormous pyramid with the Emperor at the top,
served by his imperial Chancellery, imperial Secretariat
and Department of State Affairs. The latter supervised
six ministries: of officials, finance, rites, army, justice
and public works.

Sun Yat-sen

Mao Zedong

Chinese Communist troops marching through Beijing after taking over
the city in early 1949

Deng Xiaoping in the 1970s

Scene from a "jingxi" (Beijing Opera) performance

Agricultural produce market in northern Beijing

Looking north from the Forbidden City, Beijing

Some of the excavated statues of the Terracotta Army at the Qin tomb

The Great Goose Pagoda, an example of Tang Dynasty architecture

The Great Wall

Bank of China Tower, Hong Kong, designed by I.M. Pei, 1989

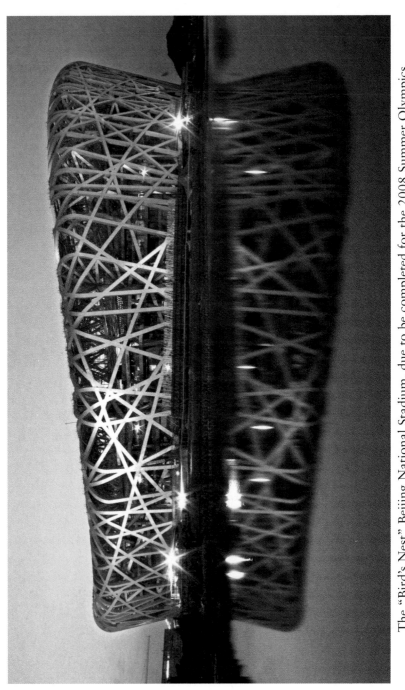

The "Bird's Nest" Beijing National Stadium, due to be completed for the 2008 Summer Olympics

Both physically and culturally the Tang was a period of expansion. Through military campaigns and diplomatic negotiations Chinese influence was extended out into the north-west along the Silk Road, and good relations were established with the Tibetans. The Koreans and Japanese—forced to admire the cultural domination of China with its complex government system, elegant architecture, flourishing literature and marvellous handicrafts combining in an extremely elegant lifestyle—borrowed hugely, beginning with the script. The walled capital of the Tang, Chang'an (today's Xi'an), was enormous, covering an area far greater than that delineated by the surviving Ming city wall. Apart from the local population, a considerable number of foreign traders from the Middle East also lived in the city and had their own mosques and Zoroastrian and Manichean temples. They came for silks and the newly perfected porcelain and luxury goods and, in turn, they brought luxuries: pearls, Arab horses for the Emperor's games of polo, grapes and melons, precious stones and handicrafts.

The great legacy of the Tang was both governmental and cultural. The pattern of imperial government was established, to change little in succeeding centuries, and the poetry of the dynasty is still considered China's greatest. The two best known poets are Li Bai (Li Po in Wade-Giles) and Du Fu (Tu Fu). The former is known as a great drinker and his best-known poem describes drinking with the moon and his shadow for company. Du Fu is regarded as a more profound observer for his poems reflect the misery of exile (he fled to Sichuan during the An Lushan rebellion and was occasionally out of favour with his bureaucratic superiors) and the

sufferings of the poor at the gates of the rich men's
mansions. Bai Juyi (Po Chü) was another Tang poet who
addressed himself to political problems, comparing the
current regime unfavourably with the days of the
founding Emperor. As it was dangerous to attack the
Emperor directly, Bai Juyi went through contortions to
make his point. One of his poems points out that the
elephant in the imperial zoo, a tribute gift from the
small neighbouring state of Burma, was moribund,
whilst the elephants in the zoo during the enlightened
reign of the dynastic founder enjoyed very good health.
The implication was that everything, including
elephants, was currently rotten and the Emperor was
personally to blame. Wang Wei (701–61 CE) was a
painter as well as a poet and though his work is only
known through copies, his writings are part of the
development of Chinese painting towards the depiction
of the nature of things rather than their exterior
appearance.

Period Of Division: Five Dynasties and Ten Kingdoms, 907–79 CE

The period of division following the collapse of the Tang
is known as the Five Dynasties and Ten Kingdoms.

The Song Dynasty: 960–1279 CE

The Song dynasty was founded by the leader of the
Imperial Guard of one of the Five Dynasties in the
north, Shao Kuangyin.

The main things to remember about the Song dynasty
are that it was a divided dynasty and that, culturally, it
was very different from the Tang. The Tang was
outward-looking, absorbing other influences like the

baggy female clothing of Central Asia, and one of the greatest Tang poets, Li Bai, was born in what is today Soviet Central Asia. Ceramic designs had incorporated non-Chinese design elements (putti playing amongst grape arbours) and reflected, in the ceramic models of loaded camels, the openness to foreign trade. The Song, by contrast, was a period of productive introspection, a search for the roots of the Chinese tradition, not that of the outside world. Confucianism was re-evaluated and updated and many of the ceramic designs are based on ancient bronzes and jades, for Song scholars were discovering Chinese antiquity, in a sort of equivalent of the Gothic revival.

The division of the Song into the northern Song (960–1127 CE) and southern Song (1127–1279 CE) reflects the move of the capital from Kaifeng on the Yellow River southwards to Hangzhou. The move was forced by the increasing military power of the northern peoples, most notably the Khitan, Jurched and Tanguts (and, later, the Mongols).

Foreign trade overland was made difficult by the alien rulers in the north and north-west but the sea trade from the southern coastal ports (most notably Quanzhou in Fujian, which now has a maritime trade museum) flourished. Silks and porcelain were shipped in long, narrow boats to south-east Asia, Korea, Japan, and the boats returned loaded with spices, ivory, luxury timbers and medicinal herbs. Ships were powered by both oars and sails and, for safety, were already divided by bulkheads (or watertight compartments to prevent complete disaster in case of a localized leak).

Despite the forced move south, life in the Song capitals was very different from that of the Tang.

During the Tang, cities were divided internally by walls,
whose gates locked at the evening curfew, and many of
the popular love stories of the Tang tell of young men
locked out of their ward at night after an assignation.
This system had disappeared by the Song when only the
outer gates by the city walls were closed at night whilst
inhabitants were free to wander to the pleasure boats
moored on the river (where they were entertained by
sing-song girls) or to the many theatres, wine-shops and
tea-houses. A marvellous painting of Kaifeng as the
capital has survived, Zhang Zeduan's "Qingming Festival
on the River" (late eleventh to early twelfth century).
Painted in a vivid realistic style, this depicts the bustling
streets with their open-fronted shops (similar to the
small shops that line the streets in small towns today)
and the variety of road traffic: officials with "eared
hats" on horses, the characteristic Chinese wheelbarrow
with the weight over the central wheel, loaded carts,
ladies in sedan chairs with brightly patterned curtains
and pedlars with baskets on carrying poles. Many of the
buildings have an upper storey circled by a veranda, and
the internal courtyards behind the shops can be
glimpsed. The way that the women are concealed within
the sedan chairs is an indication of the increasing
enclosure of women, which was reinforced by the new
fashion of foot-binding. This strange practice, which has
persisted well into the twentieth century, was at first
an upper-class fashion which gradually spread to all but
the very poor, who depended on the work of women as
well as men. When girls were about seven, their feet
were tightly wrapped in wet strips of cloth, bending all
but the big toe underneath the sole of the foot. A small
block of wood was bandaged under the heel to enable

the victim to walk in a strange, stiff-legged way. Once
the feet were deformed in this way, a woman had to
keep her bindings on, to be able to move at all, and
even in pornographic paintings otherwise naked women
are depicted with little leggings and foot-bindings.

Mongul Yuan Dynasty: 1279–1368 CE

The sudden arrival of the Mongols in the twelfth century
and their conquest of everything that lay between Vienna
and Beijing is still something of a mystery. It has been
suggested that Central Asia suddenly became drier and
less hospitable to these nomads, but this theory has not
stood close examination. Others suggest that a purely
nomadic society such as that of the Mongols suffered from
economic instability, for nomadism without pastoralism
could not provide the grains needed to supplement the
milk and mean diet, nor did nomads pause to indulge in
mining and smelting of the iron that was essential to their
horsemanship. Their iron stirrups (in use by the fourth
century CE, if not earlier) enabled them to stabilize
themselves on horseback so that they could shoot their
iron-tipped arrows with accuracy. Both stirrups and
arrows had to be purchased from sedentary mining
communities. However, need for supplies was constant
and would not on its own provoke the immense growth
of the Mongol empire. It must have been a combination of
such factors together with the divided and unstable
leadership of Chinggis (or Genghis) Khan (c.1167–1227).
He gradually subdued all the other Mongol clans and
groups and began the apparently inexorable conquering
expansion.

It was one of his grandsons, Khublai Khan (1215–94),
who supervised the conquest of south China,

overthrowing the Song dynasty and establishing the Yuan. The name means "first", "beginning" or "fundamental principal" and it was the first time that a dynastic name was chosen for its meaning; all previous ones had something to do with surnames or place-names of significance.

The Yuan capital was established in the north, in Beijing, where, there, an entirely new city was built on the ideal Chinese grid system. By using the Yellow River, the Grand Canal was extended northwards to reach Beijing and supply the capital with grain from rice-producing south China.

Ming Dynasty: 1368–1644 CE

Zhu Yuanzhang, founder of the Ming ("Bright") dynasty, was born into a poor tenant family in Fengyang, Anhui province, in 1328.

After the alien rule of the Mongols, Zhu Yuanzhang and his supporters looked back deliberately to the great Chinese dynasties of Han, Tang and Song and used them as conscious models. Even in ceramics, there was a revival of the three-colour earthenware of the Tang with a new Ming palette.

It was during the Ming that the Great Wall, once again a crucial defensive barrier, was faced with brick, as can still be seen today. Also during the reign of the Yongle Emperor a series of grand maritime expeditions were launched under the command of the eunuch admiral Zheng He from Yunnan. Between 1405 and 1433 (before the Europeans really got going on their maritime explorations), seven expeditions set out to the Persian Gulf, South-east Asia and the eastern coast of Africa. The expense of the expeditions was one reason

for their cancellation and China never regained the
same status as a maritime power.

The Qing Dynasty: 1644–1911 CE

The Manchus, who established the Qing ("Pure")
dynasty, were from the north-eastern part of China.

The Qing did not gain full control over south China
for a couple of decades, and the last Ming stronghold,
the island of Taiwan, was not captured until 1683. The
Qing also pursued a policy of conquest and control in
Turkestan, Mongolia and Tibet, areas which had fallen
out of the Chinese sphere of interest.

Despite their tactical adoption of Chinese methods,
the Manchus were keen to remain separate. They
remained different in appearance for they wore their
own costume and their women never bound their feet.
Chinese men were forbidden to wear the standard Ming
hairstyle (a bun on top of the head) and had to follow
the Manchu male custom of shaving the front of the
head and braiding the rest of the hair into a long plait.
A Ming hairstyle was a mark of resistance (incidentally,
if you see any Taoist priests, they still wear the Ming
hairstyle), just as cutting off their long plaits became a
mark of anti-Qing resistance for young men at the
beginning of the twentieth century.

Two Qing emperors generally classed as "great
leaders" are the Kangxi ("Vigorous and splendid")
Emperor (1654–1722) and his grandson, the Qianlong
("Lasting eminence") Emperor (1711–99). It was the
Kangxi Emperor who, though young, presided over the
capture of the south. Not long after, he settled border
disputes with the Russians, signing a treaty of peace in
1689, before personally leading armies into Outer

Mongolia and Turkestan to subdue threatening neighbours. He made six tours of inspection in south China, particularly to examine water-conservancy projects, and was concerned with improving communications via the Grand Canal and with making the Yellow River safe.

The Emperor supervised the construction of the wonderful Summer Palace at Chengde, about 150 kilometres north-east of Beijing. The Bishu shan zhuang (or "Mountain village where you can escape the heat"), a hunting park dotted with pavilions and pools, surrounded by the eight "outer temples" which are almost stage-sets in the Tibetan style, is one of the places where you can actually feel how extraordinary the scale of Qing grandeur can be. The entire valley is brought into the composition. The use of Tibetan style for some of the outer temples was a matter both of politics and taste; the buildings were used to receive Tibetan and Mongolian dignitaries.

It was the Kangxi Emperor who appointed Jesuit missionaries to run the Imperial Board of Astronomy (the Jesuit observatory can still be seen in Beijing just west of the Friendship Store) and he made use of Jesuit missionaries like Gerbillon as interpreters during negotiations with Russia. Jesuits and Chinese made maps for him, showing the areas of his conquests, and Matteo Ricci engraved them. Many poems were attributed to the Kangxi Emperor but it is impossible to know whether he actually wrote them; in the memoirs of the Jesuit Matteo Ripa (1628–1745), there is a slightly clearer view of the Emperor: "The Emperor supposed himself to be an excellent musician and a still better mathematician, but though he had a taste for the sciences . . . he knew nothing of music and scarcely understood the first elements of mathematics . . . ''

Like his grandfather, with whom he went hunting as a child, the Qianlong Emperor led many campaigns, particularly in Central Asia, Burma and Vietnam, which, with the exception of the Central Asian campaigns, were unsuccessful and enormously expensive. They virtually wiped out the government reserves, leaving China quite unable in the succeeding century to withstand foreign encroachments. There are other intimations of impending disaster in the Qianlong period: the fruitless embassy of Lord Macartney, sent to try and open China to foreign (or at least British) trade (1793) was granted an audience by the Emperor but no concessions. The Emperor was not unaware of the possible consequences of this rebuttal for he instructed officials in Guangzhou to try and prevent other European merchants from ganging up with the English.

Like his grandfather, the Qianlong Emperor made use of the special talents of the Jesuit missionaries (who seem to have spent more time ingratiating themselves with the court and teaching European sciences and arts than gathering converts, a fact which contributed to the dissolution of the order in 1773). He particularly favoured the painter Castiglione and Father Benoit, who contributed the "European" palaces and Italianate gardens to the Emperor's summer palace (the "Old Summer Palace"), the Garden of Perfect Brightness on the outskirts of Beijing (whose ruins can still be seen despite destruction by French and foreign troops in 1860).

The last character of the Qing was the Dowager Empress Cixi (1835–1908), whose name, rather

inappropriately, meant "Motherly and auspicious". She
entered the palace in 1851 as a concubine to the
Emperor, whose only son she bore, consequently raising
her status. The Emperor died in 1861 and Cixi, together
with the senior consort, acted on her son's behalf.
There were eight official regents but Cixi had managed
to get hold of the imperial seal required for all edicts.
Using the pretext of their weakness over the British
and French invasion of 1860, Cixi managed to get one
regent executed and the rest punished. She is credited
with killing her son but he actually died of smallpox in
1875, whereupon she chose her younger sister's son as
the heir apparent. This was a flagrant breach of both
protocol (the decision was not hers to make) and
practice (the next emperor should always be of the next
generation to avoid confusion of relative positions
within the imperial clan), but, by now, few disagreed
with Cixi. Her daughter-in-law, who was pregnant by
the Emperor, committed suicide. Even when the new
Tongzhi Emperor reached his majority and she had no
official position, she continued to manoeuvre her
associates into positions close to him. When he began to
associate with reformers in 1898 and pledged to
modernize and reinvigorate China in the face of foreign
incursion and evident incapacity to face the twentieth
century, she had him imprisoned in the new Summer
Palace which she had been improving (apparently with
money designated for, and badly needed by, the navy).
When the Boxers rebels reached Beijing, a Japanese
diplomat was murdered by Chinese troops and the
foreign diplomats requested military protection from
their governments. As an eight-nation army assembled
on the coast, the Empress asked all foreign diplomats to

leave and the German minister was killed by imperial troops. It became clear that the court was actively supporting the Boxers, and the siege of the foreign legations in Beijing was laid by both Boxers and imperial troops. When the allied army finally arrived, the Empress Dowager fled to Xi'an. A protocol was signed by which the Chinese government paid reparation for the loss of life. Cixi eventually returned to Beijing and began to give a series of receptions for foreigners who were, surprisingly, captivated by the "old Buddha". A few modest reforms (similar to those proposed in 1898) were initiated, establishing modern schools and sending students to study abroad. In 1908, the Emperor died and Cixi died the next day, having appointed a three-year-old successor, Puyi.

Cixi's extraordinary career took place as the Qing collapsed in the face of internal rebellion, complicated by the impact of the outside world. The Qing did not long survive the death of Cixi. In 1911, a rather chaotic rebellion, starting in Wuhan, overthrew the Qing and proclaimed the Republic of China.

7

THE ARTS

The present political boundaries of China, which include Tibet, Inner Mongolia, Xinjiang, and the north-eastern provinces formerly called Manchuria, embrace a far larger area of East Asia than will be discussed here. "China Proper", as it has been called, consists of 18 historical provinces bounded by the Tibetan Highlands on the west, the Gobi to the north, and Myanmar (Burma), Laos, and Vietnam to the south-west; and it is primarily the arts of this area that will concern us here.

The first communities that can be identified culturally as Chinese were settled chiefly in the basin of the Huang He (Yellow River). Gradually they spread out, influencing other tribal cultures until, by the Han dynasty (206 to 220 BCE), most of China proper was dominated by the culture that had been formed in the "cradle" of northern Chinese civilization. Over this area there slowly spread a common written language, as well as a common belief in the power of heaven and the ancestral spirits to influence the living and in the importance of ceremony and sacrifice to achieve harmony among heaven, nature, and humankind. These beliefs were to have a great influence on the character of Chinese art.

Chinese civilization, contrary to the popular notion, is by no means the oldest in the world: those of Mesopotamia and Egypt are far older. But, while the early Western cultures died, became stagnant, or were transformed to the point of breaking all continuity, the culture of China has grown continuously from prehistoric settlements into the great civilization of today.

The Chinese themselves were among the most historically conscious of all the major civilizations and were intensely aware of the strength and continuity of their cultural tradition. They viewed history as a cycle of decline and renewal associated with the succession of ruling dynasties. Both the political fragmentation and social and economic chaos of decline and the vigour of dynastic rejuvenation could stimulate and colour important artistic developments. Thus, it is quite legitimate to think of the history of Chinese art, as the Chinese themselves do, primarily in terms of the styles of successive dynasties.

General Characteristics

One of the outstanding characteristics of Chinese art is the extent to which it reflects the class structure that has existed at different times in Chinese history. Up to the Warring States period (475–221 BCE), the arts were produced by anonymous craftsmen for the royal and feudal courts. During the Warring States and the Han dynasty, the growth of a land-owning and merchant class brought new patrons; and after the Han there began to emerge the concept of "fine art" as the product of the leisure of the educated gentry, many of whom were amateur practitioners of the arts of poetry, music, calligraphy, and, eventually, painting. At this time a distinction began to arise between the lower-class professional and the elite amateur artist that was to have a great influence on the character of Chinese art in later times. Gradually one tradition became increasingly identified with the artists and craftsmen who worked for the court or sold their work for profit. Identified with another tradition, the scholarly amateurs looked upon such people with some contempt, and the art of the literati became increasingly refined and rarefied to the point that, from the Song dynasty (960–1279) onward, an assumed awkwardness in technique was admired as a mark of the amateur and gentleman.

One effect of the revolutions of the twentieth century has been the breaking down of the class barriers between amateur and professional and even, during the Great Proletarian Cultural Revolution of 1966–76, an emphasis on anonymous, proletarian-made art like that of the Tang dynasty (618–907) and earlier.

Since the third century CE, calligraphy, or writing as a fine art, has been considered supreme among the visual arts in China. Not only does it require immense skill and fine judgment, but it is regarded as uniquely revealing of the character and breadth of cultivation of the writer. Since the time when inscribed oracle bones and tortoise shells (China's oldest extant writing) were used for divination in the Shang dynasty (seventeenth to eleventh centuries BCE), calligraphy has been associated with spiritual communication and has been viewed in terms of the writer's own spiritual attunement. To fully appreciate calligraphy, as to produce it, requires lofty personal qualities and unusual aesthetic sensitivity. To understand its finer points requires experience and sensibility of a high order.

The Chinese painter uses essentially the same materials as

the calligrapher—brush, ink, and silk or paper—and the Chinese judge his work by the same criteria, basically the vitality and expressiveness of the brush stroke itself and the harmonious rhythm of the whole composition. Painting in China, therefore, is essentially a linear art. The painters of most periods were concerned less with striving for originality or conveying a sense of reality and three-dimensional mass through such aids as shading and perspective, concentrating instead on transmitting to silk or paper, through the rhythmic movement of the brush stroke, an awareness of the inner life of things.

The aesthetics of line in calligraphy and painting have had a significant influence on the other arts in China. In the motifs that adorn the ritual bronzes, in the flow of the drapery over the surface of Buddhist sculpture, in the decoration of lacquerware, pottery, and cloisonné enamel, it is the rhythmic movement of the line, following the natural movement of the artist's or craftsman's hand, that to a large extent determines the form and gives to Chinese art as a whole its remarkable harmony and unity of style.

In early times this sense of attunement involved submission to the Will of Heaven through ritual and sacrifice, and it was the function of Chinese art to serve these ends. Archaic bronze vessels were made for sacrifices to heaven and to the spirits of clan ancestors, who were believed to influence the living for good if the rites were properly and regularly performed. Chinese society, basically agricultural, has always laid great stress on the need for humans to understand the pattern of nature and to live in accordance with it. The world of nature was seen as the visible manifestation of the workings of the Great Ultimate through the generative interaction of the yin–yang (female–male) dualism. As it developed, the purpose of Chinese art turned from propitiation and sacrifice to the expression of human understanding of these forces through the painting of landscape, bamboo, birds, and flowers. This might be called the metaphysical, Taoist aspect of Chinese painting.

Particularly in early times, art also had social and moral functions. The earliest paintings, referred to in ancient texts, depicted on the walls of palaces and ancestral halls benevolent emperors, sages, virtuous ministers, loyal generals, and their evil opposites as examples and warnings to the living. Portrait painting also had this moral function, depicting not the features of the subject so much as his character and his role in society. Court painters were called upon to depict auspicious and memorable events. This was the ethical, Confucian function of painting.

High religious art as such is foreign to China. Popular folk religion was seldom an inspiration to great works of art, and Buddhism, which indeed produced many masterpieces of a special kind, was a foreign importation.

Human relationships have always been of supreme importance in China, and a common theme of figure painting is that of gentlemen enjoying scholarly pursuits together or the poignant partings and infrequent reunions that were the lot of officials whose appointments took them the length and breadth of the country.

Among the typical themes of Chinese art there is no place for war, violence, the nude, death, or martyrdom. Nor is inanimate matter ever painted for art's sake: the very rocks and streams are felt to be alive, visible manifestations of the invisible forces of the universe. No theme would be accepted in Chinese art that was not inspiring, noble, refreshing to the spirit, or at least charming. Nor is there any place in the Chinese artistic tradition for an art of pure form divorced from content, and the Chinese cannot conceive of a work of art of which the form is beautiful while the subject matter is un-edifying.

In the broadest sense, therefore, all Chinese art is symbolic, for everything that is painted reflects some aspect of a totality of which the painter is intuitively aware. At the same time Chinese art is full of symbols of a more specific kind, some with various possible meanings. Bamboo suggests the spirit of the scholar, which can be bent by circumstance but never broken, and jade symbolizes purity and indestructibility. The dragon, in remote antiquity perhaps an alligator or rain deity, is the wholly benevolent symbol of the emperor; the crane, of long life; paired mandarin ducks, of wedded fidelity. Popular among the many symbols drawn from the plant world are the orchid, a Confucian symbol of purity and loyalty; the winter plum, which blossoms even in the snow and stands for irrepressible purity, in either a revolutionary political or a spiritual sense; and the gnarled pine tree, which may represent either survival in a harsh political environment or the uncon-querable spirit of old age.

The character of Chinese painting and calligraphy is closely bound up with the nature of the medium. The basic material is ink, formed into a short stick of hardened pine soot and glue, which is rubbed to the required consistency on an inkstone with a little water. The calligrapher or painter uses a pointed-tipped brush made of the hair of goat, deer, or wolf set in a shaft of bamboo. He writes or paints on a length of silk or a sheet of paper, the surface of which is absorbent, allowing no erasure or correction. He must therefore know beforehand what he intends to do, and the execution demands confidence, speed, and a mastery of technique acquired only by long practice. For example, to broaden the brush stroke, the calli-grapher or painter applies downward pressure on the brush.

Such subtle action of the highly flexible but carefully controlled brush tip determines the dynamic character of the brushwork and is the primary focus of attention of both the artist and critical viewers.

In painting, colour is added, if at all, to make the effect more true to life or to add decorative accent and rarely as a structural element in the design, as in Western art. Brighter, more opaque pigments derived from mineral sources (blue from azurite, green from malachite, red from cinnabar or lead, yellow from orpiment or ochre, all produced in various intensities) are preferred for painting on silk, while translucent vegetable pigments predominate in painting on paper (indigo blue, red from safflower or madder, vegetable green, rattan and sophora plant yellow) and produce a lighter, more delicate effect.

While painting on dry plaster walls or screens is an ancient art in China, more common formats in the past millennium have been the vertical hanging scroll, perhaps derived from the Buddhist devotional banner, and the horizontal hand scroll, which may be of any length up to about 15 metres (50 feet). Other forms are fan painting and the album leaf. The artist's carefully placed signature, inscription, and seals are an integral part of the composition. In Chinese eyes a picture may gain considerably in interest and value from the colophons added by later connoisseurs on the painting itself or, in the case of a hand scroll, mounted after it. The mounting of paintings and calligraphy is a highly skilled craft and, if carefully done, will enhance the appearance of a scroll and ensure its preservation for many centuries.

Other major art forms of China include pottery, jade carving, metalwork (including gold and silver inlay and cloisonné enamel), textiles, and lacquerware. In several of these, China can claim a long priority over the rest of the world. True pottery glazes were developed in China before the end of the second millennium BCE and porcelain by the sixth century, more than 1,000 years before its discovery in Europe; jade carving, sericulture (the raising of silkworms), and weaving of silk go back to Neolithic times and lacquer painting to the Shang dynasty. Bronze casting, while not so ancient as that of the Middle East, reached by 1000 BCE a perfection of beauty and craftsmanship not matched in the ancient Western world. In point of style, all these arts share with sculpture a debt to pictorial art and an aesthetic based on the rhythmic movement of the line.

Jade occupies a special place in Chinese artistic culture, valued as gold is in the West but hallowed with even loftier moral connotations. The *Shuowen jiezi* ("Discussions of Writings and Explanations of Characters") of Xu Shen defined jade (*yu*) as follows:

"A stone that is beautiful, it has five virtues. There is warmth in its lustre and brilliance; this is its quality of kindness; its soft interior may be viewed from the outside revealing [the goodness] within; this is its quality of rectitude; its tone is tranquil and high and carries far and wide; this is its quality of wisdom; it may be broken but cannot be twisted; this is its quality of bravery; its sharp edges are not intended for violence; this is its quality of purity."

Because of this and the belief in its indestructibility, jade from early times was lavishly used not only for dress ornaments but also for ritual objects, both Confucian and Taoist, and to protect the dead in the tomb.

The jade stone used since ancient times in China is nephrite, a crystalline calcium magnesium silicate, which in its pure state is white but may be green, cream, yellow, brown, grey, black, or mottled owing to the presence of impurities, chiefly iron compounds. Generically, the Chinese used the term *yu* to cover a variety of related "jade" stones, including nephrite, bowenite, and jadeite. In the Neolithic period, by the mid-fourth millennium BC, jade from Lake Tai (in Jiangsu province) began to be used by south-eastern culture groups, while deposits along the Liao River in the north-east (called "Xiuyan jade", probably bowenite) were utilized by the Hongshan culture.

In historic times, China's chief source of nephrite has been the riverbeds of Yarkand and Hotan in present-day Xinjiang Autonomous Region in north-western China, where jade is found in the form of boulders. Since the eighteenth century, China has received from northern Myanmar (upper Burma) a brilliant green jadeite (also called *feizui*, or "kingfisher-feathers") that is a granular sodium-aluminium silicate harder than but not quite so tough as nephrite. Having a hardness like that of steel or feldspar, jade cannot be carved or cut with metal tools but has to be laboriously drilled, ground, or sawed with an abrasive paste and rotational or repetitive-motion machinery, usually after being reduced to the form of blocks or thin slabs.

The Chinese had discovered as early as the Shang dynasty that the sap of the lac tree, a naturally occurring polymer, could be used to form hard but lightweight vessels when built up in very thin layers through the repeated dipping of a core of carved wood, bamboo, or cloth. With the addition of pigments, most commonly red and black, less frequently green and yellow, it could also be used for painting and decorating the outer layers of these vessels. Being sticky, painted lacquer must be applied slowly with the brush, giving rise to prolonged motions and fluid, often elegantly curvilinear designs. Because lacquer is almost totally impervious to water, vessels and wine cups have been excavated in perfect condition from waterlogged graves of the late fifth-century BCE Zeng state in

Suixian, of the fourth–third century BCE Chu state in Jiangling (now Shashi), and of the early second century BCE Han dynasty in Changsha. Such works ranged from large-scale coffins to bird- or animal-shaped drum stands to such daily utensils as nested toiletry boxes and food-serving implements. By the Warring States period, lacquerwork had developed into a major industry; and, being approximately 10 times more costly than their bronze equivalents, lacquer vessels came to rival bronzes as the most esteemed medium for providing offerings in ancestral ceremonies among the wealthy aristocracy.

It was the Chinese who first discovered that the roughly 1 km (1,000 yards) of thread that constitutes the cocoon of the silkworm, *Bombyx mori*, could be reeled off, spun, and woven; and sericulture soon became an important feature of the Chinese rural economy. Its place in Chinese culture is indicated by the legend that it was the wife of the mythical Yellow Emperor, Huangdi, who taught the Chinese people the art and by the fact that in historic times the empress was ceremonially associated with it. The weaving of damask probably existed in the Shang dynasty, and the fourth–third century BCE tombs at Mashan near Shashi (Hubei province, excavated in 1982) have provided outstanding examples of brocade, gauze, and embroidery with pictorial designs as well as the first complete garments. Although transportation westward across Central Asia's trade route brought Chinese silks to many parts of the Mediterranean region, knowledge of silk production techniques did not reach the area until the sixth century CE.

8

CALLIGRAPHY AND PAINTING

Chinese calligraphy is a form of pure art and derives from the written form of the Chinese language. Chinese is not an alphabetical language; each character is composed of a number of differently shaped lines within an imaginary square. The early Chinese written words, like the Egyptian hieroglyphs, were pictorial images, though not so close to the objects they represented as in the ancient Egyptian writing. Rather, they were simplified images, indicating meaning through suggestion or imagination. These simple images were flexible in composition, capable of developing with changing conditions by means of slight variations.

The earliest known Chinese logographs are engraved on the shoulder bones of large animals and on tortoise shells. For this reason, the script found on these objects is commonly called *jiaguwen*, or shell-and-bone script. It seems likely that each of the ideographs was carefully composed before it was engraved. Although the figures are not entirely uniform, they do not vary greatly in size. The figures must have evolved from rough and careless scratches in the still more distant past. Because the literal content of most *jiaguwen* is related to ancient religious, mythical prognostication or to rituals, *jiaguwen* is also known as oracle bone script. Archaeologists and paleographers have demonstrated that this early script was widely used in the Shang dynasty (*c.* eighteenth–eleventh century BCE). Nevertheless, the 1992 discovery of a similar inscription on a potsherd at Dinggongcun in Shandong province demonstrates that the use of a mature script can be dated to the late Neolithic Longshan culture (*c.* 3000–1500 BCE).

Jiaguwen was followed by a form of writing found on bronze vessels associated with ancestor worship and thus known as *jinwen* ("metal script"). Wine and raw or cooked food were placed in specially designed and cast bronze vessels and offered to the ancestors in special ceremonies. The inscriptions, which might range from a few words to several hundred, were incised on the insides of the vessels. The words could not be roughly formed or even just simple images; they had to be well worked out to go with the decorative ornaments outside the bronzes, and in some instances they almost became the chief decorative design in themselves.

Although they preserved the general structure of the bone-and-shell script, they were considerably elaborated and beautified. Each bronze or set of them may bear a different type of inscription, not only in the wording but also in the manner of writing. Hundreds were created by different artists. The bronze script—which is also called *guwen* ("ancient script"), or *dazhuan* ("large seal") script—represents the second stage of development in Chinese calligraphy.

When China was united for the first time, in the third century BCE, the bronze script was unified and regularity enforced. Shihuangdi, the first emperor of Qin, gave the task of working out the new script to his prime minister, Li Si, and permitted only the new style to be used. This third stage in the development of Chinese calligraphy was known as *xiaozhuan* ("small seal") style. Small-seal script is characterized by lines of even thickness and many curves and circles. Each word tends to fill up an imaginary square, and a passage written in small-seal style has the appearance of a series of equal squares neatly arranged in columns and rows, each of them balanced and well-spaced.

This uniform script had been established chiefly to meet the growing demands for record-keeping. Unfortunately, the small-seal style could not be written speedily and therefore was not entirely suitable, giving rise to the fourth stage, *lishu*, or official style. (The Chinese word *li* here means "a petty official" or "a clerk"; *lishu* is a style specially devised for the use of clerks.) Careful examination of *lishu* reveals no circles and very few curved lines. Squares and short straight lines, vertical and horizontal, predominate. Because of the speed needed for writing, the brush in the hand tends to move up and down, and an even thickness of line cannot be easily achieved.

Lishu is thought to have been invented by Zheng Miao (240–207 BCE), who had offended Shihuangdi and was serving a 10-year sentence in prison. He spent his time in prison working out this new development, which opened up seemingly endless possibilities for later calligraphers. Freed by *lishu* from earlier constraints, they evolved new variations in the shape of strokes and in character structure. The words in *lishu* style tend to be square or rectangular with a greater width than height. While stroke thickness may vary, the shapes remain rigid; for instance, the vertical lines had to be shorter and the horizontal ones longer. As this curtailed the freedom of hand to express individual artistic taste, a fifth stage developed— *zhenshu* (*kaishu*), or regular script. No individual is credited with inventing this style, probably during the period of the Three Kingdoms and Western Jin (220–317). The Chinese write in regular script today; in fact, what is known as modern Chinese writing is almost 2,000 years old, and the written words of China have not changed since the first century of the Common Era.

"Regular script" means "the proper script type of Chinese writing" used by all Chinese for government documents, printed books, and public and private dealings in important matters ever since its establishment. Since the Tang period (618–907 CE), each candidate taking the civil service examination was required to be able to write a good hand in regular style. This Imperial decree deeply influenced all Chinese who wanted to become scholars and enter the civil service. Although the examination was abolished in 1905, most Chinese up to the present day try to acquire a hand in regular style.

In *zhenshu* each stroke, each square or angle, and even each dot can be shaped according to the will and taste of the calligrapher. Indeed, a word written in regular style presents an almost infinite variety of problems of structure and composition and, when executed, the beauty of its abstract design can draw the mind away from the literal meaning of the word itself.

The greatest exponents of Chinese calligraphy were Wang Xizhi and his son Wang Zianzhi in the fourth century. Few of their original works have survived, but a number of their writings were engraved on stone tablets and woodblocks, and rubbings were made from them. Many great calligraphers imitated their styles, but none ever surpassed them for artistic transformation.

Wang Xizhi not only provided the greatest example in the regular script, but also relaxed the tension somewhat in the arrangement of the strokes in the regular style by giving easy movement to the brush to trail from one word to another. This is called *xingshu*, or running script. This, in turn, led to the creation of *caoshu*, or grass script, which takes its name from its resemblance to windblown grass—disorderly yet orderly. The English term *cursive writing* does not describe grass script, for a standard cursive hand can be deciphered without much difficulty, but grass style greatly simplifies the regular style and can be deciphered only by seasoned calligraphers. It is less a style for general use than for that of the calligrapher who wishes to produce a work of abstract art.

Technically speaking, there is no mystery in Chinese calligraphy. The tools for Chinese calligraphy are few—an ink stick, an ink stone, a brush, and paper (some prefer silk). The calligrapher, using a combination of technical skill and imagination, must provide interesting shapes to the strokes and must compose beautiful structures from them without any retouching or shading and, most important of all, with well-balanced spaces between the strokes. This balance needs years of practice and training, for which reason, in part, calligraphy is regarded as a form of philosophical training very much like the martial arts; indeed, many master fighters over history have also been master calligraphers.

The fundamental inspiration of Chinese calligraphy, as of all arts in China, is nature. In regular script each stroke, even each dot, suggests the form of a natural object. As every twig of a living tree is alive, so every tiny stroke of a piece of fine calligraphy has the energy of a living thing. Printing does not admit the slightest variation in the shapes and structures, but strict regularity is not tolerated by Chinese calligraphers, especially those who are masters of the *caoshu*.

A finished piece of fine calligraphy is not a symmetrical arrangement of conventional shapes but, rather, something like the coordinated movements of a skilfully composed dance—impulse, momentum, momentary poise, and the interplay of active forces combining to form a balanced whole.

The Historical Context

Calligraphy and painting came together in the fifth century. The Sinicization of the Turkic rulers of the Northern Wei and the reunification of China under the Sui and Tang a century later paved the way for an infusion of southern taste at the court in the north and, gradually, for a synthesis of southern and northern styles. Calligraphy became a court activity and the emperor himself was a keen brush master as well as collector.

It was during Xuanzong's reign (716–756 CE) that Chinese calligraphy reached a definitive period. The three greatest masters involved in synthesizing southern and northern tendencies, blending fluid brush movement and expressive power, were Zhang Xu (known for his "delirious cursive" writing) and his pupils Yan Zhenqing and the monk Huaisu (the latter practising a "wild cursive", or *kuangcao*, style). They helped establish a new aesthetic standard that would soon pervade painting as well as calligraphy, more fully than ever before realizing in visual form the ancient aesthetic principles of "natural" emotionality and "sincerity" in rendering. Their preference for rugged, intentionally awkward, or altogether surprising forms was quite different from the elegant polish of the earlier, southern Chinese styles; and their emphasis on expressing character and emotion was handed down through Liu Gongquan of the next century and enshrined as the dominant manner of the Song dynasty by Su Shi, Huang Tingjian, and Mi Fu of the eleventh century.

Painting also flourished under the emperor's patronage. A number of royal patrons, including Kublai, the emperors Buyantu and Tog-temür, and Kublai's great-granddaughter Sengge, built an Imperial collection of important early works and also sponsored paintings that emphasized such themes as architecture and horses. Still, their activities were not a match for Song royal patronage, and it was in this period that the amateur art of painters of the scholar class first came to dominate Chinese painting standards.

The restriction of the scholars' opportunities at court and the choice of many of them to withdraw into seclusion rather than serve the Mongols created a heightened sense of class identity and individual purpose, which in turn inspired their art. Eremitic rather than courtly values now shaped the art of painting as never before, and a stylistic gulf sprang up between literati painters and court professionals that was not bridged until the eighteenth century.

Whereas most painting had previously displayed technical refinement and had conservatively transmitted the heritage of the immediate past, gradually evolving through modest individual departures, the literati thenceforth typically based their styles on a wide-ranging knowledge of distant stylistic precedents, selectively chosen and radically transformed by means of expressive calligraphic brushwork. Style and subject were both intended to reflect closely the artist's own personality and mood rather than conforming to the wishes of a patron. Typical were the simply brushed orchid paintings of Zheng Sixiao, who painted this traditional symbol of political loyalty without any ground beneath as a comment on the grievous loss of China to foreign domination.

Qian Xuan was among the first to define this new direction. From Wuxing in Zhejiang, he steadfastly declined an invitation to serve at court, as reflected in his painting style and themes. A conservative painter before the Mongol conquest, especially of realistic flowers and birds, he altered his style to incorporate the primitive qualities of ancient painting, favouring the Tang blue-and-green manner in his landscape painting, stiff or peculiarly mannered renditions of vegetation and small animals, and the archaic flavour of clerical script in his brush-work.

Calligraphy became a part of his design and frequently confirmed through historical references a link between subject matter and his eremitic choice of lifestyle. Like many Chinese scholars who espoused this amateur ideal, Qian Xuan was obliged by demeaning circumstances to exchange his paintings in return for his family's livelihood. The most distinguished of the scholar-painters was Zhao Mengfu, a fellow townsman and younger follower of Qian Xuan who became a high official and president of the Imperial Hanlin Academy. In his official travels he collected paintings by Northern Song masters that inspired him to revive and reinterpret the classical styles in his own fashion.

The Yuan produced many fine calligraphers, including Zhao Mengfu, who was the most influential, Yang Weizhen, and Zhang Yu. The period was less innovative in calligraphy than in painting, however, and Zhao's primary accomplishment was to sum up and resynthesize the past. His well-studied writing style was praised in his time for its breadth of historical understanding, and his standard script became the national model for book printing, but he was later criticized for a lack of daring or expression of personality, for a brush style too sweet and pleasing.

Other gentlemen-painters who worked at the Yuan court perpetuated more conservative Song styles, often rivalling or even surpassing their Song predecessors in the process. Ren Renfa worked in great detail and was perhaps the last of China's great horse painters; he defended his court service through both the style and theme of his paintings. Li Kan carefully studied the varieties of bamboo during his official travels and wrote a systematic treatise on painting them; he remains unsurpassed as a skilled bamboo painter. Gao Kegong followed Mi Fu and Mi Yuren in painting cloudy landscapes that symbolized good government. Wang Mian, who served not the Mongols but anti-Mongol forces at the end of the dynasty, set the highest standard for the painting of plums, a symbol of irrepressible purity and, potentially, of revolutionary zeal.

In retrospect, however, it was the ideals of the retired scholars that had the most lasting effect on later Chinese art. This may be summed up as individuality of expression, brushwork more revealing of the inner spirit of the subject—or of the artist himself—than of outward appearance, and suppression of the realistic and decorative in favour of an intentional plainness, understatement (*pingdan*), and awkwardness (*zhuo*), which marks the integrity of the gentleman suspicious of too much skill. Four masters of the middle and later Yuan, all greatly influenced by Zhao Mengfu, came to be regarded as the foremost exponents of this philosophy of painting in the Yuan period.

Huang Gongwang, a Taoist recluse, was the oldest. His most revered and perhaps only authentic surviving work is the hand scroll "Dwelling in the Fu-ch'un Mountains" (National Palace Museum, Taipei), painted with dynamic brushwork during occasional moods of inspiration between 1347 and 1350. Unlike the academicians, Huang Gongwang did not hesitate to go over his brushwork, for expression, not representation, was his aim. The cumulative effect of his masterpiece is obtained not by its fidelity to visible forms but by a profound feeling of oneness with nature that set an ideal standard for later scholarly painting.

This scholarly serenity was also expressed in the landscapes of Wu Zhen, a poor Taoist diviner, poet, and painter who, like Huang Gongwang, was inspired by Dong Yuan and Juran, whose manner he rendered, in landscapes and bamboo painting alike, with blunt brushwork, minimal motion, and utmost calm. His bamboo paintings are also superb, and, in an album in the National Palace Museum (Taipei), he pays tribute to his Song dynasty predecessors Su Dongpo (Su Shi) and Wen Tong.

The third of the Four Masters of the Yuan dynasty was Ni Zan, a prosperous gentleman and bibliophile forced by crippling taxation to give up his estates and become a wanderer. As a landscapist he eliminated all depictions of human beings. He thus reduced the compositional pattern of Li Cheng (symbolizing lofty gentlemen in isolation from the court) to its simplest terms, achieving as Wu Zhen had a sense of austere and monumental calm with the slenderest of means. He used ink, it was said, as sparingly as if it were gold.

Quite different was the technique of the fourth Yuan master, Wang Meng, a grandson of Zhao Mengfu. His brushwork was dense and energetic, derived from Dong Yuan but tangled and hoary and thereby imbued with a feeling of great antiquity. He often drew heavily from Guo Xi or from what he perceived as Tang traditions in his landscape compositions, which he filled with scholarly retreats. He sometimes used strong colours as well, which added a degree of visual charm and nostalgia to his painting that was lacking in the other three masters' work.

The combination in the Four Masters of a consistent philosophical and political attitude and a wide range of ink techniques made them models for later scholar-painters, both in their lives and in their art. It is impossible to appreciate the work of the landscape painters of the Ming and Qing dynasties unless one is aware of how acutely conscious they were of their debt to the Yuan masters and how frequently they paid tribute to them both in their style and in their inscriptions. Thenceforward, indeed, the artist's own inscription, as well as the colophons of admirers and connoisseurs, became an integral part of the total work of art.   .

Calligraphy continued to thrive in the Ming period, especially in the sixteenth and early seventeenth centuries, and new
developments, such as the appearance of calligraphic hanging
scrolls, testified to the increasing popularity of writing as a
decorative art form. Dong Qichang, in calligraphy as in
painting, came to be regarded as a leader for his time (sometimes paired with Wen Jingming, of the previous generation).
He developed a style as historically conscious as, yet somewhat
more individualized than, that of Zhao Mengfu of the Yuan,
the previous acknowledged master.

But Dong, like Zhao, was subjected to criticism for too
attractive a style. Furthermore, he was surrounded by numerous middle to late Ming masters who greatly enriched the art
of the period with strikingly personal styles (especially in the
execution of cursive and semicursive scripts) that showed the
influence of the middle Tang and Northern Song dynasty
individualists. They included Chen Xianzhang, Zhu Yunming,
Chen Shun, Wang Wen, Xu Wei, Zhang Ruitu, Ni Yuanlu,
Huang Daozhou, Shi Kefa, and Wang Duo.

Those who straddled the Ming–Qing transition continued
to explore individualistic calligraphic styles (particularly in
cursive and semicursive scripts) and included many who also
excelled at painting, such as Fu Shan, Fa Ruozhen, Zhu Da,
and Dao Ji. The chief contribution of Qing calligraphers came
later, however, with a resurgence in the importance of seal and
clerical scripts (which had survived primarily in seal carving
and in the writing of titled frontispieces for painted hand
scrolls). This was based on a renewed scholarly interest in
inscribed Zhou dynasty bronzes and in northern stelae of the
Han, Six Dynasties, and Tang periods.

While an indication of Chinese calligraphers' interest in seal
and clerical type scripts can already be seen in the early Qing
writings of Fu Shan, Zhu Da, and Dao Ji, a more scientific

study of bronze and stone inscriptions (*jinshixue*) was begun in the early to mid-eighteenth century by such scholar-calligraphers as Wang Shu. Thereafter, practitioners could be divided among imitative calligraphers and those who were more creative in their adaptation of these ancient scripts.

Among the latter were the eighteenth-century Yangzhou painters Jin Nong and Gao Fenghan, as well as the eighteenth- and nineteenth-century calligraphers Deng Shiru, Yi Bingshou, Ruan Yuan, and Wu Dazheng.

The interest in ancient styles continued in the early twentieth century, when the paleographer Dong Zuobin and other calligraphers pioneered the adaptation to the modern brush of the script used to inscribe Shang dynasty divinations, which had recently been excavated.

Printing and Painting since 1912

Western artistic styles in painting did not enter China until the nineteenth century. It was only after the 1842 opening of Shanghai that more modern innovations began to influence traditional arts and a new wealthy clientele with money to support the emerging market came into being. Within a decade, however, a Shanghai regional style appeared, led by Ren Xiong, his more popular follower Ren Yi (better known as Ren Bonian), and Ren's follower Wu Changshi.

The new style of painting drew its inspiration from a series of individualist artists of the Ming and Qing, including Xu Wei, Chen Shun, Chen Hongshou, Zhu Da, and Dao Ji; it focused on birds and flowers and figural themes more than the old landscape tradition; and it emphasized decorative qualities, exaggerated stylization, and satiric humour rather than refined brushwork and sober classicism. Under Wu Changshi's influence, this style was passed on to Beijing through the art of Chen Hengke (or Chen Shizeng) and Qi Baishi in the first years after the revolution.

Many members of this new generation of artists drew their inspiration from Japan, which had already been forced to adapt to the West. Gao Jianfu studied art for four years in Japan, beginning in 1898; during a second trip there, he met Sun Yat-sen, and subsequently, in Guangzhou, he participated in the uprisings that paved the way for the fall of Imperial rule and the establishment in 1912 of a republic. Inspired by the "New Japanese Style", Gao and his brother and Chen Shuren inaugurated a "New National Painting" movement, which in turn gave rise to a Cantonese (or "Lingnan") regional style that incorporated Euro-Japanese characteristics. Their work was a significant harbinger and continued to thrive in Hong Kong, practised by such artists as Zhao Shao Ang. The first establishment of Western-style art instruction also dates from this period. A small art department was opened in Nanjing High Normal School in 1906, and the first art academy, later to become the Shanghai Art School, was founded in the year of the revolution, 1911, by the 16-year-old Liu Haisu, who in the next decade pioneered the first public exhibitions (1913) and the use of live models, first clothed and then nude, in the classroom.

Increasingly, by the mid-1920s, young Chinese artists were attracted not just to Japan but also to Paris and German art centres. A trio of these artists brought back some understanding of the essential contemporary European traditions and movements. Liu Haisu was first attracted to Impressionist art, while Lin Fengmian, who became director of the National Academy of Art in Hangzhou in 1928, was inspired by post-impressionist experiments in colour and pattern by Henri Matisse and the Fauvists. Lin advocated a synthesis combining

Western techniques and Chinese expressiveness and left a lasting mark on the modern Chinese use of the brush. Xu Beihong, head of the National Central University art department in Nanjing, eschewed European modernist movements in favour of Parisian academism. He developed his facility in drawing and oils, later learning to imitate pencil and chalk with the Chinese brush; the monumental figure paintings he created served as a basis for Socialist Realist painters after the communist revolution of 1949.

By the 1930s, all these modern trends were clearly developed and institutionalized. Although most of the major artists of the time advocated modernism, two continued to support more traditional styles: Qi Baishi, who combined Shanghai style with an infusion of folk-derived vitality, and the relatively conservative landscapist Huang Binhong, who demonstrated that the old tradition could still produce a rival to the great masters of the seventeenth century.

Socialism produced a new set of artistic demands that were first met not by painting but by the inexpensive mass medium of woodblock prints (which had been invented in China and first used in the Tang dynasty to illustrate Buddhist sutras). Initially stimulated by the satiric leftist writer Lu Xun, printmakers flourished during the 1930s and 1940s under the dual influence of European socialist artists like Käthe Kollwitz and the Chinese folk tradition of New Year's prints and papercuts. Among the most prominent print artists were Li Hua and Gu Yuan, who attained a new standard of political realism in Chinese art.

In 1942, as part of the CCP's first intellectual rectification movement, Mao Zedong delivered two speeches at the Yenan Forum on Literature and Art that became the official party dictates on aesthetics for decades to come. Mao emphasized the subordination of art to political ends, the necessity for popularization of styles and subjects in order to reach a mass audience, the need for artists to share in the lives of ordinary people, and the requirement that the party and its goals be treated positively rather than subjected to satiric criticism. "Art for art's sake" was strictly denounced as a bourgeois liberal attempt to escape from the truly political nature of art. Although Mao later defended a place for the artistic study of nude models, a staple of Western naturalism, the tone he set led to severe limitations in the actual practice of this.

The Sino-Japanese War of 1937–45 led many artists of varied persuasions to flee eastern China for the temporary Nationalist capital in Chongqing, Sichuan province, bringing a tremendous mixing of styles and artistic ferment, but the opportunity for innovation which this promised was thwarted by subsequent events. After the 1949 revolution, Communist Party control of the arts was firmly established by the place-ment of the academies under the jurisdiction of the Ministry of Culture, by the creation of artists' federations and associations (which served as an exclusive pathway to participation in exhibitions and other means of advancement) under the man-agement of the party's Department of Propaganda, by the establishment of a strict system of control over publications, and by the virtual elimination of the commercial market for contemporary arts.

Throughout the 1950s, as Socialist Realist standards were gradually implemented, oil painting and woodblock printing were favoured and political cartoons and posters were raised to artistic status. Artists in the traditional media—with their basis in the Individualist art of the old "feudal" aristocracy—struggled institutionally for survival, eventually succeeding only as a result of the nationalist fervour that accompanied China's ideological break with the Soviet Union late in the decade. The internationalist but relatively conservative Xu

Beihong was installed as head of the new Central Academy of Fine Arts in Beijing but died in 1953. Other older-generation leaders passed on shortly afterward (Qi Baishi and Huang Binhong) or were shunted aside (Liu Haisu and Lin Fengmian), and a younger generation soon came to the fore, ready to make the necessary compromises with the new regime.

The talented landscapist Li Keran, who had studied with Qi Baishi, Lin Fengmian, Huang Binhong, and Xu Beihong, combined their influences with realistic sketching to achieve a new naturalism in the traditional medium. A leading figure painter was Cheng Shifa, a descendant of the Shanghai school who brought that style to bear in politically polished depictions of China's minority peoples. Many talented artists, including Luo Gongliu and Ai Zhongxin, painted in oils, which, because of their link to the Soviet Union and Soviet art advisers, held a favoured position until the Sino-Soviet split of the late 1950s.

While the early 1960s provided a moment of political relaxation for Chinese artists, the Cultural Revolution of 1966–76 brought unprecedented hardships, ranging from forced labour and severe confinement to death. Destruction of traditional arts was especially rampant in the early years of the movement. Only those arts approved by a military-run apparatus under the sway of Mao's wife, Jiang Qing, could thrive; these followed the party's increasingly strict propagandist dictates and were often created anonymously as collective works. In the early 1970s, when China first reopened Western contacts, Premier Zhou Enlai attempted to restore government patronage for the traditional arts. When Zhou's health declined, traditional arts and artists again suffered under Jiang Qing, including being publicly denounced and punished at "black arts" exhibitions in Beijing, Shanghai, and Xi'an in 1974.

The passing of Mao and Maoism after 1976 brought a new and sometimes refreshing chapter in the arts under the leadership of Deng Xiaoping. The 1980s were characterized by decreasing government control of the arts and increasingly bold artistic experimentation. Three phenomena in 1979 announced this new era: the appearance of Cubist and other Western styles, as well as nude figures, in the murals publicly commissioned for the new Beijing airport (although the government "temporarily" covered the nudes); a private arts exhibition by The Stars art group at the Beijing Art Gallery; and the rise of a truly realistic oil painting movement, which swept away the artificiality of Socialist Realist propaganda. A resurgence of traditional Chinese painting and woodblock printing occurred in the 1980s, featuring the return of formerly disgraced artists, including Li Keran, Cheng Shifa, Shi Lu, Zhao Yannian and Huang Yongyu, and the emergence of such fresh talents as Wu Guanzhong, Jia Youfu, and Li Huasheng.

After 1985, as an increasingly bold avant-garde movement arose, the once-threatening traditional-style painting came to seem to the government like a safe alternative. In the final months before the June 1989 imposition of martial law in Beijing, an exhibition of nude oil paintings from the Central Academy of Fine Arts at the Chinese National Gallery and an avant-garde exhibition featuring installation art, performance art (which lacked the necessary permit for a public gathering), and the mockery of the government through printed scrolls full of unreadable pseudo-characters drew record crowds. The latter was closed by police, and both exhibits were eventually denounced as having lowered local morals, helping to precipitate the tragic events that followed in June 1989. New limitations on artistic production, exhibition, and publication ensued. At the conclusion of these events, a number of leading artists, including Huang Yongyu, fled China, joining others who had previously fled or abandoned China to establish centres of Chinese art throughout the world.

Among the leading Chinese artists outside mainland China have been Chao Wu-chi (Zao Wou-ki), who settled in Paris; Chang Dai-chien in Taiwan, Brazil, and the USA; Wang Chi-ch'ien (C.C. Wang) and Tseng Yu-ho in the USA; Liu Kuo-sung, Ch'en Ch'i-kwan, and Ho Huai-shuo in Taiwan; Fang Chao-lin in Hong Kong and London; and Lin Feng-mien in Hong Kong.

A number of young artists have achieved recognition within China today. Among them are Chen Qiulin, an installation artist who blends performance art and photography; Wu Jungyong, a fine-arts animator; Lu Peng, a painter whose work often carries critiques of both China's authoritarian past and its market economy present; and Shen Fan, an abstract artist at the centre of a Shanghai-based artistic circle. Each artist weds Western and Chinese techniques—and, as with so many artists of the past, each regularly tests the limits of governmental tolerance.

9

ARCHITECTURE

Until the modern era, the Chinese built their homes chiefly of timber and rammed earth; these remain the principal building materials in the countryside. Both are vulnerable to fire and the ravages of time, with the result that little ancient architecture has survived. The oldest datable timber building is the small main hall of the Nanchan Temple, on Mount Wutai in Shanxi province, built sometime before 782 and restored in that year. Brick and stone are used for defensive walls, the arch for gates and bridges, and the vault for tombs. Only rarely has the corbelled dome (in which each successive course projects inward from the course below it) been used for temples and tombs. Single-storey architecture predominates throughout northern and much of eastern China, although multistorey building techniques date to the late Zhou dynasty (eleventh century to 221 BCE).

The basic elements in a Chinese timber building are the platform of pounded earth faced with stone or tile on which the building stands; the post-and-lintel frame (vertical posts topped by horizontal tie beams); the roof-supporting brackets and truss; and the tiled roof itself. The walls between the posts, or columns, are not load-bearing, and the intercolumnar bays (odd-numbered along the front of the building) may be filled by doors (usually doubled) or by brick or such material as bamboo wattle faced with plaster, or they may be left open to create peristyles. The flexible triangular truss is placed transverse to the front side of the building and defines a gable-type roof by means of a stepped-up series of elevated tie beams (*tailiang*, for which this entire system of architecture is named); the beams are sequentially shortened and alternate with vertical struts that bear the roof purlins and the main roof beam.

The flexible proportions of the gable-end framework of struts and beams permits the roof to take any profile desired, typically a low and rather straight silhouette in northern China before the Song, and increasingly elevated and concave in the Song, Yuan, Ming, and Qing. The gable-end framework is typically moved inward in a prominent building and partially masked in a hip-and-gable (or half-hip) roof and completely masked in a full-hipped roof. The timber building is limited in depth by the span of the truss; in theory, however, it may be of any length, although it rarely exceeds 11 bays in practice.

The origin of the distinctive curve of the roof, which first appeared in China about the sixth century CE, is not fully understood, although a number of theories have been put forward. The most likely is that it was borrowed, for purely aesthetic reasons, from China's Southeast Asian neighbours, who cover their houses with atap (leaves of the nipa palm) or split bamboo, which tend to sag naturally, presenting a picturesque effect. The swept-up eaves at the corners of the Chinese roof, however, do have a structural function in reducing what would otherwise be an excessive overhang at that point.

In the "pavilion concept," whereby each building is conceived of as a freestanding rectilinear unit, flexibility in the overall design is achieved by increasing the number of such units, which are arranged together with open, connecting galleries around courtyards; diversity is achieved through design variations that individualize these courtyard complexes. In the private house or mansion, the grouping of halls and courtyards is informal, apart from the axial arrangement of the entrance court with its main hall facing the gateway; but in a palace such as the gigantic Forbidden City in Beijing, the principal halls are ranged with their courtyards behind one another on a south-to-north axis, building up to a ceremonial climax and dying away to lesser courts and buildings to the north. Ancestral halls and temples follow the palatial arrangement. The scale of a building, the number of bays, the unit of measure used for the timbers, whether bracketing is included or not, and the type of roof (gabled, half- or full-hipped, with or without prominent decorative ridge-tiling and prominent overhang) all accord with the placement and significance of the building within a courtyard arrangement, with the relative importance of that courtyard within a larger compound, and with the absolute status of the whole building complex. The entire system, therefore, is modular and highly standardized.

The domination of the roof allows little variation in the form of the individual building; thus, aesthetic subtlety is concentrated in pleasing proportions and in details such as the roof brackets or the plinths supporting the columns. Tang architecture achieved a "classic" standard, with massive proportions yet simple designs in which function and form were fully harmonized. Architects in the Song dynasty were much more adventurous in playing with interlocking roofs and different levels than were their successors in later centuries. The beauty of the architecture of the Ming dynasty (1368–1644) and Qing dynasty (1644–1911/12) lies rather in the lightweight effect and the richness of painted decoration.

The Historical Context

Traditional Housing

The basic structure of the Chinese house has remained almost unchanged at least from the Shang dynasty (seventeenth to eleventh century BCE). In all types of buildings the roof is the most important feature, and by the Tang dynasty (618–907 CE) the characteristic upturned eaves and heavy glazed and coloured tile covering had developed. The roof is chiefly supported by timber posts on stone or bronze bases, and the walls of the building serve merely as screens in brick or timber. Floors are often of beaten earth packed tightly into a timber border. Usually, a family house was composed of a series of buildings or pavilions enclosing a garden courtyard and surrounded by a wall. The courtyard played an immensely important part, because of the ever-present ideal that man should live in harmony with nature: a small pool with a lotus plant, a tree, and large rocks symbolized the whole natural landscape, and it was on these features that most care was lavished.

The supporting pillars and brackets of important buildings were carved and painted, many of the designs being similar to those made familiar by Chinese pottery and porcelain. The yellow dragon symbolizes the power of the spirit, the tiger the forces of animal life. Windows were latticed with strips of wood in varying patterns over which translucent white paper was stretched. In addition to the lattice-work patterns, the windows themselves took on great variety of outline, for instance that of a diamond, fan, leaf, or flower. Doorways, too, were fancifully shaped in the form of the moon, a lotus petal, pear, or vase, for structural support was not required from the light panel-type walls. Some walls may have been removable altogether, as they were subsequently in the Japanese house; others were of painted wood, hung with tapestries or paintings on silk and other materials.

A description of a Ming home of the leisured class mentions ceilings with cloisons (compartments) in yellow reed work, papered walls and pillars, black polished flagstones, and silk hangings. Richly coloured rugs, chair covers, and cushions contrasted with dark furniture, which was arranged according to the strict ideas of asymmetrical balance.

Materials are very different from those of the West. The Chinese have always been masters of the ceramic art, and their skill spread northward to Korea, north-eastward to Japan, and south to the countries of Southeast Asia. Nearly all the more important techniques—majolica excepted—came from China. The Tang dynasty was renowned for fine earthenwares; the Song dynasty (960–1279) for superb stonewares; and from the Yuan dynasty (1206–1368) onward the Chinese have led the world in the manufacture of porcelain, the secret of which reached Europe only after the porcelain had been imported for several centuries. Bronze was employed for vessels rather than figure sculpture. Originally purely religious in connotation, bronze vessels were given as gifts of emperors to their favoured subjects by the Zhou dynasty, and from that time on were commonly employed for secular purposes. During the Tang dynasty, handsome mirrors as well as such useful and decorative things as toilet-boxes were commonly made.

China was known for its silk in the West in ancient Roman times. Fragments of silk were found in Chinese Turkistan dating to the first century BCE with motifs of design strongly resembling those of the twentieth century. The Chinese have always been noted for superb silk embroideries, highly detailed in a manner requiring a multitude of tiny stitches. Painted silks have been produced in large quantities. Velvet weaving, usually in long strips as chair covers, was an art probably learned from the West, but the art of tapestry (*kesi*), may go back as far as the Han dynasty (206 BCE–220 CE). Carpet-knotting of the highest quality, no doubt learned from Persia, cannot be proved to date before the seventeenth century, but it may have started much earlier. Rare carpets are knotted with silk and gold, but those with a woollen pile are of fine quality. Pillar-carpets, woven to encircle pillars, are a distinctively Chinese type. Motifs of decoration are those common to other materials.

Jade (nephrite and jadeite) is carved in China into objects with many different purposes. In early times, like bronze, it was mainly used for religious purposes, but it later came to be employed for a variety of secular objects, principally those intended to furnish the scholar's table, such as brush-pots, ink-slabs, water-droppers, table-screens, and paper-weights. In the eighteenth century especially, bowls and covers, handsomely carved and pierced with a variety of motifs and patterns, were made for interior decoration as incense burners.

Lacquer, the solidified sap of a tree (*Rhus vernicifera*), has been widely employed for a variety of decorative purposes on a foundation of wood or, less often, hempen fabric. Lacquer is employed as a form of paint, or applied in thick layers that can be carved with knives. It is also used to decorate structural timbers in the interior. The finest lacquer came from Japan in the seventeenth and eighteenth centuries.

Enamelling on metal is an art that the Chinese learned from Europe but, in the eighteenth century especially, some very large bronze vessels in a variety of ornamental forms were covered with enamel utilizing the cloisonné technique. Painted enamels came from Guangzhou (Canton) in the eighteenth century, and resemble in style contemporary porcelain enamelling from the same place.

Little is known of early Chinese furniture, apart from what may be gathered from paintings and similar sources. Low stools and tables were in early use, and chairs, dressing tables, altar tables, and canopied beds were common by the Western (early) Han dynasty (206 BCE–25 CE). Designs and materials changed very little in the intervening years. Rosewood has always been widely employed, and in the palaces elaborate pieces were encrusted with gold and silver, jade, ivory, and mother-of-pearl.

The Chinese interior was more extensively furnished with chairs, tables, couches, beds, and cabinets of cupboards and drawers than was the custom elsewhere in the East. As in Europe, the chair with arms was thought to be a seat of honour. The woods employed are native to the country and were hardly ever exported to the West, though Chinese rosewood is fairly well known in the West because most exported furniture was in this wood. Carved lacquer furniture, like the throne of the Qing emperor Qianlong in the Victoria and Albert Museum, London, was reserved for the emperor and high officials, and the massive incised lacquer screens, known in the West as Coromandel screens, were occasionally exported. Furniture of bamboo, principally intended for garden use, has hardly survived, but barrel-shaped seats of porcelain for the same purpose are not uncommon. Carved decoration on furniture is nearly always extremely simple in design and limited to some form of interlacing fret.

Temples and Tombs

The Sui-Tang period (581–907 CE) saw some of China's most lavish royal tomb building, before the onset of a relative modesty in the Song and a decline of qualitative standards in later periods. Excavated royal tombs at Changling, north of the capital, include three built for close relatives of Wuhou who were being degraded or executed by her on her way to the throne and reburied amid much pomp and splendour in 706 after the restoration of the Tang royal lineage. In each, the subterranean sepulchre is surmounted by a truncated pyramidal tumulus and is approached through a sculpture-lined "spirit way" (*lingdao*).

Inside, painted corridors and incised stone sarcophagi provide a lingering record of Tang splendour, with colourful renderings of palatial settings, foreign diplomats, servants-in-waiting, and recreation at polo and the hunt. Along the corridor, niches that had served temporarily as ventilating shafts are stuffed with ceramic figurines, riders and entertainers, Tang horses and other fabulous animals, mostly done in bold tricolour glazes. The corridor leads to two domed vaults serving as an antechamber and burial hall.

The tombs of some Tang rulers were so grand that artificial tomb mounds no longer sufficed, and funerary caverns were carved out beneath large mountains. The huge tomb of Emperor Gao Zong and his empress, Wuhou (China's only joint burial of rulers), also at Changling, has yet to be excavated but appears to be intact.

The Sui and the first half of Tang were also great periods of temple building. The first Sui emperor distributed relics throughout the country and ordered that pagodas and temples be built to house them, and the early Tang monarchs were equally lavish in their foundations. Apart from masonry pagodas, however, very few Tang temple buildings have survived. The oldest yet identified is the main hall of Nanchan Temple at Mount Wutai (before 782); the largest is the main hall of nearby Foguang Temple (857). The Great Buddha Hall (Daibutsu-den, 752) of the Todai Temple (Todai-ji) at Nara in Japan, 88 metres long and 51.5 metres wide, built in the Tang style, is today the largest wooden building in the world; however, it is small compared with the lost Tang temple halls of Luoyang and Chang'an.

Tang and later pagodas show little of the Indian influence that was so marked in earlier years. Tang wooden pagodas have all been destroyed, but graceful examples survive at Nara, Japan, notably at Horyu Temple, Yakushi Temple, and Daigo Temple. Masonry pagodas include the seven-storey, 58-metre high Big Wild Goose Pagoda, Xi'an, on which the successive stories are marked by corbelled cornices, and timber features are simulated in stone by flat columns, or pilasters, struts, and capitals.

In this period, the cave-temples at Dunhuang were increasingly Sinicized, abandoning the Indianesque central pillar, the circumambulated focus of worship which in Six Dynasties caves was sculpted and painted on all four sides with Buddhist paradises; in the Tang, major Buddhist icons and paradise murals were moved to the rear of an open chamber and given elevated seating, much like an emperor enthroned in his palace or like any Chinese host.

By the end of the Tang, the traditional Chinese techniques of architectural siting had been synthesized into geomantic systems known as *fengshui* or *kanyu* (both designating the interactive forces of Heaven and Earth). These had origins reaching back at least to earliest Zhou times and were undertaken seriously by architects in all periods.

Practised by Taoist specialists, northern Chinese traditions emphasized the use of a magnetic compass and were especially concerned with the conjoining of astral and earthly principles according to months and seasons, stars and planets, the hexagrams of the *Yiching* divinatory text, and a "five phases" theory of fire, water, wood, metal, and earth that was first propagated in the Han dynasty; while in the south, where landscape features were more irregular, a "Form school" emphasized the proper relationship of protective mountains (the northern direction representing dark forces and requiring barriers, the south being benign and requiring openness) and a suitable flow of water. In later periods, elements of both schools could be found in use throughout China.

The Age of Royal Palaces

Little remains of Yuan architecture today. The great palace of Kublai Khan in the Yuan capital Dadu ("Great Capital"; now Beijing) was entirely rebuilt in the Ming dynasty. Excavations demonstrate that the Yuan city plan is largely retained in that of the Ming; originally conceived under the combined influence of Liu Bingzhong and non-Chinese Muslims such as Yeheidie'er, it appears to be thoroughly Chinese in concept. More detailed information survives only in first-generation Ming dynasty court records and in the somewhat exaggerated description of Marco Polo.

The first Ming emperor established his capital at Nanjing, surrounding it with a wall more than 30 km in length, one of the longest in the world. The palace he constructed no longer exists. In 1402, a son of the founding Ming emperor enfeoffed at the old Yuan capital usurped the throne from his nephew, the second Ming ruler, and installed himself as the Yongle Emperor. He rebuilt the destroyed Mongol palaces and moved the Ming capital there in 1421, renaming the city Beijing ("Northern Capital").

His central palace cluster, the Forbidden City, is the foremost surviving Chinese palace compound, maintained and successively rebuilt over the centuries. In a strict hierarchical sequence, the palaces lie centred within the bureaucratic auspices of the Imperial City, which is surrounded by the metropolis that came to be called the "inner city," in contrast to the newer (1556) walled southern suburbs, or "outer city". A series of eight major state temples lay on the periphery in balanced symmetry, including temples to the sun (east) and moon (west) and, to the far south of the city, the huge matched temple grounds of heaven (east) and agriculture (west).

Close adherence to the traditional principles of north–south axiality, walled enclosures and restrictive gateways, systematic compounding of courtyard structures, regimentation of scale, and a hierarchy of roofing types were all intended to satisfy classical architectural norms, displaying visually the renewed might of native rulers and their restoration of traditional order.

Central to this entire arrangement are three great halls of state, situated on a high, triple-level marble platform (the number three, here and elsewhere, symbolic of heaven and of the Imperial role as chief communicant between Heaven and Earth). The southernmost of these is the largest wooden building in China (roughly 65 by 35 metres), known as the Hall of Supreme Harmony. (The names and specific functions of many of the main halls were changed several times in the Ming and Qing.)

To their north lies a smaller-scale trio, the main halls of the Inner Court, in which the emperor and his ladies resided. The entire complex now comprises some 9,000 rooms (of an intended 9,999, representing a perfect yang number). The grandeur of this palatial scheme was matched by the layout of a vast Imperial burial ground on the southern slopes of the mountain range to the north of Beijing, not far from the Great Wall, which eventually came to house 13 royal mausoleums, with an elaborate "spirit way" and accompanying ritual temple complexes.

In its colossal scale, the monumental sweep of its golden-tiled roofs, and its axial symmetry, the heart of the Forbidden City is unsurpassed as a symbol of Imperial power. In architectural technique, however, the buildings represent a decline from the adventurous planning and construction of the Song period. Now the unit is a simple square or rectangular pavilion with few projections (or none), and the bracketing system is reduced to a decorative frieze with little or no structural function. Instead, emphasis is placed upon carved balustrades, rich colour, and painted architectural detail. This same lack of progress shows in Ming temples also.

Exceptional is the Hall of Prayer for Good Harvests (Qiniandian) at the Temple of Heaven, a descendant of ancient state temples like the Mingtang. It took its present circular form about 1530. Its three concentric circles of columns, which range up to 18 metres in height, symbolize the four seasons, the 12 months, and the 12 daily hours; in a remarkable feat of engineering, they support the three roof levels (a yang number) and, in succession, a huge square brace representing Earth, a massive circular architrave denoting Heaven, and a vast interior cupola decorated with golden dragons among clouds.

Gardens of Delight

Qing dynasty work in the Forbidden City was confined chiefly to the restoration or reconstruction of major Ming buildings, although the results were typically more ornate in detail and garish in colour than ever before.

The Manchu rulers were most lavish in their summer palaces, created to escape the heat of the city. In 1703 the Kangxi Emperor began a series of palaces and pavilions set in a natural landscape near the old Manchu capital, Chengde.

Engravings of these made by the Jesuit father Matteo Ripa in 1712–13 and brought by him to London in 1724 are thought to have influenced the revolution in garden design that began in Europe at about this time.

About 1687 the Kangxi Emperor had begun to create another garden park north-west of Beijing, which grew under his successors into the enormous Yuanming Yuan ("Garden of Pure Light"). Here were scattered many official and palace buildings, to which the Qianlong Emperor moved his court semi-permanently. In the northern corners of the Yuanming Yuan, the Jesuit missionary and artist Giuseppe Castiglione (known in China as Lang Shining) designed for Qianlong a series of extraordinary Sino-Rococo buildings, set in Italianate gardens ornamented with mechanical fountains designed by the Jesuit priest Michel Benoit.

Today the Yuanming Yuan has almost completely disappeared, the foreign-style buildings having been burned by the French and British in 1860. To replace it, the empress dowager Cixi greatly enlarged the new summer palace (Yihe Yuan) along the shore of Kunming Lake to the north of the city.

The finest architectural achievement of the period, however, occurred in private rather than institutional architecture— namely, in the scholars' gardens of south-eastern China, in such towns as Suzhou, Yangzhou, and Wuxi. As these often involved renovations carried out on Yuan and Ming dynasty foundations, it remains difficult to discern the precise outlines of their innovations.

With the aid of paintings and Ji Cheng's *Yuanye* ("Forging a Garden", 1631–34), it becomes evident that, as in the worst of Qing architecture, these gardens became ever more ornate. The best examples, however, remain well within the bounds of good taste owing to the cultivated sensibility of scholarly taste, and they were distinguished by an inventive imagination lacking in Manchu court architecture. Such gardens were primarily Taoist in nature, intended as microcosms invested with the capacity to engender tranquillity and induce longevity in those who lodged there.

The chief hallmark of these gardens was the combination of a central pond, encompassing all the virtues of yin in the Chinese philosophical system, with the extensive use of rugged and convoluted rockery, yang, which summed up the lasting Chinese adoration of great mountain chains through which flowed the vital energy of the Earth. (The most precious rocks were harvested from the bottom of Lake Tai near Suzhou.)

Throughout this urban garden tradition, where the scale was necessarily small and space was strictly confined, designers attempted to convey the sense of nature's vastness by breaking the limited space available into still smaller but ever varied units, suggesting what could not otherwise literally be obtained, and expanding the viewer's imagination through inventive architectural design. Among those gardens still preserved today, the Liu Garden in Suzhou offers the finest general design and the best examples of garden rockery and latticed windows, while the small and delicate Garden of the Master of Nets (Wangshi Yuan), also in Suzhou, provides knowledgeable viewers a remarkable series of sophisticated surprises.

Modern Architecture

Until the mid-1920s official and commercial architecture were chiefly in the eclectic European style of such treaty ports as Guangzhou, Xiamen, Fuzhou, and Shanghai, much of it designed by foreign architects. In 1925, however, a group of foreign-trained Chinese architects launched a renaissance movement to study and revive traditional Chinese architecture and to find ways of adapting it to modern needs and techniques.

In 1930 they founded Zhongguo Yingzao Xueshe, the Society for the Study of Chinese Architecture, which was joined in the following year by Liang Sicheng, the dominant figure in the movement for the next 30 years. The fruits of their work can be seen in new universities and in major government and municipal buildings in Nanjing and Shanghai. The war with Japan put an end to further developments along these lines, however.

Since 1949, the movement has largely found extremely conservative expression in such buildings as the Institute of Chinese Culture and the National Palace Museum in Taipei, Taiwan. Tunghai University in Taichung, Taiwan, designed by the Chinese-born American architect I.M. Pei, is a much more successful synthesis of Chinese spirit and modern techniques.

Pei was also responsible for the impressive triangular glass skyscraper in Hong Kong, the China Bank Tower, completed in 1989. It houses the Hong Kong headquarters of the Beijing-based central Bank of China, together with other tenants. At 1,209 feet (369 metres), the skyscraper was for a few years the tallest building in the world outside the USA. The tower has a distinctive three-dimensional triangular shape (quadrilateral at the bottom and trilateral at the top) which, according to Pei, transfers "all vertical stress to the four corners of the building, making it very stable and wind resistant" (an important consideration in typhoon-threatened Hong Kong). The interior floors are irregular, ending in points and angles, and are completely sided by windows, with multiple views. The 70-storey building is topped by twin poles, though these are a purely decorative flourish.

With the increasing demands of an emerging market economy, urban renewal projects associated with the 2008 Olympic Games, and the constant need for new housing and other structures, Beijing and other big cities have been transformed by spectacular planning projects, but an awareness of the traditional role of symbolism in architecture has been retained and adapted to communist propaganda purposes. Large portions of the Forbidden City in Beijing have been restored and established as a public museum, but a section has been given over to residences for the new ruling elite. A new primary thoroughfare (Changan Boulevard) has been established, running east and west in front of the old palaces, contrary to the old north–south axis. A vast square for public political activity has been created in front of the Gate of Heavenly Peace (Tiananmen, entryway to the Imperial City), flanked on one side by the Museum of Chinese History and the Revolution and on the other by the Great Hall of the People, built in Soviet style in 1959 during the Great Leap Forward.

Most of the city's magnificent walls were torn down before or during the Cultural Revolution on the pretext that they impeded the flow of traffic. (The walls of Xi'an Gate are largely intact and suggest just how magnificent Beijing's once were.) Finally, the regime's founder, Mao Zedong, who died in 1976, was buried in a mausoleum bearing a striking resemblance to the Lincoln Memorial in Washington, DC; the tomb is located in the centre of the city at the south end of Tiananmen Square, where it obstructs the north–south axis in flagrant violation of traditional geomantic principles.

With the remaking of China's cities, including the wholesale modernization of Shanghai and the massive growth of new towns throughout the southern coastal regions, architecture remains vibrant. Ancient principles of siting and construction blend with the most modern practices, so that it is not unusual to see the girders of a skyscraper rising into the sky, sur-rounded by a scaffolding of bamboo. Some of the world's tallest buildings grace Chinese skylines today, and the world's leading architectural firms increasingly find themselves doing business throughout the country.

10

MUSIC

One always approaches any survey of Chinese music history with a certain sense of awe—for what can one say about the music of a varied, still active civilization whose archaeological resources go back to 3000 BCE and whose own extensive written documents refer to endless different forms of music in connection with folk festivals and religious events as well as in the courts of hundreds of emperors and princes in dozens of different provinces, dynasties, and periods? If a survey is carried forward from 3000 BCE, it becomes clear that the last little segment of material, from the Song dynasty (960–1279 CE) to today, is equivalent to the entire major history of European music. For all the richness of detail in Chinese sources, it is only for this last segment that there is information about the actual music itself. Yet the historical, cultural, instrumental, and theoretical materials of earlier times are equally informative and fascinating.

Chinese writings claim that in 2697 BCE the legendary emperor Huangdi sent a scholar, Ling Lun, to the western mountain area to cut bamboo pipes that could emit sounds matching the call of the phoenix bird, enabling the creation of music properly pitched for harmony between his reign and the universe, in keeping with Huangdi's establishment of uniform weights and measures to the same end. Even this charming symbolic birth of music dates far too late to aid in discovering the melodies and instrumental sounds accompanying the rituals and burials that occurred before the first historically verified dynasty, the Shang (eighteenth to eleventh century BCE). The beautiful sounds of music are evanescent, and before the invention of recordings they disappeared at the end of a performance. The remains of China's most ancient music are found only in those few instruments made of sturdy material. Archaeological digs have uncovered globular clay ocarinas (*xun*), tuned stone chimes (*qing*), and bronze bells (*zhong*); and the word *gu*, for drum, is found incised on Shang oracle bones.

The earliest surviving written records are from the next dynasty, the Zhou (1066–221 BCE). Within the famous Five Classics of that period, it is in the *Liji* ("Record of Rites") of the second century BCE that one finds an extensive discussion of music. The *Yijing* ("Classic of Changes") is a diviner's handbook built around geometric patterns, cosmology, and magic numbers that indirectly may relate to music. The *Chunqiu* ("Spring and Autumn") annals, with its records of major events, and the *Shujing* ("Classic of History"), with its mixture of documents and forgeries, contain many references to the use of music, particularly at court activities. There are occasional comments about the singing of peasant groups, an item that is rare even in the early historical materials of Europe. The *Shijing* ("Classic of Poetry") is of equal interest, for it consists of the texts of 305 songs dating from the tenth to the seventh centuries BCE. Their great variety of topics (love, ritual, political satire, etc.) reflect a viable vocal musical tradition quite understandable to modern radio or record listeners. The songs also include references to less durable musical relics such as the flutes, mouth organ (sheng) and, apparently, two forms of the zither (the *qin* and the *se*).

The Chinese talent for musical organization was by no means limited to pitches. Another important ancient system called the eight sounds (*bayin*) was used to classify the many kinds of instruments used in Imperial orchestras. This system was based upon the material used in the construction of the instruments, the eight being stone, earth (pottery), bamboo, metal, skin, silk, wood, and gourd.

Stringed instruments of ancient China belong to the silk class because their strings were never gut or metal but twisted silk. Drums are skin instruments, whereas percussive clappers are wood. One of the most enjoyable members of the wooden family is the *yu*, a model of a crouching tiger with a serrated ridge or set of slats along its back that were scratched by a bamboo whisk in a manner recalling the various scratched gourds of Latin American bands. The Chinese category of gourd is reserved for one of the most fascinating of the ancient instruments, the *sheng* mouth organ. Seventeen bamboo pipes are set in a gourd or sometimes in a wooden wind chest. Each pipe has a free metal reed at the end encased in the wind chest. Blowing through a mouth tube into the wind chest and closing a hole in a pipe with a finger will cause the reed to sound, and melodies or chord structures may be played. Many variants of this instrumental principle can be found in Southeast Asia, and it is not possible to know for definite where this wind instrument first appeared. Western imitations of it are found in the reed organ and, later, in the harmonica and the accordion.

Modern information on the actual performance of music has suffered because of the destruction of many books and musical instruments under the order of Shihuandi, emperor of the Qin dynasty. Yet there are several survivals from the Han dynasty that do give some insight into how the musical events took place. In the court and the Confucian temples there were two basic musical divisions: banquet music (*yanyueh*) and ritual music (*yayueh*). Dances in the Confucian rituals were divided into military (*wuwu*) and civil (*wenwu*) forms. The ensembles of musicians and dancers could be quite large, and ancient listings of the content of their performances were often printed in formation patterns similar to those of football marching bands in America today. Rubbings from Han tomb tiles show more informal and apparently very lively music and dance presentations at social affairs.

The Han dynasty empire expanded and at the same time built walls between its national core and western Asia. But these actions were paralleled by an increasing flow of foreign ideas and materials. Buddhism entered from India to China in the first century CE, whereas booty, goods, and ideas came from Central Asian Gandharan, Yuezhi, and Iranian cultures along the various desert trade routes. Desert ruins and Buddhist caves from this period and later reveal a host of new musical ensembles and solo instruments. Two stringed instruments of particular interest are the angle harp (*konghu*) and the pear-shaped plucked lute (*pipa*). The harp can be traced back across Central Asia to the ancient bas-reliefs of Assyria. The lute also seems to have West Asian ancestors but is a more "contemporary" instrument. Variants of this instrument have continued to enter or be redesigned in China down to the present day.

New percussion instruments are evident in the celestial orchestras seen in Buddhist iconography. One apparent accommodation between old Chinese and West Asian tradition is the *fangxiang*, a set of 16 iron slabs suspended in a wooden frame in the manner of the old sets of tuned stones. Knobless gongs related to the present-day Chinese *luo* seem to have entered the Chinese musical scene before the sixth century from South Asia, while the cymbals (*bo*) may have come earlier from India via Central Asian groups. One of the most sonorous Buddhist additions was a bronze bell in the form of a basin (*qing*) that, when placed rim up on a cushion and struck on the rim, produces a tone of amazing richness and duration. Among the varied new instruments pictured in heavenly ensembles, one can still find occasional "old-time" instruments such as a set of narrow wooden clappers (*chongdu*) tied together at one end like ancient wooden books. The clappers were sounded by compressing them quickly between the hands. Variants of this Zhou dynasty instrument are still heard in all three major East Asian countries.

Not all the new influences in China came via religious or trade activities. During the Six Dynasties period (220–589 CE) China was rent by internal strife and border wars. The constant confrontations with the Tatars of the north caused an increased interest in the musical signals of the enemy via drums, trumpets, and double reeds. Although related instruments were equally evident to the south and west, there can be little doubt that the creation of cavalry bands with double kettledrums are direct imitations of the musical prowess of the horseback terrorists against whom the walls of China were built. With great effort and much blood, China gradually reunified under the Sui dynasty (581–618), and older courtly music and the latest musical fads were consolidated.

The few centuries of the Tang dynasty (618–907) are supersaturated with brilliant Imperial growth and cultural flourishing as well as military and natural disasters. Such a rich loam of good and bad nourished one of the most fascinating eras of

music history in the world. The more formal Imperial ceremonies revitalized the ancient orchestras of bells, stone chimes,
flutes, drums, and zithers, plus large bands of courtly dancers.
With the rise of foreign trade Persians, Arabs, Indians, and
Malayans were found in the foreign quarters of port towns,
while every trade caravan brought in masses of new faces and
modes of living.

There was hardly a tavern in the capital of Chang'an (now
Xi'an, Shaanxi province) that could compete without the aid
of a western dancing or singing girl with an accompanying set
of foreign musicians. One set of girls from Sogdiana (centred in
modern Uzbekistan) won the support of the emperor Xuanzong (712–756) because they were costumed in crimson robes,
green pants, and red deerskin boots and twirled on top of balls.
Other girls from the area today called Tashkent inspired a poet
of the ninth century, Bai Juyi, with their dance, which began
with their emergence from artificial lotuses and ended with
them pulling down their blouses to show their shoulders, a
style not unfamiliar to old Western burlesque connoisseurs.

In addition to all the commercial musical enterprises of the
Tang dynasty period, there was another equally extensive
system under government supervision. The Tang emperor
Xuanzong seemed particularly keen on music and took full
advantage of the various musical "tributes" or "captives" sent
to him by all the nations of Asia. This plethora of sounds was
further enriched by the special palace district in Chang'an called
the Pear Garden (Liyuan), in which hundreds of additional
musicians and dancers were trained and in which the emperor
himself was most active. Such trainees were often female. They
followed in an earlier tradition of court girls (*gongnu*) whose
basic duties were to entertain distinguished guests.

The mass of different foreign musical styles in the capital
was too much for the government musical bureaucracy. A

distinction had already been made between court music (*yayueh*) and common music (*suyueh*); but Tang nomenclature added a third kind—foreign music (*huyueh*). Eventually officials organized Imperial music into the ten kinds of systems (*shibuji*). Of these categories, one represented instrumentalists from Samarkand, whereas another group came from farther west in Bukhara (in modern Uzbekistan). Kashgar, at the mountain pass between the east and west, sent yet a different group. Musical ensembles also were presented to the emperor from the eastern Turkistan trade centres of Kucha and Turfan, India and two recently defeated kingdoms of Korea.

Official court music is the best chronicled genre within this classification system. Ritual presentations are generally divided into two types: so-called standing music, performed without strings and apparently in the courtyard; and sitting music, for a full ensemble played inside a palace. There are lists of the names of some pieces in these categories with their authorship usually credited to the emperor or empress of the time. Those familiar with music in the courts of Henry VIII and Louis XIV or with the songs always ending in praise of Queen Elizabeth I may recognize the cultural context of such music.

Later-dynasty copies of Tang paintings show ladies entertaining the emperor with ensembles of strings, winds, and percussion; and many of the choreographic plans of the larger pieces are also available in books. According to some sources, court orchestra pieces began with a prelude in free rhythm that set the mood and mode of the piece and introduced the instruments. This was followed by a slow section in a steady beat, and the piece ended in a faster tempo. Documents also tell much about the instrumentation and the colour and design of each costume of the musicians and dancers. No orchestral scores are to be found, however.

One solo piece for *qin* survives, and 28 ritual melodies for *pipa* were discovered in the hidden library of the Buddhist caves of Dunhuang (Cave of the Thousand Buddhas), but the grand musical traditions of Tang remain frustratingly elusive. Even so, approximations of that music, most with a vaguely Middle Eastern air, are the standard fare at tourist venues in Xi'an and the surrounding region.

The Chinese Opera

Chinese drama can be noted as far back as the Zhou dynasty, but it was really the Tang period Pear Garden school that quite literally set the stage for Chinese opera. Regional music-drama flourished throughout the Song empire, but the two major forms were the southern drama (*nanqu* or *nanxi*) and the northern drama (*zaju* or *beiju*). The *ci* poetical form was popular in both, although the southern style was held to be softer. The northern style is said to have used more strings, and in general to have been bolder in spirit. According to period writers, each of the four acts of a northern drama was set in a specific mode in which different tunes were used, interspersed with dialogue. The southern style was more lyrical.

Credit for the beginning of Beijing opera is given to actors from Anhui province appearing in Beijing in the 1790s. However, Beijing opera really combines elements from many different earlier forms and, like Western grand opera, can be considered to be a nineteenth-century product. In addition to all the instruments mentioned above, many others may be found.

The most common melodic instrument for opera is some form of fiddle, or bowed lute (*huqin*). It comes in several different forms, such as the *jinghu* and *erhu*. Although the shape of the body may be different, all traditional Chinese fiddles exhibit certain specific structural characteristics. The small body has a skin or wooden soundboard and an open back. The two strings pass over a bridge and then are suspended above a pole to the pegs, which are inserted from the rear of the scroll (not from the sides as on a Western violin). Such a system places one string above the other rather than parallel to it (as on a banjo or a *pipa*). Because of this, the bow passes between the strings, playing one string by pressing down and the other by pulling up. The fingerings of tunes are done by sideways pressure, along the strings; they are too far from the pole for it to serve as a fingerboard, which, because of the vertical stringing, would be a nuisance in any case. It is this unique manner of fiddle construction that helps one determine the source of many of the bowed lutes of Southeast Asia.

Like any theatrical music, the tunes of Beijing opera must conform to the text structure and the dramatic situation. In the latter case, one finds that a majority of Beijing aria texts are based on series of couplets of 7 or 10 syllables each. Beijing melodies themselves tend to fall into two prototypes called *xipi* and *erhuang*. Within each of these general types there are several well-known tunes, but the word "prototype" has been used to define them, as each opera and each situation is capable of varying the basic melody greatly. Although both examples are set at a standard tempo (*yuanban*), the *erhuang* is faster and its rhythm denser, as it is a male aria, while the *xipi* is female and slower.

Both pieces could be played at a slower (*manban*) or faster (*kuaiban*) tempo, however, or could be accompanied by other special rhythms. Such choices often cause changes in the melody itself. In general, the choice of both tune and rhythm style is guided by the text and the character. In most arias each sentence is separated by an instrumental interlude.

Beijing opera is also characterized by colourful costumes and striking character-identifying makeup as well as acrobatic combats and dances. These conventions of Chinese opera are similar to those of eighteenth-century European traditions, though the sounds are certainly quite different. The need to communicate in music or in theatre requires the repeated use of aural and visual conventions if an audience is to understand and be moved by the event. Although it was heavily suppressed during the Cultural Revolution, Beijing opera has seen a resurgence in the last two decades: it boasts a great many practitioners and fans among the Chinese today and is a staple of any tourist visit to the capital.

Music in the Twentieth Century

Under the influence of missionary and modernization movements, many musical experiments occurred in the last dynasty, but these were greatly increased by the rise of the first republic in 1911 and the establishment of the People's Republic in 1949. During the period of the republic and of the Japanese war, a plethora of new songs were created in "modern" style. "March of the Volunteers" was written in 1934 by Nie Er to text by the modern Chinese playwright Tian Han as a patriotic march and was adopted as the national anthem in 1949.

Chinese and Western composers continued to try out bits of each other's traditions with only occasional success, and individual Chinese artists have become famous for their performance on Western instruments. Chinese instruments in turn have been subjected to many modernizations, such as the building of a family of *erhu* fiddles by the creation of bass and alto versions. In conjunction with this movement there was the appearance of concerti for such instruments accompanied by a mixed Western and Chinese orchestra.

As was noted earlier, under the People's Republic many completely traditional forms continued, particularly in foreign Chinese communities. The special point of interest since 1949, however, is the application of Marxist doctrine to the musical scene of China. The first obvious area of change is found in the ever-popular forms of regional and Beijing opera. Although the appeal of traditional tales of emperors, princesses, or mythological characters could not be suppressed, the emphasis of all new operas was on workers, peasants, soldiers, and socialism. Thus, *Sanguozhi yanyi* (*Romance of the Three Kingdoms*) or *Kongchengji* (*The Ruse of an Empty City*) tend to be replaced by *Qixi Baihutuan* (*Raid on the White Tiger Regiment*) or *Honghu chiwei dui* (*Red Guards of Hung Lake*). Aria topics also vary, such as "Looking Forward to the Liberation of the Working People of the World" or "Socialism is Good".

As part of the encouragement of people's music, the national government emphasized regional folk music. Provincial and national research institutes were created to collect and study such music, and folk songs were incorporated into primary as well as advanced and Western music education. In general, folk music was "reconstructed" away from its former individualistic nature into collectives of choruses or folk orchestras. The topics of such regional songs were also reconstructed so that they reflected the new socialist life. The most famous new folk song from Shaanxi province is "Red is the East", while the Miao people were credited with "Sing in Praise of Chairman Mao".

During the Maoist period, more than 50 minority groups and provincial Chinese ensembles had at least one song directly in praise of Chairman Mao, while other songs dealt with local industries and accomplishments. Such songs are sometimes performed in regional style with traditional accompaniments, although they may often be found arranged Western-style for use in the public schools of the nation. This effort, in addition to the number of recordings that are available, make it possible for a Chinese citizen to become aware, perhaps for the first time in history, of the great variety of local music traditions in his large country, even though such music appears now in Marxist reconstructions.

Marxist defence of this changed folk music is that music of a given period must reflect the views and aspirations of the masses (as understood by the government) and must be based on idioms of the people. Composers of concert music have produced many folk orchestra compositions along with symphony, piano, and military band music based on this basic Marxist musical principle, called Socialist Realism. When dealing with traditional instruments and vocal styles, the composers have sometimes created extremely original and interesting pieces despite the general conservatism of government aesthetics policies. Vocal and choral music are preferred because of their ability to communicate specific national goals more efficiently than, for example, *The Sacred War Symphony*.

Although Western music of all kinds, but particularly rock music, was condemned and suppressed during the years of the Cultural Revolution, Chinese youth developed forms of the genre that sometimes blended traditional Chinese themes with Western beats. In the 1980s, when the ban on Western and Westernized music began to lift, artists and groups such as Cui Jian, Tang Dynasty, and Zang Tianshuo gained followings throughout the country. The 1990s saw commercialization of the music, with artists such as Dou Wei and Zhang Cu finding huge audiences through television and radio. At the same time, tentative efforts have been made to use contemporary Western idioms in Chinese concert music. As in the West, the music market in China was more fragmented in the early years of the twenty first century, with something to appeal to just about every taste available for sale.

11

LITERATURE

Chinese literature is one of the major literary heritages of the world, with an uninterrupted history of more than 3,000 years, dating back at least to the fourteenth century BCE.

The graphic nature of the written aspect of the Chinese language has produced a number of noteworthy effects upon Chinese literature and its diffusion: Chinese literature, especially poetry, is recorded in handwriting or in print and purports to make an aesthetic appeal to the reader that is visual as well as aural. This visual appeal of the graphs has in fact given rise to the elevated status of calligraphy in China, where it has been regarded for at least the last 16 centuries as a fine art comparable to painting. Scrolls of calligraphic renderings of poems and prose selections have continued to be hung alongside paintings in the homes of the common people as well as the elite, converting these literary gems into something to be enjoyed in everyday living.

On the negative side, such a writing system has been an impediment to education and the spread of literacy, thus reducing the number of readers of literature; for even a rudimentary level of reading and writing requires knowledge of more than 1,000 graphs, together with their pronunciation. On the other hand, the Chinese written language, even with its obvious disadvantages, has been a potent factor in perpetuating the cultural unity of the growing millions of Chinese people, including assimilated groups in far-flung peripheral areas. Different in function from recording words in an alphabetic–phonetic language, the graphs are not primarily indicators of sounds and can therefore be pronounced in variant ways to accommodate geographical diversities in speech and historical phonological changes without damage to the meaning of the written page.

As a result, the major dialects in China never developed into separate written languages as did the Romance languages, and, although the reader of a Confucian Classic in southern China might not understand the everyday speech of someone from the far north, Chinese literature has continued to be the common asset of the whole Chinese people. By the same token, the graphs of China could be utilized by speakers of other languages as their literary mediums.

The pronunciation of the Chinese graphs has also influenced the development of Chinese literature. The fact that each graph had a monophonic pronunciation in a given context created a large number of homonyms, which led to misunderstanding and confusion when spoken or read aloud without the aid of the graphs. One corrective was the introduction of tones or pitches in pronunciation. As a result, metre in Chinese prosody is not concerned with the combination of syllabic stresses, as in English, but with those of syllabic tones, which produce a different but equally pleasing cadence. This tonal feature of the Chinese language has brought about an intimate relationship between poetry and music in China.

All major types of Chinese poetry were originally sung to the accompaniment of music. Even after the musical scores were lost, the poems were, as they still are, more often chanted—in order to approximate singing—than merely read.

Chinese poetry, besides depending on end rhyme and tonal metre for its cadence, is characterized by its compactness and brevity. There are no epics of either folk or literary variety and hardly any narrative or descriptive poems that are long by the standards of world literature. Stressing the lyrical, as has often been pointed out, the Chinese poet refrains from being exhaustive, marking instead the heights of his ecstasies and inspiration or the depths of sorrow and sympathy. In that aesthetic, verbal economy is highly desirable. Generally, pronouns and conjunctions are omitted, and one or two words often allude to highly complex thoughts or situations. This explains why many of these highly formalized lyric poems have been differently interpreted by learned commentators and competent translators.

The line of demarcation between prose and poetry is much less distinctly drawn in Chinese literature than in other national literatures. This is clearly reflected in three genres. The *fu*, for example, is on the borderline between poetry and prose, containing elements of both. It uses rhyme and metre and not infrequently also antithetic structure, but, despite occasional flights into the realm of the poetic, it retains the features of prose without being necessarily prosaic. This accounts for the variety of labels given to the *fu* in English by writers on Chinese literature—poetic prose, rhyme prose, rhapsody, and prose poetry.

Another genre belonging to this category is *pianwen* ("parallel prose"), characterized by antithetic construction and balanced tonal patterns without the use of rhyme; the term is suggestive of "a team of paired horses", as is implied in the Chinese word *pian*. Despite the polyphonic effect thus produced, which approximates that of poetry, it has often been made the vehicle of proselike exposition and argumentation. Another genre, a peculiar mutation in this borderland, is the *baguwen* ("eight-legged essay"). Now generally regarded as unworthy of classification as literature, for centuries (from 1487 to 1901) it dominated the field of Chinese writing as the principal yardstick in grading candidates in the official civil-service examinations. It exploited antithetical construction and contrasting tonal patterns to the limit by requiring pairs of columns consisting of long paragraphs, one responding to the other, word for word, phrase for phrase, sentence for sentence.

History

The oldest specimens of Chinese writing extant are inscriptions on bones and tortoise shells dating back to the last three centuries of the Shang dynasty (seventeenth–eleventh centuries BCE) and recording divinations performed at the royal capital. These inscriptions, like those engraved on ceremonial bronze vessels toward the end of the Shang period, are usually brief and factual and cannot be considered literature. Nonetheless, they are significant in that their sizable vocabulary (about 3,400 characters, of which nearly 2,000 have been reliably deciphered) has proved to be the direct ancestor of the modern Chinese script.

Early Chinese literature does not present, as the literatures of certain other world cultures do, great epics embodying mythological lore. What information exists is sketchy and fragmentary and provides no clear evidence that an organic mythology ever existed; if it did, all traces have been lost. Attempts by scholars, Eastern and Western alike, to reconstruct the mythology of antiquity have consequently not advanced beyond probable theses.

Nevertheless, during the latter period of the twelfth century BCE Zhou, Chinese mythology began to undergo a profound transformation. In effect, an entirely new mythological world was created. The old gods, to a great extent already forgotten, were gradually supplanted by a multitude of new ones, some of whom were imported from India with Buddhism or gained popular acceptance as Taoism spread throughout the empire. In the process, many early myths were totally reinterpreted to the extent that some deities and mythological figures were rationalized into abstract concepts and others were euhemerized into historical figures. Above all, a hierarchical order, resembling in many ways the institutional order of the empire, was imposed upon the world of the supernatural.

These new gods generally had clearly defined functions and definite personal characteristics and became prominent in literature and the other arts. The myth of the battles between Huangdi ("The Yellow Emperor") and Chiyou ("The Wormy Transgressor"), for example, became a part of Taoist lore and eventually provided models for chapters of two works of vernacular fiction, *Shuihuzhuan* ("The Water Margin", also translated as "All Men Are Brothers") and *Xiyouji* (1592; "Journey to the West", also partially translated as "Monkey").

Historical personages were also commonly taken into the pantheon, for Chinese popular imagination has been quick to endow the biography of a beloved hero with legendary and eventually mythological traits. Qu Yuan, the ill-fated minister of the state of Chu (771–221 BCE), is the most notable example. Mythmaking consequently became a constant, living process in China. It was also true that historical heroes and would-be heroes arranged their biographies in a way that lent themselves to mythologizing.

*   *   *

The first anthology of Chinese poetry, known as the *Shijing* ("Classic of Poetry") and consisting of temple, court, and folk songs, was given definitive form somewhere around the time of Confucius (551–479 BCE). But its 305 songs are believed to range in date from the beginning of the Zhou dynasty to the time of their compiling.

The high regard in which this anthology has been held in China results both from its antiquity and from the legend that Confucius himself edited it. It was elevated in 136 BCE to the position of a major classic in the Confucian canon. The *Shijing* is generally accounted the third of the Five Classics (*Wujing*) of Confucian literature, the other four of which are the *Yijing* ("Classic of Changes"), a book of divination and cosmology; the *Shujing* ("Classic of History"), a collection of official documents; the *Liji* ("Record of Rites"), a book of rituals with accompanying anecdotes; and the *Chunqiu* ("Spring and Autumn") annals, a chronological history of the feudal state of Lu, where Confucius was born, consisting of topical entries of major events from 722 to 481 BCE. The Five Classics have been held in high esteem by Chinese scholars since the second century BCE.

The poems of the *Shijing* were originally sung to the accompaniment of music; and some of them, especially temple songs, were accompanied also by dancing. (In all subsequent periods of Chinese literary history, new trends in poetry were profoundly influenced by music.) Most of the poems of the *Shijing* have a preponderantly lyrical strain whether the subject is hardship in military service or seasonal festivities, agricultural chores or rural scenes, love or sports, aspirations or disappointments of the common folk and of the declining aristocracy. Apparently, the language of the poems was relatively close to the daily speech of the common people, and even repeated attempts at refinement during the long process of transmission have not spoiled their freshness and spontaneity. In spite of this, however, when the songs are read aloud and not sung to music their prevailing four-syllable lines conduce to monotony, hardly redeemed by the occasional interspersion of shorter or longer lines.

If there ever was an epic tradition in ancient China comparable to that of early India or the West, only dim traces of it persist in the written records. The *Shijing* has a few narrative poems celebrating heroic deeds of the royal ancestors, but these are rearranged in cycles and only faintly approximate the national epics of other peoples. One cycle, for example, records the major stages in the rise of the Zhou kingdom, from the supernatural birth of its remote founder to its conquest of the Shang kingdom. These episodes, which, according to traditional history, cover a period of more than 1,000 years, are dealt with in only about 400 lines. Other cycles, which celebrate later military exploits of the royal Zhou armies, are even briefer.

The *Shijing* exerted a profound influence on Chinese poetry that, generally speaking, has stressed the lyrical rather than the narrative element; a dependence more on end rhymes for musical effect than on other rhetorical devices; regular lines, consisting of a standard number of syllables; and the utilization of intonation that is inherent in the language for rhythm, instead of the alternation of stressed and unstressed syllables as is the norm in Western poetry.

Prior to the rise of the philosophers in the sixth century BCE, brief prose writings were reported to be numerous; but of these only two collections have been transmitted: the *Shu*, or *Shujing* ("Classic of History"), consisting of diverse kinds of primitive state papers, such as declarations, portions of charges to feudal lords, and orations; and the *Yi* or *Yijing*, a fortune-telling manual. Both grew by accretion and, according to a very doubtful tradition, were edited by Confucius himself. Neither can be considered literature, but both have exerted influence on Chinese writers for more than 2,000 years as a result of their inclusion in the Confucian canon.

The earliest writings that can be assigned to individual "authorship", in the loose sense of the term, are the *Laozi*, or *Daodejing* ("Classic of the Way of Power"), which is attributed to Laozi, who is credited with being the founder of Taoism and who might have been an older contemporary of Confucius; and the *Lunyu* ("Conversations"), or *Analects* (selected miscellaneous passages), of Confucius. Neither of the philosophers wrote extensively, and their teachings were recorded by their followers.

Thus, the *Laozi* consists of brief summaries of the sage Laozi's sayings, many of which are in rhyme and others in polished prose to facilitate memorization. Likewise, the *Analects* is composed of collections of the sage's sayings, mostly as answers to questions or as a result of discussions because writing implements and materials were expensive and scarce. The circumstances of the conversations, however, were usually omitted; and as a consequence the master's words often sound cryptic and disjointed, despite the profundity of the wisdom.

By about 400 BCE, writing materials had improved, resulting in a change in prose style. The records of the discourses became longer, the narrative portions more detailed; jokes, stories, anecdotes, and parables, interspersed in the conversations, were included. Thus, the *Mencius*, or *Mengzi*, the teachings of Mencius, not only is three times longer than the *Analects* of Confucius but also is topically and more coherently arranged. The same characteristic may be noticed in the authentic chapters of the *Zhuangzi*, attributed to the Taoist sage Zhuangzi, who "in paradoxical language, in bold words, and with subtle profundity, gave free play to his imagination and thought . . . Although his writings are inimitable and unique, they seem circuitous and innocuous. Although his utterances are irregular and formless, they are unconventional and readable . . ." (from the epilogue of the *Zhuangzi*).

Following the unification of the empire by the Jin dynasty (221–206 BCE) and the continuation of the unified empire under the Han, literary activities took new directions. At the Imperial and feudal courts, the *fu* genre, a combination of rhyme and prose, began to flourish. Long and elaborate descriptive poetic compositions, the *fu* were in form a continuation of the Chu elegies, now made to serve a different purpose—the amusement of the new aristocracy and the glorification of the empire—by dwelling on such topics as the low table and the folding screen or on descriptions of the capital cities. But even the best *fu* writing, by such masters of the art as Mei Sheng and Sima Xiangru, bordered on the frivolous and bombastic. Another major *fu* writer, Yang Xiong, in the prime of his career remorsefully realized that the genre was a minor craft not worthy of a true poet. Nonetheless, the *fu* was almost universally accepted as the norm of creative writing, and nearly 1,000 pieces were produced.

A more important contribution to literature by the Han government was the reactivation in 125 BCE of the Yue Fu, or Music Bureau, which had been established at least a century earlier to collect songs and their musical scores. Besides temple and court compositions of ceremonial verse, this office succeeded in preserving a number of songs sung or chanted by the ordinary people, including songs from the border areas, which reveal alien influences. This category—called *yuefu*, for the Music Bureau—includes not only touching lyrics but also charming ballads.

Prose literature was also developed during the Jin and Han dynasties. In addition to a prolific output of philosophers and political thinkers, history writing became an important part of literature. Outstanding among these is the *Shiji* (*c.* 85 BCE; "Historical Records", Eng. trans., *The Records of the Grand Historian of China*, 2 vol.) by Sima Qian. A masterpiece that took 18 years to produce, it deals with major events and personalities of about 2,000 years (down to the author's time), comprising 130 chapters and totalling more than 520,000 words. The *Shiji* was not only the first general history of its kind attempted in China, but it also set a pattern in organization for dynastic histories of subsequent ages.

An artist as well as a historian, Sima Qian succeeded in making events and personalities of the past into living realities for his readers; his biographies subsequently became models for authors of both fiction and history. Sima's great successor, the poet-historian-soldier Ban Gu, author of the *Hanshu* ("Han Documents"), a history of the former Han dynasty containing more than 800,000 words, performed a similar tour de force but did not equal Sima Qian in either scope or style.

After the fall of the Han dynasty, there was a long period of political division (220–589 CE). Despite the social and political confusion and military losses, however, the cultural scene was by no means dismal. Several influences on the development of literature are noteworthy. First Buddhism, introduced earlier, had brought with it religious chants and Indian music, which helped to attune Chinese ears to the finer distinctions of tonal qualities in their own language. Second, aggressive northern tribes, who invaded and dominated the northern half of the country from 316, were being culturally absorbed and converted. Third, the political division of the empire between the south and the north (as a result of the domination of non-Chinese in the north) led to an increase in cultural differences and to a subsequent rivalry to uphold what was regarded as cultural orthodoxy, frequently resulting in literary antiquarianism.

As orthodox Confucianism gradually yielded to Taoism and later to Buddhism, nearly all of the major writers began to cultivate an uninhibited individuality. Lu Ji, third-century poet and critic, in particular emphasized the importance of origin-ality in creative writing and discredited the long-established practice of imitating the great masters of the past. Still, his celebrated essay on literature (*Wen fu*), in which he enunciated this principle, was written as a *fu*, showing after all that he was a child of his own age.

The third/fourth-century Taoist philosopher Ge Hong in-sisted that technique is no less essential to a writer than moral integrity. The revolt of the age against conventionality was revealed in the new vogue of *qingtan* ("pure conversation"), intellectual discussions on lofty and non-mundane matters, recorded in a fifth-century collection of anecdotes entitled *Shishuo Xinyu* ("A New Account of Tales of the World") by Liu Yiqing.

Though prose writers as a whole continued to be most concerned with lyrical expression and rhetorical devices for artistic effect, there were notable deviations from the prevail-ing usage in the polyphonic *pianwen* ("parallel prose"). In this form, parallel construction of pairs of sentences and counter-balancing of tonal patterns were the chief requirements. *Pian-wen* was used especially in works concerned with philosophical disputes and in religious controversies; but it was also used in the first book-length work of literary criti-cism, *Wenxin diaolong* ("The Literary Mind and the Carving of the Dragon"), by the sixth-century writer Liu Xie.

*   *   *

Chinese literature reached its golden age during the Tang dynasty (618–907). In poetry, the greatest glory of the period, all the verse forms of the past were freely adopted and refined, and new forms were crystallized. One new form was perfected early in the dynasty and given the definitive name *lüshi* ("regulated verse"). A poem of this kind consists of eight lines of five or seven syllables—each line set down in accordance with strict tonal patterns—calling for parallel structure in the middle, or second and third, couplets.

Another verse form much in vogue was the *jueju* ("truncated verse"). An outgrowth and a shortened version of the *lüshi*, it omitted either the first four lines, the last four lines, the first two and the last two lines, or the middle four lines. Thus, the tonal quality of the *lüshi* was retained, whereas antithetic structure was made optional. These poems of four lines, each consisting of five or seven words (syllables or characters), had to depend for their artistry on suggestiveness and economy comparable to the *roba'iyat* ("quatrains") of Omar Khayyam and the Japanese haiku.

The fine distinctions of tonal variations in the spoken language had reached their height during this period, with eight tones; and rules and regulations concerning the sequence of lighter and heavier tones had been formulated. But since the observance of strict rules of prosody was not mandatory in the *gushi* ("ancient style") form still in use, it was possible for an individual poet to enjoy conformity or freedom as he saw fit.

Of the more than 2,200 Tang poets whose works—totalling more than 48,900 pieces—have been preserved, only a few can be mentioned.

Generally considered the greatest poet of China was Du Fu, a keen observer of the political and social scene who criticized injustice wherever he found it and who clearly understood the nature of the great upheaval following the rebellion of dissatisfied generals in 755, which was a turning point in the fortunes of the Tang. As an artist, Du Fu excelled in all verse forms, transcending all rules and regulations in prosody while conforming to and exploiting them. His power and passion can perhaps be suggested by a single line (translated by Robert Payne): "Blue is the smoke of war, white the bones of men."

At the end of the Tang and during the Five Dynasties, another new verse form developed. Composed normally of lines of irregular length and written as lyrics to musical tunes, this form came to be known as *ci*. Because the lines in a *ci* might vary from one to nine or even 11 syllables, they were comparable to the natural rhythm of speech and therefore easily understood when sung. First sung by ordinary folk, they were popularized by professional women singers and, during the Tang, attracted the attention of poets.

It was not, however, until the transitional period of the Five Dynasties (907–960), a time of division and strife, that *ci* became the major vehicle of lyrical expression. The greatest *ci* poet of the period was Li Yu, last monarch of the Southern Tang, who was seized in 976 as the new Song dynasty consolidated its power. Li Yu's *ci* poetry is saturated with a tragic nostalgia for better days in the south; it is suffused with sadness—a new depth of feeling notably absent from earlier *ci*, which had been sung at parties and banquets.

Besides the early *ci*, the end of the Tang saw the evolution of another new folk form: *bianwen* ("popularizations", not to be confused with *pienwan*, or parallel prose), utilizing both prose and verse to retell episodes from the Buddha's life and, later, non-Buddhist stories from Chinese history and folklore.

The Song dynasty (960–1279 CE), was marked by cultural advancement and military weakness. During this period, literary output was spectacularly increased, thanks mainly to the improvement of printing (invented in the eighth century) and to the establishment of public schools throughout the empire (from 1044). Yet this was challenged with the arrival of outsiders.

Fleeing from the Jin (Juchen) Tatars, who captured their capital in 1127, the Song officials and courtiers retreated southward. For almost a century and a half, China was again divided. And in spite of political reunification by Kublai Khan, founder of the Yuan, or Mongol, dynasty (beginning in 1206 in the north and comprising the whole of China by 1280), the cultural split persisted.

In the south, where China's historic traditions found asylum, racial and cultural homogeneity persisted. In fact, the centre of Chinese philosophy and traditional literature never again returned north of the Chang Yangtze (Jiang) delta. But in the north new developments arose, which led to wholly new departures. First, the migration and fusion of the various ethnic groups gave birth to a common spoken language with fewer tones, which later was to become the basis of a national language; second, with the southward shift of the centre of traditional culture, the prestige of the old literature began to decline in the north, especially in the eyes of the conquerors. Thus, in contrast to the south, North China under the Yuan dynasty provided a unique milieu for unconventional literary activities.

In this period, dramatic literature came into a belated full flowering. The skits and vaudeville acts, the puppet shows and shadow plays of previous ages had laid the foundation for a full-fledged drama; but the availability of Indian and Iranian models during the Yuan dynasty may have been a more immediate cause for its accelerated growth. Many Chinese men of letters refused to cooperate with the alien government, seeking refuge in painting and writing. As the new literary type developed—the drama of four or five acts, complete with prologue and epilogue and including songs and dialogue in language fairly close to the daily speech of the people—many men of letters turned to playwriting. Between 1234 and 1368, more than 1,700 musical plays were written and staged, and 105 dramatists were recorded; moreover, there is an undetermined number of anonymous playwrights whose unsigned works have been preserved but discovered only in the twentieth century.

Similarly, fiction writers who wrote in a semi-vernacular style began to emerge, continuing the tradition of storytellers of the past or composing lengthy works of fiction written almost entirely in the vernacular. All of the early pieces of this type of book-length fiction were poorly printed and anonymously or pseudonymously published. Although many early works were attributed to such authors as Luo Guanzhong, there is little reliable evidence of his authorship in any extant work. These novels exist in numerous, vastly different versions that can best be described as the products of long evolutionary cycles involving several authors and editors. The best known of the works attributed to Luo are *Sanguozhi yanyi* ("Romance of the Three Kingdoms"), *Shuihuzhuan* ("The Water Margin"), and *Pingyaozhuan* ("The Subjugation of the Evil Phantoms"). The best of the three from a literary standpoint is the *Shuihuzhuan*, which gives full imaginative treatment to a long accretion of stories and anecdotes woven around a number of enlightened bandits—armed social and political dissenters.

It was in vernacular literature that the writers of the Ming dynasty (1368–1644) made a real contribution. In drama, a tradition started in the Song dynasty and maintained in southern China during the period of Mongol domination was revitalized. This southern drama, also musical and known

nqi ("tales of marvels"), had certain special traits: (1) a
nqi play contains from 30 to 40 changes of scene; (2) the
change of end rhymes in the arias is free and frequent; (3) the
singing is done by many actors instead of by the hero or
heroine alone; (4) many plots, instead of being extracted from
history or folklore, are taken from contemporary life.

Because there were no rules regulating the structure of the
chuanqi, playlets approaching the one-act variety were also
written. This southern theatre movement, at first largely
carried on by anonymous amateurs, gradually won support
from the literati until finally, in the sixteenth century, a new
and influential school was formed under the leadership of the
poet-singer Liang Chenyu and his friend, the great actor Wei
Liangfu. The Kun school, initiating a style of soft singing and
subtle music, was to dominate the theatre to the end of the
eighteenth century.

Aside from drama and *daqu* (a suite of melodies sung in
narration of stories), which in the south were noticeably
modified in spirit and structure, becoming more ornate and
bookish—it was prose fiction that made the greatest progress
in the sixteenth century. Two important novels took shape at
that time. Wu Cheng'en's *Xiyouji* is a fictionalized account of
the pilgrimage of the Chinese monk Xuanzang to India in the
seventh century. The subject matter was not new; it had been
used in early *huaben*, or "vernacular story", books and Yuan
drama; but it had never been presented at length in such a
lively and rapid-moving narration. Of all the 81 episodes of
trial and tribulation experienced by the pilgrim, no two are
alike. Among the large number of monsters introduced, each
has unique individuality. Like the *Shuihuzhuan*, it reveals the
influence of the style of the oral storytellers, for each chapter
ends with the sentence "in case you are interested in what is to
follow, please listen to the next instalment, which will reveal

it." Unlike the *Shuihuzhuan*, which was written in a kind of semi-vernacular, the language used was the vernacular of the living tongue. For the author the choice must have been a deliberate but difficult one, for he had the novel first published anonymously to avoid disapproval. Besides eliciting numerous commentaries and "continuations" in China, it has two English translations.

The title of the second novel, *Jin Ping Mei* (the author of which is unknown), is composed of graphs from the names of three female characters. Written in an extremely charming vernacular prose style, the novel is a well-knit, long narrative of the awful debaucheries of the villain Ximen Qing. The details of the different facets of life in sixteenth century China are so faithfully portrayed that it can be read almost as a documentary social history of that age. The sexual perversions of the characters are so elaborately depicted that several Western translators have rendered a number of indelicate passages in Latin. The novel has been banned in China more than once, and all copies of the first edition of 1610 were destroyed.

By the early nineteenth century, China could no longer ward off the West and, after the first Opium War (1839–42), China's port cities were forcibly opened to increased foreign contacts. In due course, many Western works on diverse subjects were translated into Chinese. The quality of some of these was so outstanding that they deserve a place in the history of Chinese literature. One distinguished translator was Yen Fu, who had studied in Great Britain and whose renderings of Western philosophical works into classical Chinese were acclaimed as worthy of comparison, in literary merit, with the Zhou philosophers. Another great translator was Lin Shu, who, knowing no foreign language himself but depending on oral interpreters, made available to Chinese readers more than 170 Western novels, translated into the literary style of Sima Qian.

Modern Chinese Literature

Following the overthrow of the Manchu dynasty and the establishment of the Republic in 1912, many young intellectuals turned their attention to the overhauling of literary traditions, beginning with the language itself. In January 1917 an article by Hu Shih, a student of philosophy at Columbia University, entitled *Wenxuegailiang chuyi* ("Tentative Proposal for Literary Reform") was published in the Beijing magazine *Xinqingnian* ("New Youth"). In it Hu called for a new national literature written not in the classical language but in the vernacular, the living "national language" (*guoyu*).

The literary reform movement that began with these and other "calls to arms" was a part of the larger May Fourth Movement for cultural and sociopolitical reform, whose name commemorates a 1919 student protest against the intellectual performance of the Chinese delegates to the Paris Peace Conference formally terminating World War I. At the outset, the literary reformers met with impassioned but mostly futile opposition from classical literati such as the renowned translator Lin Shu, who would largely give up the battle within a few years.

The first fruits of this movement were seen in 1918 and 1919 with the appearance in *Xinqingnian* of such stories as *Kuangren riji* ("The Diary of a Madman"), a Gogol-inspired piece about a "madman" who suspects that he alone is sane and the rest of the world is mad, and *Yao* ("Medicine"), both by Zhou Shuren. Known by the pseudonym Lu Xun, Zhou had studied in Japan and, with his younger brother, the noted essayist Chou Tso-jen, had become a leader of the literary revolution soon after returning to China. Lu Xun's acerbic, somewhat westernized and often satirical attacks on China's feudalistic traditions, established him as China's foremost critic and writer. His *A-Q zhengzhuan* (1921; "The True Story of Ah Q"), a damning critique of early twentieth-century conservatism in China, is the representative work of the May Fourth period and has become an international classic.

These early writings provided the impetus for a number of youthful intellectuals to pool their resources and promote shared ideals by forming literary associations. The Wenxue vanjiu-hui ("Literary Research Association"), generally referred to as the "realist" or "art-for-life's-sake" school, assumed the editorship of the established literary magazine *Xiaoshuo yuebao* ("Short Story Monthly"), in which most major fiction writers published their works throughout the 1920s. The socially reflective, critical-realist writing that characterized this group held sway in China well into the 1940s, when it was gradually eclipsed by more didactic, propagandistic literature.

Members of the smaller Chuangzaoshe ("Creation Society"), on the other hand, were followers of the "Romantic" tradition, who eschewed any expressions of social responsibility by writers, referring to their work as "art for art's sake". In 1924, however, the society's leading figure, Guo Moruo, converted to Marxism, and the Creation Society evolved into China's first Marxist literary society.

Much of the energy of members of both associations was expended in translating literature of other cultures, which largely replaced traditional Chinese literature as the foundation upon which the new writing was built. This was particularly true in drama and poetry, in which figures such as Henrik Ibsen and Rabindranath Tagore, respectively, were as well known to Chinese readers as indigenous playwrights and poets.

Political events of the mid-1920s, in which Nationalist, Communist, and warlord forces frequently clashed, initiated a shift to the left in Chinese letters, culminating in 1930 in the founding of the Zuoyizuojia lianmeng ("League of Leftist Writers"), whose membership included most influential writers. Lu Xun, the prime organizer and titular head throughout the league's half-decade of activities, had stopped writing fiction in late 1925 and, after moving from Beijing to Shanghai in 1927, directed most of his creative energies to translating Russian literature and writing the bitingly satirical random essays (*zawen*) that became his trademark. Among the many active pre-war novelists, the most successful were Mao Dun, Lao She, and Ba Jin.

Mao Dun, a founder of the Literary Research Association, was the prototypical Realist. The subjects of his socially mimetic tableaux included pre-May Fourth urban intellectual circles, bankrupt rural villages, and, in perhaps his best known work, *Ziye* (1933; "Midnight"), metropolitan Shanghai in all its financial and social chaos during the post-Depression era.

Lao She, modern China's foremost humorist, whose early novels were written while he was teaching Chinese in London, was deeply influenced by traditional Chinese storytellers and the novels of Charles Dickens. His works are known for their episodic structure, racy northern dialect, vivid characterizations, and abundant humour. Yet it was left to him to write modern China's classic novel, the moving tale of the gradual degeneration of a seemingly incorruptible denizen of China's "lower depths"—*Luotuo Xianggzi* (1936; "Camel Hsiang-tzu", published in English in a bowdlerized translation as "Rickshaw Boy", 1945).

Ba Jin, a prominent Anarchist, was the most popular novelist of the period. A prolific writer, he is known primarily for his autobiographical novel *Jia* (1931; "The Family"), which traces the lives and varied fortunes of the three sons of a wealthy, powerful family. The book is a revealing portrait of China's oppressive patriarchal society, as well as of the awakening of China's youth to the urgent need for social revolution.

The 1930s also witnessed the meteoric rise of a group of novelists from Northeast China (Manchuria) who were driven south by the Japanese annexation of their homeland in 1932. The sometimes rousing, sometimes nostalgic novels of Xiao Jun and Xiao Hong and the powerful short stories of Duanmu Hongliang became rallying cries for anti-Japanese youth as signs of impending war mounted.

Poetry of the 1930s underwent a similar politicization, as more and more students returned from overseas to place their pens in the service of the "people's resistance against feudalism and imperialism". The lyrical verse of the early Crescent Moon poets was replaced by a more socially conscious poetry by the likes of Ai Qing, Tian Chien, and Zang Kejia that appealed to the readers' patriotic fervour. Others, particularly those who had at first gravitated toward the Crescent Moon Society, began striking out in various directions: notable works of these authors include the contemplative sonnets of Feng Zhi, the urbane songs of Beijing by Bian Zhilin, and the romantic verses of He Qifang. Less popular, but more daring, were Dai Wangshu and Li Jinfa, poets of the Xiandai ("Contemporary Age") group, who wrote very sophisticated, if frequently baffling, poetry in the manner of the French Symbolists.

While fiction reigned supreme in the 1930s, as the art of the short story was mastered by growing numbers of May Fourth writers, and novels were coming into their own, the most spectacular advances were made in drama, owing largely to the efforts of a single playwright. Although realistic social drama written in the vernacular had made its appearance in China long before the 1930s, primarily as translations or adaptations of Western works, it did not gain a foothold on the popular stage until the arrival of Cao Yu, whose first play, *Leiyu* (1934; "Thunderstorm"), a tale of fatalism, retribution, and incestuous relations among members of a rich industrialist's family, met with phenomenal success. It was followed over the next several years by other critically and popularly acclaimed plays, including *Richu* (1936; "Sunrise") and *Yuanye* (1937; "Wilderness"), all of which examined pressing social issues and universal human frailties with gripping tension and innovative dramaturgy. Political realities in future decades would force a steady decline in dramatic art, so that Cao Yu's half-dozen major productions still stand as the high-water mark of modern Chinese theatre. Yet even though movies, television, and other popular entertainments would weaken the resiliency of this literary form, it would still serve the nation as an effective propaganda medium, particularly during the war of resistance.

During the Sino-Japanese War, most writers fled to the interior, where they contributed to the war effort by writing patriotic literature under the banner of the All-China Anti-Japanese Federation of Writers and Artists, founded in 1938 and directed by Lao She. All genres were represented, including reportage (*baogao wenxue*), an enormously influential type of writing that was a natural outgrowth of the federation's call for writers to go to the countryside and the front lines. Literary magazines were filled with short, easily produced and adaptable plays, topical patriotic verse, and war-zone dispatches. Among the major writers who continued to produce work of high quality during this period were Ba Jin, Cao Yu, Mao Dun, and Ding Ling. The cast's fictional explorations of the female psyche and the social condition of women had caught the public's imagination in the 1920s, and in the late 1930s she established herself as the major literary figure in the Communist stronghold of Yan'an.

The growing dissatisfaction of intellectuals with the Nationalist government in Chongqing surfaced dramatically during the civil war that raged throughout China following Japan's surrender, ending with the Nationalists' retreat to Taiwan and the establishment, in October 1949, of the People's Republic of China. Most writers, feeling intense pride and welcoming the challenge, chose to remain on the mainland and serve the new government.

Literature on the China mainland since 1949 has largely been a reflection of political campaigns and ideological battles. This state of affairs can be traced to Mao Zedong's 1942 "Talks at the Yenan Forum on Literature and Art", in which he articulated his position that literature, which existed to serve politics, was to be popularized while the people's level of literary appreciation was gradually being elevated. Mao's call for a truly proletarian literature—written by and for workers, peasants, and soldiers—gave rise to a series of rectification campaigns that further defined and consolidated party control over literary activities. In 1949, the First National Congress of Writers and Artists was convened, and the All-China Federation of Literature and Art Circles was founded, with Guo Moruo elected as its first chairman.

Mao's literary ideals had first been realized in the 1940s by Zhao Shuli, whose early stories, such as *Li Youcai banhua* ("The Rhymes of Youcai"), were models of proletarian literature, both in form and in content. As the civil war neared its conclusion, novels of land reform, such as Ding Ling's prize-winning *Taiyang zhao zai Sangganhe shang* (1949; "The Sun Shines over the Sangkan River") and Zhou Lino's *Baofeng zouyu* (1949; "The Hurricane"), became quite popular. Few of the established May Fourth writers continued to produce fiction after 1949, for their experience as social critics did not prepare them for Socialist Realism, a method of composition borrowed from the Soviet Union, according to which society is described as it should be, not necessarily as it is. Many of the older poets, however, were successful during the early post-liberation years, writing poetry in praise of land reform, modernization, and Chinese heroes of the Korean War. Playwrights were also active, introducing more proletarian themes into their works, some of which incorporated music. By this time, Lao She had begun writing plays, such as *Longxugou* (1951; "Dragon Beard Ditch"), which earned him the prestigious title of People's Artist. Another very popular play, *Baimaonü* (1953; "White-Haired Girl") by He Jingzhi, was taken from a contemporary folk legend.

During the mid-1950s, an experiment in liberalization—the Hundred Flowers Campaign—was abruptly terminated as criticism of the party went beyond all expectations; it was followed by an anti-rightist movement that purged the cultural ranks of most pre-liberation writers and artists. The literary nadir, however, was not reached until the Cultural Revolution (1966–76), when the only literature available was a few carefully screened works by Lu Xun, a handful of model revolutionary Beijing operas, and the revolutionary-romantic novels of Hao Jan. After the death of Mao and the fall of the Gang of Four, literature made a comeback and most surviving writers were rehabilitated, although the progress was as rocky as the political scene Chinese literature continued to reflect.

The accusatory "scar literature", a sort of national catharsis that immediately followed the 10-year "holocaust", gave way to more professional and more daring writing, as exemplified in the stories of Wang Meng, with their stylistic experiments in stream of consciousness; the symbolic "obscure" poetry of Bei Dao and others; the relatively bold dramas, both for the stage and for the screen, of several playwrights; and the innovative investigative reportage of Liu Binyan. In addition to translated literature from the West, literature from Taiwan also began to reach mainland writers and readers as literary restrictions continued to fall gradually. Even so, in the wake of the Tiananmen Square incident of 1989 and other repressive episodes, many leading contemporary Chinese writers, among them Bei Dao, Yang Lian, Gao Xingjian, and Da Chen, now live in the West. The journal *Jintian*, which Bei Dao edits from California, has become a leading organ for this literature in exile.

12

EVERYDAY LIFE IN MODERN CHINA

Chinese culture—predominantly that of the Han people, who constitute the vast majority of China's population—has evolved over the course of 5,000 years. Many of its most popular cultural expressions, including music and dance, have changed little over the millennia; apart from a few changes in instrumentation, for example, many of the folk songs that Chinese sing today are, note for note, those that their ancestors sang during the Tang dynasty, arguably China's greatest period of artistic expression.

To anyone not born into it, much of Chinese culture is difficult to understand. In part this is a linguistic obstacle, for the Chinese language, made up of thousands of homophones differentiated by tones, presents a formidable barrier. Just so, traditional Chinese music uses scales and tunings unlike those of the West and of Africa, while the Chinese ideographic alphabet, containing more than 50,000 symbols, takes years of study to master. Chinese scholars have remarked that these differences serve much the same purpose as the Great Wall: they keep barbarians out of Zhongguo, "the middle kingdom" or "the centre of the world", and they assert the centrality of China and its people.

The Chinese prize tradition and cultural continuity. In keeping with Confucian ideals, one of the vehicles for maintaining tradition and excellence has been education. Despite a universal public education system that is reeling under the weight of too many students and too few facilities, ordinary Chinese are well educated relative to most of the rest of the world, and they consistently score well in tests of maths and science, at least in part because their teachers are well trained, in part because much Chinese education consists of constant drill and memorization that serves well in testing situations. Chinese students excel in other fields as well; musical instruction is widespread, with piano and violin being popular instruments and music reading ability common. Most younger Chinese study and have some knowledge of English, instruction in which was made universal during the modernization programs of Deng Xiaoping. The demand for English instruction is growing with China's continuing integration into the world economy, and demand is high for native speakers as teachers.

As with every other culture of the world, daily life in China draws on universal themes, among them work, food, sport, health, leisure, and the organization of time. It is also marked, as elsewhere, by tensions between the traditional and the modern. Although China rightly prizes its regional cuisines, for example, it cannot but be noticed that many street corners seem to be sprouting a Western-owned or at least Western-style fast-food franchise. Traditional markets are less popular than shopping malls, at least among the young, who are keenly interested in imported music, film, and fashion and who are technologically sophisticated (even if the government does its best to control what is available on the Internet). As elsewhere, finally, the rapid changes wrought by technology and the global economy have formed a gulf between old and young, roughly classed as, respectively, those who can remember the Cultural Revolution and those who cannot. It can be said that in many ways these two groups inhabit two quite different Chinas, observing customs and rituals that bewilder the other.

Food

Chinese culture can best be understood through the vehicle of food. Chinese cuisine, like Chinese philosophy, is organized along Taoist principles of opposition and change: hot is balanced by cold, spicy by mild, fresh by cured. The cooking of Sichuan province in central China is distinguished by the use of hot peppers. The lush southern interior of the country prizes fresh ingredients; Cantonese cuisine in particular is a symphony of subtle flavours from just-picked vegetables and lightly cooked meats. No matter what the region, foods of all kinds are viewed as an accompaniment to grains, the staple of the Chinese diet.

Apart from French *haute cuisine*, the highest expression of the gastronomic art is generally regarded to be that of the Chinese. It is no accident that China and France should have produced the world's most distinctive and respected cuisines. Both countries were naturally blessed with an abundance and rich variety of raw ingredients. In each of these countries gastronomy traditionally commanded great interest and respect.

The intellectual, artistic, political, and financial leaders of China and France traditionally attached great importance to good eating. It has already been noted how this worked in the case of the Bourbon kings of France and with statesmen of such eminence as Talleyrand. In ancient China the preparation and service of food played an important part in court rituals. The first act of many emperors was to appoint a court chef, and once they were on the job these chefs strove mightily to outdo each other.

In ancient China, hunting and foraging supplied much of the food. Wild game such as deer, elk, boar, muntjac (a small deer), wolf, quail, and pheasant, was eaten, along with beef, mutton, and pork. Vegetables such as royal fern, smartweed, and the leafy thistle (*Sonchus*) were picked off the land. Meats were preserved by salt-curing, pounding with spices, or fermenting in wine. To provide a contrast in flavours the meat was fried in the fat of a different animal.

As Chinese agriculture developed, styles of food were determined to a great degree by the natural resources available in certain parts of the country, thus the vastly different ways of cooking and the development of distinctive regional cuisines. As a more varied fare began to emerge, tastes grew more refined. By the time of Confucius, gastronomes of considerable sophistication had appeared on the scene. Confucius wrote of one of these fastidious eaters: "For him the rice could never be white enough. When it was not cooked right, he would not eat. When the food was not in season, he would not eat. When the meat was not cut correctly, he would not eat. When the food was not served with the proper sauce, he would not eat."

Like all other forms of haute cuisine, classic Chinese cooking is the product of an affluent society. By the second century CE the Chinese court had achieved great splendour, and the complaint was heard that idle noblemen were lounging about all day, feasting on smoked meats and roasts.

By the tenth or eleventh century a distinctive cuisine had begun to emerge, one that was developed with great attention to detail. It was to reach its zenith in the Qing dynasty (1644–1911/12). This cuisine was a unique blend of simplicity and elegance. The object of cooking and the preparation of food was to extract from each ingredient its unique and most enjoyable quality.

As in the case of the French cuisine, the hors d'oeuvre set the tone of the meal. "The hors d'oeuvre must look neat," say the Chinese gastronomic authorities Lin Zuifeng and her daughter Lin Xiangru. They are best served in matching dishes, each containing one item. Many people like to garnish the dishes with parsley and vegetables cut in the shape of birds, fish, bats, etc., or even to make baskets of flowers from food. These are all acceptable if kept under control, and if the rest of the meal is served in the same florid style. The worst offence would be to start with a florid display of food and then suddenly change style midway.

The theory of balancing *fan* (grains and rice) with *cai* (vegetables and meat) is one of the factors that distinguish Chinese gastronomy from that of all other nations. This refined proportion of harmony and symmetry of ingredients was practised whenever possible in households throughout the ages and is not limited to formal or high cuisine or to meals served on special occasions.

In addition to taste that pleases (a most elemental require-ment in China), astrological, geographical, and personal char-acteristics had to satisfy the complex system of the yin–yang balance of hot and cold. According to this theory, every foodstuff possesses an inherent humour; thus, consuming foods and beverages at proper and complementary temper-atures can adjust the possible deviation of the normal state of the two intertwining forces.

Certain foods and culinary traditions are prevalent through-out most of the country. Rice is the staple except in the north, where wheat flour takes its place. Fish is extremely important in all regions. Pork, chicken, and duck are widely consumed, as well as large quantities of such vegetables as mushrooms, bamboo shoots, water chestnuts, and bean sprouts. The Chinese season their dishes with monosodium glutamate and soybean sauce, which takes the place of salt. Another distinctive feature of Chinese cooking is the varied and highly imaginative use of fat, which is prepared in many different ways and achieves the quality of a true delicacy in the hands of a talented Chinese cook. The Chinese take tea with their meals, whether green or fermented. Jasmine tea is served with flowers and leaves in small-handled cups.

The Great Chinese Schools

Traditionally, China is divided into five gastronomic regions, three of which are characterized by the great schools of Chinese cooking, Beijing, Sichuan, and Zhejiang-Jiangsu. The other two regions, Fujian and Guangdong, are less important from a gastronomic point of view.

Beijing is the land of fried bean curd and water chestnuts. Among foods traditionally sold by street vendors are steamed bread and watermelon seeds. Vendors also dispensed buns called *baozi* that were stuffed with pork and pork fat, and *jiaozi*, or crescents, cylindrical rolls filled with garlic, cabbage, pork, and scallions. Wheat cakes wrapped around a filling of scallions and garlic, and noodles with minced pork sauce are also traditional Beijing specialities.

But the greatest of all delicacies of this region is of course the Peking duck. This elaborate, world-renowned dish requires lengthy preparation and is served in three separate courses. In its preparation, the skin is first puffed out from the duck by introducing air between the skin and the flesh. The duck is then hung out to dry for at least 24 hours, preferably in a stiff, cold breeze. This pulls the skin away from the meat. Then the duck is roasted until the skin is crisp and brown. The skin is removed, painted with hoisin sauce (a sweet, spicy sauce made of soybeans), and served inside the folds of a bun as the first course. The duck meat is carved from the bones and carefully cut into slivers. Sautéed onions, ginger, and peppers are added to the duck meat and cooked with bean sprouts or bamboo slivers. This forms the second course. The third course is a soup. The duck bones are crushed and then water, ginger, and onion are added to make a broth. The mixture is boiled, then drained, and the residue is cooked with cabbage and sugar until the cabbage is tender.

The cooking of Sichuan in central China is distinguished by the use of hot peppers, which are indigenous to the region. The peppers lend an immediate sensation of fiery hotness to the food, but, once this initial reaction passes, a mingled flavour of sweet, sour, salty, fragrant, and bitter asserts itself. Fried pork slices, for example, are cooked with onions, ginger, red pepper, and soy sauce to achieve this aromatic hotness.

The provinces of Zhejiang and Jiangsu feature a broad variety of fish—shad, mullet, perch, and prawns. Minced chicken and bean-curd slivers are also specialities of these provinces. Foods are often arranged in pretty floral patterns before serving.

Fujian, which lies farther south, features shredded fish, shredded pork, and *popia*, or thin bean-curd crepes filled with pork, scallions, bamboo shoots, prawns, and snow peas.

Perhaps, the most familiar form of Chinese cooking is that of Guangdong, for Guangzhou (Canton) lies within this coastal province. Mushrooms, sparrows, wild ducks, snails, snakes, eels, oysters, frogs, turtles, and winkles are among the many exotic ingredients of the province. More familiar to Westerners are such Cantonese specialities as egg roll, egg foo yung (*furong*), and roast pork.

Martial Arts and Sport

Physical exercise is a staple of Chinese culture. Millions gather daily at dawn to practise martial arts (notably *taijiquan* [tai chi chuan]), wield swords in a graceful ballet, or (among women) perform a synchronized dance of pliés and turns.

Taijiquan is an ancient and distinctive Chinese form of exercise or attack and defence that is popular throughout the world. As exercise, *taijiquan*, whose name means "supreme ultimate fist", is designed to provide relaxation in the process of body-conditioning exercise and is drawn from the Taoist principles of *taiji*, notably including the harmonizing of the yin and yang, respectively the passive and active principles, referred to in *taiji* teachings as emptiness and solidarity, respectively. It employs flowing, rhythmic, deliberate movements, with carefully prescribed stances and positions, but in practice no two masters teach the system exactly alike. As a mode of attack and defence, *taijiquan* is a cousin of gongfu (kung fu) and is properly considered a martial art. It may be used with or without weapons.

Freehand exercise to promote health was practised in China as early as the third century, and, by the fifth century, monks at the Buddhist monastery of Shaolin were performing exercises emulating the five creatures: bear, bird, deer, monkey, and tiger. The snake was added later, and, by the early Ming dynasty (1368), the yin and yang principles had been added to harmonize the whole. An assimilation of these developments, the art of *taijiquan* was codified and named in the early Qing dynasty (1644–1911/12).

There have been many schools of *taijiquan*, and five are popular and distinctive. Depending on school and master, the number of prescribed exercise forms varies from 24 to 108 or more. The forms are named for the image created by their execution, such as "White stork displays its wings" and "Fall back and twist like monkey". All start from one of three stances, weight forward, weight on rear foot, and horse riding, or oblique.

Of China's indigenous forms of sport, the martial arts have the longest history by far. Their origin dates to at least 2,000 years ago, to a period in which contending warlords, bandits, and foreign invaders controlled large portions of China and forbade the populace to own weapons.

Martial arts can be divided into the armed and unarmed arts. The former include archery, spearmanship, and swordsmanship; the latter, which originated in China, emphasize striking with the feet and hands or grappling. In modern times, derivatives of some of the armed martial arts, principally Japanese forms such as kendo (fencing) and kyudo (archery), are practised as sports. Derivatives of the unarmed forms of combat, such as the Japanese and Korean judo, sumo, karate, and tae kwon do, are practised, as are self-defence forms, such as aikido, hapkido, and gongfu. All of these forms are subsumed under the general Chinese category of *wushu*, or "boxing".

As martial art, gongfu can be traced to the Zhou dynasty (1066–221 BCE) and even earlier. As exercise it was practised by the Taoists in the fifth century BCE. Its prescribed stances and actions are based on keen observations of human skeletal and muscular anatomy and physiology, and it requires great muscular coordination. The various movements in gongfu, most of which are imitations of the fighting styles of animals, are initiated from one of five basic foot positions: normal upright posture and the four stances called dragon, frog, horse riding, and snake. There are hundreds of styles of gongfu, and armed as well as unarmed techniques have been developed. In the latter half of the twentieth century a new genre of action films centred on gongfu techniques and philosophies emerged, largely from studios in Hong Kong, and helped to promote international interest in the art.

China has become one of the dominant countries in international sports competitions since it began participating regularly in the Olympic Games, at the 1980 Winter Games. Since then the country's finest Olympic moment came at the 2004 Summer Games. Chinese athletes took a total of 63 medals, dominating the badminton, diving, table tennis, and weightlifting events and making strong showings in a variety of others, including shooting and women's judo. Beijing was chosen to host the 2008 Summer Games. Much of the city was refurbished and cleaned to accommodate athletes and visitors, even as a new national stadium and 20 other sports facilities were built and 11 more remodelled. The 2008 programme included 28 sports and 302 events, one more event than the Olympic Games of 2004, held in Athens, Greece. These events were staged in Beijing and other major cities, with Hong Kong hosting the equestrian competitions.

Chinese Medicine

Throughout China the value of traditional medicine is stressed, especially in rural areas. All medical schools are encouraged to teach traditional medicine as part of their curriculum, and efforts are made to link colleges of Chinese medicine with Western-type medical schools. Medical education is shorter than it is in Europe, and there is greater emphasis on practical work. Students spend part of their time away from the medical school working in factories or in communes; they are encouraged to question what they are taught and to participate in the educational process at all stages. One well-known form of traditional medicine is acupuncture, which is used as a therapeutic and pain-relieving technique; requiring the insertion of brass-handled needles at various points on the body, acupuncture has become quite prominent as a form of anaesthesia.

The vast number of non-medically qualified health staff, upon whom the health-care system greatly depends, includes both full-time and part-time workers. The latter include so-called barefoot doctors, who work mainly in rural areas, worker doctors in factories, and medical workers in residential communities. None of these groups is medically qualified. They have had only a three-month period of formal training, part of which is done in a hospital, fairly evenly divided between theoretical and practical work. This is followed by a varying period of on-the-job experience under supervision.

Acupuncture

Acupuncture grew out of ancient Chinese philosophy's dualistic cosmic theory of the yin and the yang. The yin, the female principle, is passive and dark and is represented by the Earth; the yang, the male principle, is active and light and is represented by the Heavens. The forces of yin and yang act in the human body as they do throughout the natural universe as a whole. Disease or physical disharmony is caused by an imbalance or undue preponderance of these two forces in the body, and the goal of Chinese medicine is to bring the yin and the yang back into balance with each other, thus restoring the person to health.

An imbalance of yin and yang results in an obstruction of the vital life force, or *qi* (ch'i), in the body. The fundamental energy of the *qi* flows through 12 meridians, or pathways, in the body, each in turn associated with a major visceral organ (liver, kidney, etc.) and with a functional body system. Acupuncture is designed to affect the distribution of yin and yang in these channels so that the *qi* can flow freely and harmoniously.

The actual practice of acupuncture consists of inserting needles into any of hundreds of points located over the 12 basic meridians and over a number of specialized meridians. The needles used may be slightly arrowheaded or may have extremely fine points. The typical insertion is 3 to 10 mm (0.1 to 0.4 inches) in depth; some procedures call for insertions up to almost 25 cm (10 inches). Once inserted, a needle may be twisted, twirled, or connected to a low-voltage alternating current for the duration of its use. The physician frequently inserts needles at a considerable distance from the point on which they are to act; for example, a needle inserted into the pad of the thumb is expected to produce analgesia in the abdomen. Similarly, successive points on a specific meridian may affect widely different areas or conditions; e.g. the first six points of the yin lung meridian deal primarily with swollen joints, excessive heat in joints, bleeding from the nose, heart pains, mental depression, and inability to stretch the arms above the head. The location of the points is mastered by the use of innumerable diagrams and models.

Acupuncture appears somehow to be effective in relieving pain and is routinely used in China as an anaesthetic during surgery. Western visitors have witnessed ambitious (and ordinarily painful) surgical operations carried out on fully conscious Chinese patients locally anaesthetized only by acupuncture.

Several theories have been advanced to explain acupuncture's effectiveness in this regard. There is speculation that the needle insertions stimulate the body's production of such natural opiates (painkilling chemicals) as endorphins or enkephalins. Others have posited that the minor stimulation of acupuncture selectively acts on impulse transmission to the central nervous system, thus closing certain neurological "gates" and blocking the transmission of pain impulses from other parts of the body. Some Western observers studying the method have suggested that acupuncture analgesia is plainly a placebo analgesia—which does not, however, detract from its effectiveness. Chinese assertions that acupuncture can actually cure disease defy rational clinical practice and have yet to be substantiated by Western medical researchers.

The Chinese year is organized according to the lunar cycle and has been so for more than 4,500 years; indeed, it is said that the legendary emperor Huangdi introduced the zodiac and the lunar calendar at the outset of his reign in 2697 BCE. Each year is named for one of the zodiacal animals: dog, pig, rooster, dragon, ox, sheep, horse, rabbit, snake, monkey, rat, and tiger. In traditional belief, a person's character is determined by the tutelary animal of the year in which he or she is born.

The beginning of the year falls between late January and mid-February and is marked by the greatest festival in the Chinese calendar. New Year's Eve is typically spent with one's family and involves recognition of one's ancestors and, in traditional households, the gods. New Year's Day is traditionally inaugurated by dragon, lion, and tiger dancing, singing, and fireworks. The following day, married women visit their parents. The fifth day of the new year is considered especially propitious for launching new businesses or projects. The Lantern Festival, on the 15th day of the new year, marks the end of the holiday season.

China observes a number of national holidays, including New Year's Day, the Spring Festival, Youth Day (May 4), and National Day (October 1). Along with the Lantern Festival, Tomb Sweep Day (April 4 or 5) and the Mid-Autumn Festival

(October) are celebrated throughout the country. Scores of local festivals are also held at various times.

Cinema

Other Asian nations have had spotty cinematic histories, although most developed strong traditions during the late twentieth century. The film industries of mainland China, Taiwan, and Korea were marked by government restrictions for most of the twentieth century, and the majority of their output consisted of propaganda films. The loosening of many restrictions in the 1980s and 1990s resulted in a new wave of Asian directors who have attained worldwide prominence. At the turn of the twenty first century, China's "Fifth Generation Cinema" was known for such outstanding young directors as Chen Kaige, who specializes in tales of political oppression and sexual repression, and Zhang Yimou, whose work celebrates the individual's capacity to endure in the face of sweeping social change. Films such as Chen's "Farewell, My Concubine" (*Bawang bie ji*, 1993) and Zhang's "Raise the Red Lantern" (*Dahong denglong gaogao gua*, 1991) have become staples of international art houses and made stars of actors such as Gong Li, Ge You, Zhang Ziyi, and Jet Li. Ang Lee's martial-art classic "Crouching Tiger, Hidden Dragon" (*Wohu Canglong*, 2000) and Chen's "The Promise" (*Wu Ji*, 2005), both multi-million-dollar period epics, have won many international awards. A so-called Sixth Generation of film-makers is now rising, perhaps the best known of whom is Wang Xiaoshuai, whose "Shanghai Dreams" (*Qing hong*, 2005) has also been critically lauded far outside China.

PART 5

PLACES

13

THE MAJOR SITES TO VISIT

Beijing

Beijing is the capital of the People's Republic of China. Few cities in the world have served for so long as the political headquarters and cultural centre of an area as immense as China. The city has been an integral part of China's history over the past eight centuries, and nearly every major building of any age in Beijing has at least some national historical significance. It is impossible to understand China without a knowledge of this city.

The city remained the most flourishing cultural centre in China despite the frequent political changes in the country throughout the early decades of the twentieth century; Beijing's importance was fully realized, however, only when the city was chosen as the capital of the People's Republic in 1949, and this political status has added much vitality to it. Indeed, few cities have ever had such rapid growth in population and geographic area, as well as in industrial and other activities. Combining both historical relics of an ancient culture and new urban construction, ranging from fast-food franchises to plush

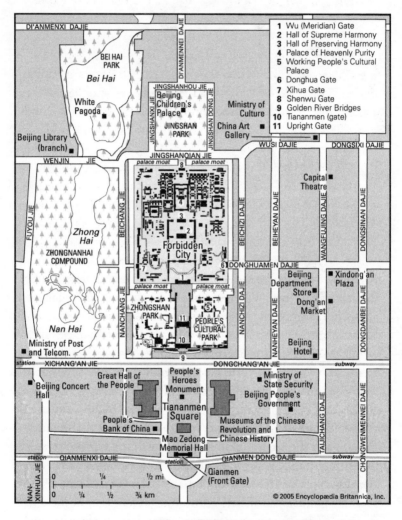

DI'ANMENXI DAJIE
DI'ANMENNEI DAJIE

BEI HAI PARK

Bei Hai

JINGSHANHOU JIE
JINGSHANXI JIE
Beijing Children's Palace
JINGSHAN DONG JIE
JINGSHAN PARK

White Pagoda

Ministry of Culture

Beijing Library (branch)

China Art Gallery

WUSI DAJIE
DONGSIXI DAJIE

WENJIN JIE

JINGSHANQIAN JIE

palace moat   palace moat

BEICHANG JIE

8

FUYOU JIE

Zhong Hai

ZHONGNANHAI COMPOUND

4

3

2

Forbidden City

Capital Theatre

BEICHIZI DAJIE

BEIHEYAN DAJIE

WANGFUJING DAJIE

DONGSINAN DAJIE

DONGDANBEI DAJIE

7

6 DONGHUAMEN DAJIE

palace moat   palace moat

Beijing Department Store

Xindong'an Plaza

1

NANCHANG JIE

ZHONGSHAN PARK

Nan Hai

11

10

PEOPLE'S CULTURAL PARK

5

NANCHIZI DAJIE

NANHEYAN DAJIE

Dong'an Market

Beijing Hotel

Ministry of Post and Telcom.

9

station   XICHANG'AN JIE

DONGCHANG'AN JIE

subway

Beijing Concert Hall

Great Hall of the People

People's Heroes Monument

Ministry of State Security

Beijing People's Government

Tiananmen Square

People's Bank of China

Museums of the Chinese Revolution and Chinese History

TAIJICHANG DAJIE

CHONGWENMENNEI DAJIE

Mao Zedong Memorial Hall

station   QIANMENXI DAJIE

station

QIANMEN DONG DAJIE

subway

NAN-XINHUA JIE

0   ¼   ½ mi

0   ¼   ½   ¾ km

Qianmen (Front Gate)

© 2005 Encyclopædia Britannica, Inc.

Legend:
1 Wu (Meridian) Gate
2 Hall of Supreme Harmony
3 Hall of Preserving Harmony
4 Palace of Heavenly Purity
5 Working People's Cultural Palace
6 Donghua Gate
7 Xihua Gate
8 Shenwu Gate
9 Golden River Bridges
10 Tiananmen (gate)
11 Upright Gate

Central Beijing

hotels for foreign tourists and corporate travellers, it has become a showplace of modern China and one of the world's great cities.

Although much of Beijing's older and more picturesque character has been destroyed in the drive since 1949 to modernize and industrialize, some parts of the city are still redolent of the past. Many fine monumental buildings, old restaurants, and centres of traditional Chinese arts and crafts remain, and the central government has taken steps to prevent the city core from being further industrialized. Broad new boulevards, replete with even newer commercial ventures, have displaced the colourful stalls and markets for which the city was once famous, but the neighbourhood life of old Beijing can still be glimpsed in the narrow *hutong* (residential alleys), with their tiny potted-plant gardens, enclosed courtyards, and (decreasingly) coal-burning stoves—some of which are still guarded by carved stone lions at their gates.

Beijing represents, better than any other existing city, the heritage of Chinese architectural achievement. During each dynasty in which the city was the capital, care was consistently taken to preserve tradition when it was rebuilt or remodelled. Few cities in the world can thus rival Beijing in the regularity and harmony of its city plan.

The urban plan, based on traditional Chinese geomantic practices, was composed about a single straight line, drawn north and south through the centre of the Forbidden City, on which the internal coherence of the city hinged. All the city walls, important city gates, main avenues and streets, religious buildings, and daily shopping markets were systematically arranged in relation to this central axis. Because the central axis has historically signified the authority of the ruling dynasty, many official buildings, public grounds, and city gates were located along this line. From north to south this line passed through the Bell Tower (Zhonglou); the Drum Tower (Gulou); Jingshan Park; the Forbidden City, including the Imperial Palaces; Tiananmen Square; Qianmen (Front Gate); the Tianqiao neighbourhood; and (no longer standing) Yongding Gate.

The symmetrical layout of the city to the east and west of this line is quite striking. In front of the palaces, the Temple of the Imperial Ancestors (now in the People's Cultural Park) on the east side of the axis is balanced by the Altar of Earth and Harvests (now in Zhongshan Park) on the west. Farther away from the palaces, the market area of Dongdan to the east was balanced by the Xidan market to the west; these still form two of Beijing's main business districts. The Tiantan (Temple of Heaven) Park to the south of the inner city is counterbalanced by the Ditan (Altar of the Earth) Park to the north of the city. Of the 16 city gates constructed in Ming times, seven were located on each side of the north–south line, and two were situated on the line itself. Only a few of the old gates still stand, but the city streets adjacent to their sites continue to carry their names.

The main avenues of the old city, whether running north–south or east–west, connected the gates on the opposite walls and divided the whole city into a rectangular grid. Within the walls, buildings were constructed around a courtyard or series of courtyards, with every important building facing south. Buildings often stood behind one another along the north–south line, with small courtyards in between. This prevailing southern orientation of buildings has a climatic functional basis, but it also appears to have been sanctified or conventionalized early in the Bronze Age in connection with ancestral ceremonies and with the worship of Heaven and Earth.

Since 1949 the greatest changes in Beijing's appearance have been the extension of its streets immediately outside the former old city walls and the accelerating pace of new construction throughout the city. On the west side of the old city, an area extending about 1 mile (1.6 km) from the spot where the Fuxing Gate stood has become an extension of the avenue Xichang'an Jie and is used primarily for government offices. Toward the Summer Palace, to the north-west, is the Haidian district, where the most important universities and research institutes of the country are located. To the north of the city, the outlying districts have been developed as a housing area adjoining the educational district in the north-west. The eastern suburb is an industrial district dominated by the manufacture of chemicals, automobiles, and agricultural machinery. Vegetable fields in the southern suburb are gradually being supplanted by industrial plants. More recently, the look of the central city, especially in the eastern sections, has been transformed by growing numbers of high-rise office and apartment buildings.

History

With only a few interruptions, Beijing has been the capital of China for some eight centuries, and in number of years as the imperial centre In prehistoric times the area around Beijing was inhabited by some of the earliest known human beings. Between 1918 and 1939 the fossil remains of Peking man (formerly *Sinanthropus pekinensis*; now known as *Homo erectus pekinensis*), who lived about 500,000 years ago, and of Upper Cave man, who lived about 50,000 years ago, were unearthed at Zhoukoudian, a village in Beijing municipality about 30 miles (50 km) south-west of the central city.

While long periods in Beijing's early history remain blank, it is certain that some 3,000 years ago Neolithic communities settled on or near the site where the city now stands. During the Zhanguo (Warring States) period (475–256 BCE) of the Zhou dynasty (1066–221 BCE), one of the powerful feudal states, the kingdom of Yan, established its capital, named Ji, near the present city of Beijing; this was the first capital city to be associated with the site. The city was destroyed by the troops of Shihuangdi, founder of the Qin dynasty (221–206 BCE).

During the Qin, the Yan capital was incorporated into one of the 36 prefectures then established throughout the country. A new town was built during the succeeding Han dynasty (206 BCE–220 CE), also known as Yan. Throughout the Han period and the turbulent centuries that followed, however, the place remained a provincial town, most of the time caught in the fateful struggle between the Han Chinese to the south and the nomadic Xiongnu, or Huns, to the north.

During the period of the Three Kingdoms (220–280 CE), the city was again called Yan. The northern border of ancient China ran close to the present city of Beijing, and northern nomadic tribes frequently broke in from across the border. Thus, the area that was to become Beijing emerged as an important strategic and a local political centre.

For nearly three centuries (from the end of the Xi [Western] Jin dynasty in 316/317 to the beginning of the Sui dynasty in 581), the northern territory, including the site where Beijing now stands, was largely under the control of invading nomads. It was not recovered by the Han people until the Tang dynasty (618–907), when it became known as Youzhou. By the middle of the Tang, measures were being taken to prevent the noma-dic Tangut tribes of Tibet, such as the Xi Xia, and the Khitans from raiding the borderlands and the local capital. The posi-tion of Youzhou consequently became increasingly important.

Between 1211 and 1215 the Mongols—under the leadership of Genghis Khan—repeatedly attacked and finally took the city from the Jin. In the battle the palaces of Zhongdu were set on fire and blazed for more than a month. When all China fell to the

Mongol hordes, Kublai Khan (1215–94), a successor to Genghis Khan, determined to build a new capital at Beijing. In 1272 he named the new capital Dadu ("Great Capital"); under the Mongols it became for the first time the political centre of all China.

Dadu was larger than any of its forerunners and was rebuilt slightly north-east of the old site. The square of the outer wall measured about 18 miles (29 km) in length and enclosed an area of more than 20 square miles (50 square km). The city walls were built with pounded earth, and once each year labourers were called in to repair them with mud. The Imperial Palace, which was approximately to the west of the modern-day one, was situated in the southern half of the capital city. The chief palace architect at the time was an Arab, appointed by Kublai. The city of Dadu exemplified the imposing and variegated architecture of the Mongol period. The square walls and the 12 gates were all modelled on the Chinese plan, but the inner chambers and living quarters were often in the styles found in Mongolia or Central Asia.

Dadu, which had magnificent imperial palaces and treasures drawn from every corner of the country, was the scene of stupendous feasts given by the khan (ruler) on state occasions. These characteristics and the well-organized post stages on the roads leading to the city astounded the Venetian traveller Marco Polo, who visited Dadu in the 1280s.

In the mid-fourteenth century a peasant revolt overthrew the Mongol dynasty and established the Ming dynasty (1368–1644). Following a coup in which the son of the Emperor took the throne the city was renamed Beijing ("Northern Capital"), and in 1421 was officially made the capital city of the Ming dynasty.

Beijing in the Ming period grew on a yet grander scale than under the Mongols. The old city of Dadu, including its palaces, was largely demolished. The new city was situated farther south-west, which left the northern part of the Mongol city derelict while at the same time slicing off one gate from the east and west walls, respectively. In 1553 an outer wall was begun, to include the increasing number of inhabitants living outside the city. However, when the entire construction was subsequently found to be too costly, the plan was abandoned on completion of the south wall; thus emerged the present shape of the old city. Unlike the city wall of pounded earth of Mongol times, the walls of the Ming city were faced with a layer of bricks to prevent weathering.

Beijing remained superficially the same throughout Qing times (1644–1911/12). The city plan was unaltered, though many palaces, temples, and pavilions were added outside the walls to the west, notably those that comprised the Old Summer Palace, built in the seventeenth century, and the Summer Palace, built in the late nineteenth century. The Old Summer Palace was completely destroyed by fire in 1860 by British and French troops during the Second Opium (or "Arrow") War (1856–60). In the same year, as a result of the treaties of Tianjin in 1858, a permanent British embassy was established in the city, and a legation quarter, situated to the south-east of the palace ground, was reserved for British and other embassies. The legation quarter was besieged for nearly two months by the Boxer rebels in 1900.

After the revolution of 1911, Beijing remained the political centre of the Republic of China until 1928, when the Nationalists moved the capital to Nanjing; Beijing was again called Beiping. The city came under increasing pressure from the Japanese, who established the puppet state of Manchukuo in Manchuria in 1931. In July 1937 fighting broke out between Chinese and Japanese troops near the Marco Polo Bridge, south-west of the city; Beiping was subsequently occupied by the Japanese until 1945. After World War II the city reverted to the Nationalists, who were defeated by the communists in the ensuing civil war. In 1949, with the establishment of the People's Republic of China, Beijing (with its old name restored) was chosen as the capital of the new regime. The city soon regained its position as the leading political, financial, and cultural centre of China.

In the 1950s and 1960s urban development projects widened the streets and established the functional districts that characterize the modern city, but political campaigns culminating in the Cultural Revolution (1966–76) delayed many of these projects. Beginning with the economic reforms of the early 1980s, the pace of change accelerated, and Beijing changed dramatically. New shopping centres and residential buildings appeared throughout the city, and high-tech industrial parks were established, especially in the suburbs. One such area, dubbed "Silicon Valley", was developed with government backing between Beijing and Qinghua universities. Another striking change, noticeable particularly in the newer shopping centres, has been the emergence of a consumption-oriented middle class similar to that found in Hong Kong, Singapore, Seoul (South Korea), and other Asian cities undergoing rapid economic growth. At the same time, Beijing, like other modern cities, has faced growing problems with air pollution, traffic congestion, and overcrowding. As Beijing prepared to host the 2008 Summer Olympic Games, its government accelerated plans to reduce pollution, improve transportation, and beautify the city.

Architecture

Beijing, the country's political and cultural centre for more than 700 years, has more buildings of historical and architectural significance than any other contemporary city in

China. Since 1949 many new government and municipal buildings, combining both traditional and Western architecture, have been constructed.

The Imperial Palaces (Palace Museum) of the Forbidden City, with their golden roofs, white marble balustrades, and red pillars, stand in the heart of Beijing and are surrounded by a moat and walls with a tower on each of the four corners. The palaces, collectively designated a World Heritage site in 1987, consist of outer throne halls and an inner court. North of the three tunnel gates that form the Wu (Meridian) Gate (the southern entrance to the Forbidden City), a great courtyard lies beyond five marble bridges. Farther north is the massive, double-tiered Hall of Supreme Harmony (Taihedian), once the throne hall. A marble terrace rises above the marble balustrades that surround it, upon which stand beautiful ancient bronzes in the shapes of cauldrons, cranes, turtles, compasses, and ancient measuring instruments. The Hall of Supreme Harmony is the largest wooden structure in China.

North of it, beyond another courtyard, is the Hall of Central (or Complete) Harmony (Zhonghedian), where the emperor paused to rest before going into the Hall of Supreme Harmony. Beyond the Hall of Central Harmony is the last hall, the Hall of Preserving Harmony (Baohedian), after which comes the Inner Court (Neiting). The Inner Court was used as the emperor's personal apartment. It contains three large halls, the Palace of Heavenly Purity (Qianqinggong), the Hall of Union (Jiaotaidian), and the Palace of Earthly Tranquillity (Kunninggong).

The Palace of Heavenly Purity is divided into three parts. The central part was used for family feasts and family audiences, audiences for foreign envoys, and funeral services; the eastern section was used for mourning rites and the western section for state business. The other two palaces, one behind the other, were Imperial family residences. The three throne halls in the Outer Court and the three main halls in the Inner Court lie along the central axis. On either side are smaller palaces, with their own courtyards and auxiliary buildings. Behind the buildings, before the northern gate of the Imperial Palaces is reached, lies the Imperial Garden. Each palace, its courtyard and side halls, forms an architectural whole.

Among the historical and religious structures in Beijing, the Temple of Heaven (Tiantan), located south of the palace compound in the old outer city, is unique both for its unusual geometric layout and because it represents the supreme achievement of traditional Chinese architecture. In 1998 it too was designated a World Heritage site. A path, shaded by ancient cypresses, runs about 1,600 feet (490 metres) from the western gate of the temple to a raised passage about 1,000 feet (300 metres) long. This broad walk connects the two sets of main buildings in the temple enclosure. To the north lies the Hall of Prayer for Good Harvests (Qiniandian) and to the south the Imperial Vault of Heaven (Huangqiongyu) and the Circular Mound Altar (Huanqiutan), all three built along a straight line. Seen from the air, the wall of the enclosure to the south is square, while the one to the north is semicircular. This pattern symbolizes the traditional Chinese belief that heaven is round and Earth square.

The Hall of Prayer for Good Harvests, built in 1420 as a place of heaven worship for the emperors, is a lofty, cone-shaped structure with triple eaves, the top of which is crowned with a gilded ball. The base of the structure is a large, triple-tiered circular stone terrace. Each ring has balustrades of carved white marble, which gives the effect of lace when seen from a distance. The roof of the hall is deep blue, resembling the colour of the sky. The entire structure, 125 feet (38 metres) high and about 100 feet (30 metres) in diameter, is supported by 28 massive wooden pillars. The four central columns, called the "dragon-well pillars", represent the four seasons; there are also two rings of 12 columns each, the inner ring symbolizing the 12 months and the outer ring the 12 divisions of day and night, according to a traditional system. The centre of the stone-paved floor is a round marble slab that has a design of a dragon and a phoenix—traditional Imperial symbols. The hall has no walls, only partitions of open latticework doors.

The Imperial Vault of Heaven, first erected in 1530 and rebuilt in 1752, is a smaller structure some 65 feet (20 metres) high and about 50 feet (15 metres) in diameter. The circular building has no crossbeam, and the dome is supported by complicated span work. Its decorative paintings still retain their fresh original colours.

South of the enclosure lies the Circular Mound Altar, built in 1530 and rebuilt in 1749. The triple-tiered white stone terrace is enclosed by two sets of walls that are square outside and round inside; thus, the whole structure forms an elaborate and integrated geometric pattern. The inner terrace is 16 feet (5 metres) above the ground and about 100 feet (30 metres) in diameter; the middle terrace is about 165 feet (50 metres) across and the lowest terrace some 230 feet (70 metres) across. Each terrace is encircled by nine rings of stones. Both the Imperial Vault of Heaven and the Circular Mound Altar were erected to portray the geometric structure of heaven, as conceived by the architects of the Ming dynasty. After 1949 the whole enclosure of the Temple of Heaven was repaired; it is now a public park.

To the east of Tiananmen Square, within the People's Cultural Park, is the Working People's Cultural Palace (formerly the Temple of the Imperial Ancestors), where the tablets of the emperors were displayed. The temple, like the Imperial Palaces in style, was built in three stonework tiers, each with double eaves. On either side are two rows of verandas surrounding a vast courtyard large enough to hold 10,000 people.

Exhibitions of economic and cultural achievements, both of China and of other countries, are frequently mounted in the three halls. Lectures by leading scholars on science, literature, and the arts are also held there.

Perhaps the most imposing structure constructed in the heart of the city since 1949 is the Great Hall of the People. Located on the western side of Tiananmen Square this is an immense building with tall columns of grey marble set on red marble bases of floral design. It has a flat roof with a golden-yellow tile cornice over green eaves shaped like lotus petals. The base of the building is of pink granite, and its walls are apricot yellow. Its frontage is 1,100 feet (335 metres) long—about the equivalent of two city blocks—and its floor space is some 1,850,000 square feet (172,000 square metres). Inside the building, the ceiling and walls are rounded. The grand auditorium, with seating for 10,000, is where the National People's Congress holds its sessions; the focus of the room's lighting system is a red star in the ceiling surrounded by golden sunflower petals. Other components are a banquet hall that can hold 5,000, huge lobbies, and scores of meeting rooms and offices for the standing committee of the congress.

Economy

One of the main differences between the imperial capital of former times and present-day Beijing is that the old city was a centre of consumption rather than production, receiving supplies of all kinds from other parts of the country. Since 1949, however, Beijing has emerged as one of China's most industrial cities, although a concern for the adverse effects of industrialization on the city's environment has, over time, curtailed expansion.

Historically, the market areas of the city were situated at two street intersections to the south-west and south-east of the

Imperial Palaces, and the Dongdan and Xidan neighbour-hoods are still major shopping centres. Since 1990, however, Western-style shopping malls and department stores have been established in various parts of the city.

One of the most vibrant retail areas is along Wangfujing Dajie, which is a few streets east of the Imperial Palaces. As part of a 20-year development plan for this shopping street that began in 1991, it was transformed in 1999 when storefronts were beautified and all vehicular traffic (except city buses) was banned. The Beijing Department Store, a state-owned enter-prise, still operates there, but it has been overtaken by gigantic, privately owned shopping malls such as in Xindong'an Plaza, an enormous complex at the southern end of Wangfujing Dajie.

Similar shopping districts can be found in other parts of the city, such as Jianguomenwai and Sanlitun, both of which are near diplomatic compounds. The Friendship Store still operates in Jianguomenwai. In the past, when it was the only place to buy Western goods, it mainly served foreign residents and visitors, although some Chinese—usually cadres or those who received foreign-currency remittances from relatives living abroad—were allowed to shop there. Although anyone can shop there now, it has been passed up by the newer commercial establishments.

Traditional markets that still serve a local function are spread around the city. They have a long history, and each has developed its own reputation for special commodities and services. The restored Liulichang Market is located just south of the Heping Gate in the old outer city. The area acquired its name (which means "glazier's shop") from the colourful glazed tiles that were made there during the Ming dynasty, but in the latter part of the eighteenth century it gradually became a market for curios, antiques, old books, paintings, works of ancient Chinese calligraphers, and paper. It is still a centre for traditional art shops.

Dazhanlan, just west of Qianmen Dajie, was rebuilt in 1998, and many of the Qing period shops there were restored. Specialities sold there include silk, tea, herbal medicines, food, and clothing. The Panjiayuan neighbourhood, just east of Longtan Park—once popular with China's national minorities but now largely patronized by Han Chinese—sells numerous items, including a wide variety of metallic ornaments.

Yabao Lu, near the Chaoyang Gate site, is popular with Russians and eastern Europeans. Most of the Chinese shop owners there speak at least some Russian, signs are written in Cyrillic, Russian food is served, and most of the products are Russian-made clothing and daily-use items. Yating Hua Niao Shichang, just outside the south-eastern corner of Tiantan Park, is a market for flowers and birds and also sells kittens and Pekinese dogs, kites, and other items.

Culture

Beijing has been the magnificent centre of traditional Chinese culture and learning since the Ming dynasty. Emperors and courtiers patronized the arts, especially painting and calligraphy. Precious objects from other parts of the empire and from foreign countries poured into the capital. This role of cultural centre was continued during the Qing dynasty, although the century of political and social upheaval that began in the mid-nineteenth century led to an overall cultural decline in both Beijing and the whole of China. In the late 1940s the Nationalists shipped a huge quantity of art treasures to Taiwan before their defeat by the Communists. On the mainland, subsequently, many family heirlooms were purchased by the state for low prices and were then sold for export or used to enhance the country's museum holdings.

The Communist government initially encouraged pursuit of traditional arts, crafts, and scholarship, but this policy abruptly ended with the onset of the Cultural Revolution. Art objects that were not deliberately smashed were confiscated (some were returned to their former owners after 1980), traditional Chinese scholarship was essentially put to an end, and many academics were sent to the countryside or imprisoned. Since that time the government has made a concerted effort to restore damaged treasures and to revive the work of traditional artists and scholars. Because much of this activity has taken place in Beijing, the capital has undergone something of a cultural renaissance and resumed its leading role in the country's cultural life.

Traditional *jingxi* (Beijing opera)—with its elaborate and stylized costumes and makeup, cacophonous music, and spectacular dance and acrobatic routines—has been revived, after an attempt during the Cultural Revolution to adapt the form to modern revolutionary themes. The opera has great appeal for older people but less for the young, who instead prefer movies, television, and popular music. A great variety of other performance styles are also found in Beijing. The city boasts a symphony orchestra and Western-style opera and ballet companies and hosts visits by foreign orchestras and performers. Concerts of traditional Chinese and Western-style popular music are also common. A variety of plays by Chinese and Western dramatists are staged each year. Venues with high reputations include the Capital, Youth Art, and Tianqiao theatres. Also popular are acrobatic performances and musical revues.

Visual arts, notably calligraphy and Chinese-style painting, have had a major resurgence in the city, and there are many shops and galleries displaying these works as well as Western-style paintings. There is also a growing market for antiques, which can be found at Liulichang near the Qianmen site and the Panjiayuan area. In addition, the city has numerous well-stocked bookshops.

The Palace Museum, housed in the main buildings of the former Imperial Palaces, contains the city's greatest collection of art treasures. Many of the halls are kept as they were in dynastic times, each constituting a museum in itself, and others are used to display some of the priceless treasures from China's past. Of special interest are its porcelains and enamels, works in embroidery and precious metals, and stone carvings and scrolls.

The Museum of Chinese History is located on the eastern side of Tiananmen Square. Thousands of historical relics and documents are on display, arranged chronologically from the appearance of the prehistoric Peking man some 500,000 years ago through the last 6,000 years of Chinese history. The Museum of the Chinese Revolution occupies a wing of the museum building and traces the country's history since the mid-nineteenth century. The Capital Museum, in the northeast near the Anding Gate site and part of the Confucian Temple complex, has exhibits on the history of the city.

Notable art collections are housed in the China Art Gallery, just north-east of the Palace Museum, and in the Xu Beihong Museum in north-western Beijing north-east of the Xizhi Gate site. Institutions devoted to the natural sciences include the Natural History Museum, in the north-western corner of Tiantan Park; the Geological Museum, just east of Bei Hai Park; and the Beijing Planetarium, west of the Xizhi Gate site and south of the Beijing Zoo. The former homes of such notable individuals as Song Qingling (Soong Ch'ing-ling), Guo Moruo, and Qi Baishi are preserved as museums.

The Beijing Library, which holds the collections of the National Library of China, is located in the southern Haidian district, just west of the zoo. The library inherited books and archives from the renowned Imperial Wenyuange library collection of the Qing dynasty that has existed for more than 500 years and that, in turn, included books and manuscripts from the library of the Southern Song dynasty, established some 700 years ago. Also in its holdings are other collections from imperial libraries of the Qing dynasty, imperial colleges, and private owners. Among them are rare copies of ancient manuscripts and books of five dynastic periods from the Song to the Qing, including a vast number of manuscript volumes on different subjects, copies of Buddhist sutras dating to the sixth century, old maps, diagrams, and rubbings from ancient inscriptions on metal and stone. In addition, it possesses the *Yongledadian* ("Great Canon of the Yongle Era") of the Ming dynasty and a copy of the *Sikuquanshu* ("Complete Library of the Four Branches of Literature"), dating from the Qing dynasty. In the late 1980s most of the National Library's collections were moved to the present site from the Beijing Library's original building just west of Bei Hai; that facility is now a branch of the main library. Other important libraries include the Beijing University Library, containing a large collection of documents on local history, and the Capital Library.

Recreation

As the residence of the imperial families through several dynastic periods, Beijing is well known for its numerous parks and playgrounds; few cities in China have as large a proportion of land within the central city allocated for recreational uses. Among the most popular of Beijing's parks are Zhongshan Park, Bei Hai Park, Jingshan Park, the Summer Palace, and the Beijing Zoo.

Zhongshan (Sun Yat-sen) Park lies just south-west of the Forbidden City; it is the most centrally located park in Beijing and encloses the former Altar of Earth and Harvests (Shejitan), where the emperors made offerings to the gods of earth and agriculture. The altar consists of a square terrace in the centre of the park. To the north of the altar is the Hall of Worship (Baidian), now the Sun Yat-sen Memorial Hall, which dates to the early fifteenth century; its simple form, masterly design, and sturdy woodwork bear the characteristic marks of early Ming architecture. The Water Pavilion, built out over a lotus pond on three sides to provide a gathering place for scholars and poets, is in the south-west corner of the park. Scattered among the park's pools, goldfish enclosures, rocky hills, weeping willows, pines, cypresses, bamboos, and flowers are pavilions, kiosks, and towers, typical of Chinese garden landscape.

Bei Hai Park lies to the north-west of the Forbidden City. It covers some 170 acres (70 hectares), half of which is water. The focus is on Bei Hai, the most northerly of the three lakes—called "seas" (*hai*)—that lie roughly north–south along the western side of the Imperial City. Pleasure grounds, lakes, and buildings have existed on the site for eight centuries. As the lakes were deepened and dredged, the excavated earth was used to build hillocks and islands of great beauty. In 1651 a Qing emperor built the White Pagoda, the most striking landmark in the park, on top of a hill. Bei Hai is crowded with rowing boats in summer, and it freezes over to become a natural ice-skating rink in winter.

Jingshan (Prospect Hill) Park, also known as Meishan (Coal Hill) Park, is a man-made hill, more than a mile (1.6 km) in circumference, located north of the Forbidden City. The hill, offering a spectacular panorama of Beijing from its summit, has five ridges, with a pavilion on each. The hill was the scene of a historical tragedy when in 1644, at the end of the Ming dynasty, the defeated Ming emperor hanged himself on a locust tree on its east slope. In the northern part of the park is Beijing Children's Palace, with recreational, athletic, and educational facilities.

The Summer Palace—called Yiheyuan in Chinese ("Garden of Good Health and Harmony")—lies close to the Western

Hills, about 6 miles (10 km) north-west of the Xizhi Gate site. Designated a World Heritage site in 1998, it is the largest park on the outskirts of Beijing and is noted for its artful landscaping, which provides an inimitable blend of woods, water, hills, and architecture. The park covers more than 800 acres (325 hectares), four-fifths of which consists of Kunming Lake and the remainder man-made hillocks. More than 100 buildings—halls, towers, pavilions, bridges, and pagodas—lie scattered throughout the park; a marble boat, two storeys high and some 80 feet (24 metres) long, is located at the northwestern corner of the lake and is one of the major attractions. A series of richly painted covered promenades connect the buildings and courts along the shore of the lake. Just east of the Summer Palace lie the ruins of the former Summer Palace (Yuanmingyuan), destroyed in 1860 by foreign troops.

To the west of the Summer Palace, on the eastern edge of the Western Hills, is Xiangshan (Fragrant Hills) Park. Long an imperial retreat, it is now a popular area of rugged woodlands and scenic vistas. Nearby to the north is the Azure Clouds Temple (Biyunsi) complex, which contains a hall where the body of Nationalist leader Sun Yat-sen was kept after he died until it could be buried in Nanjing. Farther to the north-east is the Beijing Botanical Garden, within which is a temple containing a large statue of a reclining Buddha.

The Beijing Zoo is located in the western part of the city. The zoo was established toward the end of the nineteenth century and was named the "Garden of Ten Thousand Animals" (Wanshengyuan). Its collection is actually about half that size, but it is the largest zoo in the country, with animals from all parts of China and the world; one of the zoo's most popular attractions is its collection of giant pandas.

Further Afield: The Great Wall of China

The Great Wall of China is one of the largest building construction projects ever carried out, running (with all its branches) about 4,500 miles (7,300 km) east to west from Shanhai Pass near the Bo Hai (Gulf of Zhili) to Jiayu Pass (in modern Gansu province). Without its branches and other secondary sections, the wall extends for some 4,160 miles (6,700 km), often tracing the crestlines of hills and mountains as it snakes across the Chinese countryside. Large parts of the fortification date from the seventh through the fourth century BCE. In the third century BCE Shihuangdi (Qin Shihuang), the first emperor of a united China (under the Qin dynasty), connected a number of existing defensive walls into a single system. Although lengthy sections of the wall are now in ruins or have disappeared completely, it is still one of the more remarkable structures on Earth. The Great Wall was designated a UNESCO World Heritage site in 1987.

The Great Wall developed from the disparate border fortifications and castles of individual Chinese kingdoms. For several centuries these kingdoms probably were as concerned with protection from their near neighbours as they were with the threat of "barbarian" invasions or raids.

Most of the Great Wall that stands today is the result of work done during the reign of the Hongzhi emperor (1487–1505). Starting west of Juyong Pass, this part of the wall was split into south and north lines, respectively named the Inner and Outer walls. Along the wall were many strategic "passes" (i.e. fortresses) and gates. Among them were Juyong, Daoma, and Zijing passes, the three closest to the Ming capital Beijing. Together they were referred to as the Three Inner Passes. Farther west were Yanmen, Ningwu, and Piantou passes, known as the Three Outer Passes. Both the Inner and Outer passes were of key importance in protecting the capital and were usually heavily garrisoned.

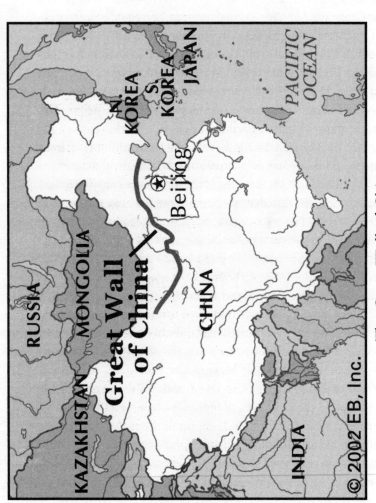

The Great Wall of China

The Great Wall had three major components: passes, signal towers (beacons), and walls. Passes were major strongholds along the wall, usually located at such key positions as intersections with trade routes. The ramparts of many passes were faced with huge bricks and stones, with dirt and crushed stones as filler. The bastions measured some 30 feet (10 metres) high and 13 to 16 feet (4 to 5 metres) wide at the top. Within each pass were access ramps for horses and ladders for soldiers. The outside parapet was crenellated, and the inside parapet, or *yuqiang* (*nüqiang*), was a low wall about 3 feet (1 metre) high that prevented people and horses from falling off the top.

In addition to serving as an access point for merchants and other civilians, the gate within the pass was used as an exit for the garrison to counterattack raiders or to send out patrols. Under the gate arch there was typically a huge wooden double door. Bolts and locker rings were set in the inner panel of each door. On top of each gate was a gate tower that served as a watchtower and command post. Usually it stood one to three storeys high and was constructed either of wood or of bricks and wood.

Signal towers were also called beacons, beacon terraces, smoke mounds, mounds, or kiosks. They were used to send military communications: beacons (fires or lanterns) during the night or smoke signals in the daytime; other methods such as raising banners, beating clappers, or firing guns were also used. Signal towers, often built on hilltops for maximum visibility, were self-contained high platforms or towers. The lower levels contained rooms for soldiers, as well as stables, sheepfolds, and storage areas.

The wall itself was the key part of the defensive system. It usually stood 21.3 feet (6.5 metres) wide at the base and 19 feet (5.8 metres) at the top, with an average height of 23 to 26 feet (7 to 8 metres), or a bit lower on steep hills. The structure of the wall varied from place to place, depending on the availability of building materials. Walls were made of tamped earth sand-wiched between wooden boards, adobe bricks, a brick and stone mixture, rocks, or pilings and planks. Some sections made use of existing river dykes; others used rugged mountain terrain such as cliffs and gorges to take the place of man-made structures.

The Great Wall has long been incorporated into Chinese mythology and popular symbolism, and in the twentieth century it came to be regarded as a national symbol. Above the East Gate (Dongmen) at Shanhai Pass is an inscription attributed to the medieval historian Xiao Xian, which is translated as "First Pass Under Heaven", referring to the traditional division between Chinese civilization and the "bar-barian" lands to the north.

Despite the wall's cultural significance, roadways have been cut through it at several points, and vast sections have suffered centuries of neglect. In the 1970s a segment near Simatai (68 miles [110 km] north-east of Beijing) was dismantled for building materials, but it was subsequently rebuilt. Other areas have also been restored, including just north-west of Jiayu Pass at the western limit of the wall; at Huangya Pass, some 105 miles (170 km) north of Tianjin; and at Mutianyu, about 55 miles (90 km) north-east of Beijing. The best-known section, at Badaling (43 miles [70 km] north-west of Beijing), was rebuilt in the late 1950s; it now attracts thousands of national and foreign tourists every day. The eastern limits of the wall, around Shanhai Pass, also had been rebuilt by the 1990s.

Shanghai and the Yangtze River Delta

Shanghai is one of the world's largest seaports and a major industrial and commercial centre of China. The city is located on the coast of the East China Sea between the mouth of the

Yangtze River (Chang Jiang) to the north and the bays of Hangzhou and Wangpan Yang to the south. The municipality's area includes the city itself, surrounding suburbs, and an agricultural hinterland.

Shanghai was the first Chinese port to be opened to Western trade, and it long dominated the nation's commerce. Since the founding of the People's Republic in 1949, however, it has become an industrial giant whose products supply China's growing domestic demands. The city has also undergone extensive physical changes with the establishment of industrial suburbs and housing complexes, the improvement of public works, and the provision of parks and other recreational facilities. Shanghai has attempted to eradicate the economic and psychological legacies of its exploited past through physical and social transformation to support its major role in the modernization of China.

History

During the Song dynasty (960–1126) Shanghai emerged from its somnolent state as a small, isolated fishing village. The natural advantages of Shanghai as a deepwater port and shipping centre were recognized as coastal and inland shipping expanded rapidly. By the beginning of the eleventh century, a customs office was established; and by the end of the thirteenth century, Shanghai was designated as a county seat and placed under the jurisdiction of Kiangsu province.

After the 1850s, the predominantly agricultural focus of the economy was quickly transformed. At this time the city became the major Chinese base for commercial imperialism by nations of the West. Following their humiliating defeat by Great Britain in 1842, the Chinese surrendered Shanghai and signed the Treaty of Nanjing, which opened the city to unrestricted foreign trade. The British, French, and Americans took possession of designated areas in the city within which they were granted special rights and privileges, and the Japanese received a concession in 1895 under the terms of the Treaty of Shimonoseki.

The opening of Shanghai to foreign business immediately led to the establishment of major European banks and multi-purpose commercial houses. The city's prospects as a leading centre of foreign trade were further enhanced when Guangzhou (Canton), a rival port in the south-eastern coastal province of Guangdong, was cut off from its hinterland by the Taiping Rebellion (1850–64). Impelled by this potential threat to the uninterrupted expansion of their commercial operations in China, the British obtained rights of navigation on the Yangtze in 1857. As the natural outlet for the vast hinterland of the lower Yangtze, Shanghai rapidly grew to become China's leading port and by 1860 accounted for about 25 per cent of the total shipping tonnage entering and leaving the country.

Shanghai did not, however, show promise of becoming a major industrial centre until the 1890s. Except for the Jiangnan Arsenal organized by the Qing dynasty (1644–1911) in the early 1860s, most industrial enterprises were small-scale offshoots of the larger foreign trading houses. As the flow of foreign capital steadily increased after the Sino-Japanese War of 1894–95, light industries were established within the foreign concessions, which took advantage of Shanghai's ample and cheap labour supply, local raw materials, and inexpensive power.

The 1920s was also a period of growing political awareness in Shanghai. Members of the working class, students, and intellectuals became increasingly politicized as foreign domination of the city's economic and political life became ever more oppressive. When the agreements signed by the UK, the USA, and Japan at the Washington Conference of 1922 failed to satisfy Chinese demands, boycotts of foreign goods were instituted. The CCP was founded in Shanghai in 1921, and four years later the Communist Party led the "May 30" uprising of students and workers. This massive political demonstration was directed against feudalism, capitalism, and official connivance in foreign imperialistic ventures. The student–worker coalition actively supported the Nationalist armies under Chiang Kai-shek, but the coalition and the Communist Party were violently suppressed by the Nationalists in 1927.

Shanghai was occupied by the Japanese during the Sino-Japanese War of 1937–45, and the city's industrial plants suffered extensive war damage. In the brief interim before the fall of Shanghai to the People's Liberation Army (PLA) in 1949, the city's economy suffered even greater dislocation through the haphazard proliferation of small, inefficient shop industries, rampant inflation, and the absence of any overall plan for industrial reconstruction.

After 1949 Shanghai's development was temporarily slowed because of the emphasis on internal regional development, especially during the period up to 1960 when close cooperation was maintained with the Soviet Union. With the cooling of relations after 1960, Shanghai has resumed its key position as China's leading scientific and technological research centre, with the nation's most highly skilled labour force.

The physical perspective of downtown Shanghai is much the same as in the pre-communist period. Because of the policy of developing integrated residential and industrial complexes in suburban areas, central city development and renewal has been given low priority. Many of the pre-World War II buildings, which housed foreign commercial concerns and diplomatic missions, still dominate the area.

Extending southward and westward from the confluence of the Wusong and Huangpu rivers, central Shanghai has a gridded street pattern and includes the area originally contained within the British concession. The area is bounded on the east along the Huangpu by Zhongshan Dong Lu (Chung-shan Tung Road), widely known as the Bund; on the west by Xizang Lu; and on the south by Yan'an Zhong Lu. Zhongshan Dong Lu has several hotels, the central administrative offices of Shanghai, and a residence for foreign seamen. On the main commercial artery, Nanjing Dong Lu, which runs westward from the eastern road, lies Shanghai's largest retail establishment—the Shanghai Number One Department Store—as well as restaurants, hotels, and the central communications building.

The Hongkou district lies to the north and east of the Wusong River. It was originally developed by American and Japanese concessionaires and in 1863 was combined with the British concession to the south to create the International Settlement. It is an important industrial area, with shipyards and factories spread out along the bank of the Huangpu in the eastern section of the district. Its best-known building, the Shanghai Daxia (Broadway Mansions Hotel), overlooks the Huangpu.

The old Chinese city, which is now part of central Shanghai, is characterized by a random and labyrinthine street pattern. Until the early twentieth century the area was surrounded by a three-mile wall. It is now circumscribed by the two streets of Renmin Lu and Zhonghua Lu, which follow the course of the original wall; and it is bisected by the main north–south artery, Henan Nan Lu (South Ho-nan Road).

Western Shanghai is primarily residential in character and is the site of the Industrial Exhibition Hall. To the south-west, the district of Xuhui, formerly Ziccawei, became a centre of Christian missionary activity in China in the seventeenth century. During the late 1800s, Jesuit priests established a major library, a printing establishment, an orphanage, and a meteorological observatory in the area.

Retail trade is concentrated in the old central business district, although the volume of trade conducted there has diminished with the establishment of the industrial satellite towns and villages on the periphery of Shanghai.

Culture

Shanghai's cultural attractions include museums, historical sites, and scenic gardens. The Shanghai Museum of Art and History houses an extensive collection of bronzes, ceramics, and other artefacts dating over several thousand years. The Shanghai Revolutionary History Memorial Hall displays photographs and objects that trace the city's evolution. The Dashijie ("Great World"), founded in the 1920s, is Shanghai's leading theatrical centre and offers folk operas, dance performances, plays, story readings, and specialized entertainment forms typical of China's national minority groups. The city also has many workers' and children's recreational clubs and several large motion-picture theatres, including the Shanghai Film Arts Centre.

The old Chinese city houses the sixteenth-century Yuyuan Garden (Garden of the Mandarin Yü), an outstanding example of late Ming garden architecture, and the Former Temple of Confucius. Other points of attraction are the Qing dynasty Longhua Pagoda, the Industrial Exhibition Hall, and the tomb and former residence of Lu Xun, a twentieth-century revolutionary writer.

The major publishing houses of Shanghai are a branch of the People's Literature Publishing House (at Beijing) and the People's Educational Publishing House. In addition to the large branch of the library of the Chinese Academy of Sciences,

Shanghai has numerous other libraries. Shanghai's art and music schools include a branch of the Central Conservatory (Tianjin), the Shanghai Conservatory, and the Shanghai Institute of Drama. There is also a variety of professional performing arts troupes, including ballet and opera companies, symphonies, and puppet troupes.

Parks, open spaces, and playing fields were notably expanded after 1949. Two of the earliest to be opened for public use were the People's Park in central Shanghai and the Huangpu Park on the shore of the Huangpu River. Every section of the city has large parks and playing fields. Among the largest are the Hongkou Arboretum and Stadium in the north; the Peace Park and playing field in the north-east; the Pudong Park in eastern Shanghai, the Fuxing Park in the south, and the Zhongshan Park on the western periphery of the central city.

Further Afield: The Yangtze River Delta

Suzhou controls the Chang Jiang (Yangtze River) delta area north and north-east of Lake Tai. The city is situated to the east of the lake, on the southern section of the Grand Canal. It is surrounded by canals on all four sides and is crisscrossed by minor canals. Suzhou is a place of great beauty, with lakes, rivers, ponds, world-famous gardens, and a string of scenic hills along the eastern shore of Lake Tai. It also lies at the centre of some of the richest agricultural land in China.

The traditional founding date of Suzhou is 514 BCE, when a city with the approximate boundaries of the present one was established by the ruler of the state of Wu (Eastern Zhou dynasty). Under the Qin dynasty (221–206 BCE), it became the seat of a county, Wujiang, and of the Kuaiji commandery, which controlled most of modern Jiangsu south of the Yangtze and of Zhejiang province. The name Suzhou dates from 589, when the Sui dynasty (581–618 CE) conquered southern China. With the building of the Grand Canal, Suzhou became an administrative and commercial centre for an area that rapidly developed into the major rice-surplus region of China.

In the thirteenth century the Venetian traveller Marco Polo visited and commented on its splendours. The Song River and Suzhou Creek gave the city direct access to the sea, and for a while Suzhou was a port for foreign shipping, until the silting of the Yangtze River delta and the irrigation and reclamation works that went on continually impeded access. Under the Ming (1368–1644) and early Qing (1644–1911/12) dynasties, Suzhou reached the peak of its prosperity. The home of many wealthy landowning families, it became a centre for scholarship and the arts. Sources of the city's wealth included the silk industry and embroidery. It also served as an important source of commercial capital and a finance and banking centre.

From 1860 to 1863, during the Taiping Rebellion of 1850–64, Suzhou was occupied by the Taiping leader Li Xiucheng. Although it was one of the few places in which Taiping reform policies seem to have been effectively carried out, the city was, nevertheless, largely destroyed. Although it was restored in the late nineteenth century, its commercial supremacy was then challenged by nearby Shanghai. Under the Treaty of Shimonoseki (concluded between China and Japan in 1896), it was opened for foreign trade but without significant results. Before World War II the area was adversely affected by foreign competition, and the silk industry, most of which was on a small handicraft scale, was hard hit. At about this time some modern factories manufacturing satins and cotton fabrics were established, and a large electric power plant was set up, but until the outbreak of the Sino-Japanese War in 1937 there was little modern industry. Suzhou was occupied by the Japanese from 1937 to 1945.

The city is a centre of learning; Suzhou University and Suzhou School of Fine Arts were established in the early twentieth century, and later the Southern Jiangsu Technical Institute and a special sericulture institute were established. Suzhou gained a reputation in the late 1950s for its training programmes for apprentice workers in traditional handicrafts. An iron and steel plant was set up in the 1950s, but there has been little significant development of heavy industry. Silk and cotton textile industries, however, have been reorganized on a large scale.

Suzhou boasts some 150 exquisite gardens with temples, pavilions, and rock sculptures. The Chinese Garden Society, re-established in 1978, organizes international academic exchanges.

Hangzhou is the provincial capital. The city stands on the north bank of the Qiantang River estuary at the head of Hangzhou Bay. It has water communications with the interior of Zhejiang to the south, is the southern terminus of the Grand Canal, and is linked to the network of canals and waterways that cover the Yangtze River delta area to the north. The city stands at the foot of a scenic range of hills, the Xitianmu Shan ("Eye of Heaven Mountains"), and on the shore of the famous Xi ("West") Lake, celebrated in poetry and paintings for its beauty and a favourite imperial retreat. Hangzhou's buildings and gardens are also renowned, and it is situated among hills and valleys in which some of the most famous monasteries in China are located.

The county of Qiantang was first established at this site under the Qin dynasty (221–206 BCE) but did not begin to develop until the fourth and fifth centuries CE when the Yangtze River delta area began to be settled. It became a major local centre with the completion of the Jiangnan Canal (then the southern section of the Grand Canal) in 609. A centre of commerce, it was visited in the late thirteenth century by the Venetian traveller Marco Polo, who called it Kinsai, or Quinsay; it then had an estimated population of 1,000,000–1,500,000.

Since 1949 Hangzhou, though it has been carefully preserved as a scenic district and tourist attraction, has also developed into an industrial centre. The silk industry has been modernized and now produces both silk and cottons. There is an electric generating plant connected by a power grid with the large Xin'an River hydroelectric project to the south-west and to Shanghai and Nanjing. A chemical industry has also been established. In the late 1950s a major tractor plant was built in Hangzhou, and a machine-tool industry subsequently developed. The city is also the centre for an industrial area engaged in grain milling, tea processing, and the production of hemp, silk, and cotton.

Hong Kong and Macau

Hong Kong developed initially on the basis of its excellent natural harbour (its Chinese name means "fragrant harbour") and the lucrative China trade, particularly opium dealing. It was the expansion of its territory, however, that provided labour and other resources necessary for sustained commercial growth that led to its becoming one of the world's major trade and financial centres.

The community remains limited in space and natural resources, and it faces persistent problems of overcrowding, trade fluctuations, and social and political unrest. Nevertheless, Hong Kong has emerged strong and prosperous, albeit with a changed role, as an entrepôt, a manufacturing and financial centre, and a vital agent in the trade and modernization of China.

Before the British arrived in the mid-nineteenth century, Hong Kong Island was inhabited only by a small fishing population, with few features to recommend it for settlement. It lacked fertile soil and fresh water, was mountainous, and was reputed to be a notorious haunt of pirates. But it was a relatively safe and undisturbed base for the British merchants who in 1821 began to use the fine harbour to anchor opium-carrying vessels. The great commercial and strategic significance of this deep, sheltered harbour, possessing east and west entrances and lying on the main trade routes of the Far East, was quickly realized.

After the first Opium War (1839–42), Hong Kong Island was ceded to Britain by the Treaty of Nanjing. The British were never satisfied with an incomplete control of the harbour, however. Less than 20 years later, after the second Opium War (1856–60), China was forced to cede Kowloon Peninsula south of what is now Boundary Street and Stonecutters Island by the Convention of Peking (1860). By the Convention of 1898, the New Territories together with 235 islands were leased to Britain for 99 years from July 1, 1898. With this expansion of territory, Hong Kong's population leapt to 120,000 in 1861 and to more than 300,000 by the end of the century.

Almost since its establishment, Hong Kong, more than any other treaty port, afforded a refuge for runaway persons and capital from China as well as an interim abode for rural emigrants destined for Southeast Asia and beyond. Such movements of Chinese people between China and Hong Kong were free and were highly responsive to the political and economic conditions in China. After the establishment of the Republic of China in 1912, proponents of emerging nationalism sought to abolish all foreign treaty privileges in China. A boycott against foreign goods particularly hurt Britain, which was well established in China. The campaign soon spread to Hong Kong, where strikes in the 1920s caused agitation.

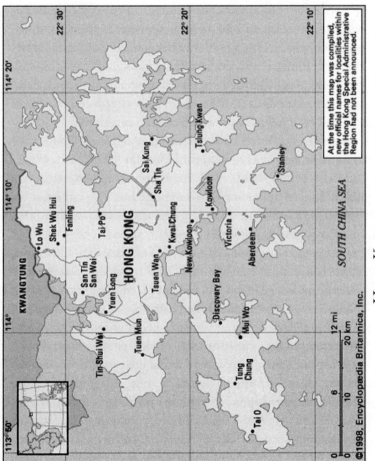

Hong Kong

At the time this map was compiled, new official names for localities within the Hong Kong Special Administrative Region had not been announced.

©1998, Encyclopædia Britannica, Inc.

KWANGTUNG

HONG KONG

SOUTH CHINA SEA

Lo Wu
Shek Wu Hui
Fanling
Tai Po
San Tin
San Wai
Yuen Long
Tin Shui Wai
Tuen Mun
Tsuen Wan
Sai Kung
Sha Tin
Kwai Chung
New Kowloon
Discovery Bay
Mui Wo
Tung Chung
Tai O
Tsiung Kwan
Kowloon
Victoria
Aberdeen
Stanley

113° 50'
114°
114° 10'
114° 20'
22° 30'
22° 20'
22° 10'

0   6   12 mi
0 10 20 km

When the Sino-Japanese War broke out in 1937, Hong Kong was once more a refuge, with thousands of Chinese fleeing to it before the advancing Japanese. With the outbreak of war in Europe in 1939, the position of the colony became even more precarious, and the Japanese attacked and occupied Hong Kong in December 1941. During the war years Hong Kong's commerce was drastically impaired; food was scarce, and many residents fled to inland China. The population, which numbered 1,600,000 in 1941, was reduced to about 650,000 by 1945 when the Japanese surrendered.

British troops returned to the city on August 30, 1945, and civil government was re-established in May 1946. Meanwhile, hundreds of thousands of Chinese and foreigners returned, and they were soon joined by economic and political refugees from China, who were fleeing the civil war between the Nationalist and Communist armies.

The United Nations embargo in 1951 on trade with China and North Korea during the Korean War seriously curtailed the entrepôt trade, the lifeline of the colony, and for several years conditions were depressed. Hong Kong began its revival based on light industries such as textiles, which were set up by immigrant capitalists and provided needed employment. These soon assumed their importance in the economy, providing as well the basis for further industrialization. But it was because much of the development depended on cheap labour, which toiled under extremely poor working conditions, that labour disputes and social discontent began to spread in the early 1960s.

Severe riots broke out in Hong Kong and Kowloon in May 1967 following a labour dispute in a plastic-flower factory. The economic and social unrest was immediately turned into violent political demonstrations, largely inspired by followers of the Cultural Revolution (1966–76) in China. When the situation stabilized toward the end of the 1960s, general working and living conditions were notably improved by labour legislation, large government housing projects, and extensive public works programmes.

Simultaneously, high-technology industries such as electronics were developed, and the property and financial markets prospered until early 1973, when the stock market collapsed as billions of dollars were drained out of Hong Kong. From the mid-1970s the economy resumed its upward trend as relations with China improved.

In the late 1970s, concern about the future of Hong Kong began to loom large, as British jurisdiction over the leased areas of the New Territories neared the 1997 expiration date. Although the lease applied only to the New Territories, the Chinese government had consistently maintained that the whole of Hong Kong was Chinese territory and considered that the question of the earlier Hong Kong–British agreements came under the category of unequal treaties and also required resolution.

Initial contacts between the two governments on the matter were made from March 1979, but formal negotiations did not start until after the visit of the British prime minister to Beijing in September 1982. Negotiations continued for two years. Finally, the Chinese–British joint declaration on the question of Hong Kong was formally signed by the heads of the two governments in Beijing on December 19, 1984. The agreement stipulated that Hong Kong (including Hong Kong Island, Kowloon, and the New Territories) would be recovered by China from July 1, 1997.

There ensued a period of often difficult negotiations between Hong Kong and Beijing on the final wording of the document by which Hong Kong would be governed under Chinese sovereignty. Despite some reservations from Hong Kong, the National People's Congress formally ratified the Basic Law on April 4, 1990, which took effect on July 1, 1997, and established the Hong Kong Special Administrative Region directly under the central government.

As in many large urban centres of the world, Hong Kong's population has increased in the last two decades. Since the 1950s the average annual rate of growth has fluctuated between about 2 and 4 per cent, the variations in some degree based on the sporadic flow of immigrants from China, which has been increasing in recent years, along with the growth of China's south coastal region at large. Immigration has been a chief cause of population increase. Birth rates have steadily declined since the late 1950s, the rate of natural increase falling below 1 per cent by the 1980s. Life expectancy, however, has been showing a gradual increase. Since the 1950s, the proportion of the population under 15 has decreased rapidly, while that between 15 and 64 has shown a marked increase and the group over 65 has more than doubled. Hong Kong is one of the world's most densely populated places.

Since 1969 Hong Kong has emerged as one of the major financial centres of the Asia-Pacific region, despite the fact that it is without the services of a central bank. The regional government delegates the functions of such an institution to certain government offices and selected commercial banks. In addition to the licensed banks in the region, there are representative offices of foreign banks, including registered deposit-taking companies.

Domestic and international currencies are traded at the Hong Kong foreign-exchange market. The stock market attracts investment from both foreign and domestic sources. Some of its major shares are also traded on the London stock market. A gold bullion market, once the world's largest, is operated by the Chinese Gold and Silver Exchange Society. The lack of exchange controls has contributed to the success of Hong Kong as a financial centre.

Culture

Hong Kong's is truly a mixed culture. Not only does the territory celebrate festivals and holidays of the East and the West, such as the Dragon Boat Festival, the Mid-Autumn Festival, the Lunar (Chinese) New Year, Christmas, the Western New Year, and others, but it also enjoys hundreds of annual cultural events ranging from traditional Cantonese and other Chinese regional operas and puppet shows to performances of ballet, theatre, and music and exhibitions of paintings and sculptures by nationally and internationally renowned performers and artists. The Hong Kong Arts Festival has become one of Asia's major cultural events, and the Hong Kong Philharmonic Orchestra, the Hong Kong Chinese Orchestra, the Chung Ying Theatre Company, and the City Contemporary Dance Company are among the best-known local artistic groups. The Hong Kong Conservatory of Music and the Hong Kong Academy of Ballet have been combined into the Hong Kong Academy for Performing Arts, offering full-time diploma courses in dance, drama, music, and technical arts.

Scores of motion pictures are produced every year in Hong Kong, many of which attain international fame; some have even started new trends in the art, such as the popular martial arts films of Hong Kong, emulated and remade by Hollywood since they emerged on the world market in the 1980s. The Hong Kong International Film Festival, inaugurated in 1977, is a major event, especially for the display of Asian films. Hong Kong is also a regional as well as an international centre in fashion design and in the cutting and design of ornamental diamonds.

Apart from the libraries of the major educational institutions, Hong Kong has a system of 25 libraries, including mobile ones. Of the museums, major ones include those specializing in history, art, science and technology, and space.

The multifunctional City Hall (a cultural centre) and the Art Centre provide the major gallery, theatrical, and concert facilities. In addition, town halls have been established in the new towns and cultural centres in some districts to serve local communities.

Hong Kong's country park system covers two-fifths of the land area, and outdoor recreation in parks is part of the way of life for many people. City-dwellers use park areas on the urban fringe for walking, running, and *taijiquan*, among other activities, while remoter locations are used for kite flying, picnicking, hiking, cycling, and camping. There are well-organized programmes of recreation and sports at the community level. The Ocean Park, one of the world's largest oceanariums, the Hong Kong Coliseum, a 12,500-seat indoor stadium that is among the largest in Asia, and the Queen Elizabeth Stadium are among the best venues for local and international sports events and musical, cultural, and entertainment programmes. For those who can afford it, the many inlets and bays in Hong Kong provide a superb setting for pleasure sailing, waterskiing, canoeing, and other water sports; the Hong Kong Yacht Club is one of the most active in the South China Sea region.

Xi'an

Located on the loess plain of the Wei River south-west of Beijing, Xi'an is important in Chinese history as the capital of several ruling dynasties and as a market and trade centre. It was also the eastern terminus of the Silk Road, the ancient trade route that connected China with the Mediterranean.

Cities have existed in the area since the eleventh century BCE. Ch'ang-an cheng ("Walled City of Chang'an"), built in 202 BCE just north-west of modern Xi'an, was the capital of the former (Western) Han dynasty and one of the greatest cities of the ancient world. It was largely destroyed during the disturbances that preceded Wang Mang's inter-regnum (9–23 CE). The later (Eastern) Han dynasty, established in 23, moved its capital to Luoyang and for several centuries Chang'an declined until it was revived by the Sui emperors (581–618), who also made it their capital.

As the capital of the Tang dynasty (618–907), Chang'an was expanded and divided into three parts—the Palace City; the Imperial City, for the officials; and the Outer City, for artisans and merchants. It soon became one of the most splendid and extravagant cities in the world. In the thirteenth century Marco Polo described the city as a thriving trade centre. The popular name Xi'ian ("Western Peace"), adopted after the Ming dynasty (1368–1644) but later changed to Siking, was restored in 1943.

From the 1920s the city was the chief port of entry for communist ideology reaching China from the Soviet Union. The city was also the site of the Xi'an Incident, of December 1936, which marked the beginning of united Chinese Nationalist and communist resistance against the Japanese.

Located in the city is the Shaanxi Provincial Museum, housed in a former Confucian temple; it is noted for its Forest of Stelae, an important collection of inscribed stelae and Buddhist sculpture. The Shaanxi History Museum houses artifacts and art objects spanning China's history, from the Paleolithic Period through the Qing dynasty. Other sites of interest in the city include the Little Wild Goose Pagoda, the Big Wild Goose Pagoda (148 feet [45 metres] high), and the Temple of Great Good Will, constructed during the Tang dynasty; the Bell Tower and Drum Tower, built during the Ming dynasty; the Great Mosque, founded in 742 with the existing buildings dating from the fourteenth century; and three well-preserved fourteenth-century city gates in the wall that surrounds the old city.

The Silk Road

The trade route from China to Asia Minor and India, known as the Silk Road, had been in existence for 1,400 years at the time of Marco Polo's travels (*c.* 1270–90 CE). It came into partial existence about 300 BCE, when it was used to bring jade from Khotan (modern Hotan, China) to China. By 200 BCE it was linked to the West, and by 100 BCE it was carrying active trade between the two civilizations. At its zenith in 200 CE this road and its western connections over the Roman system constituted the longest road on Earth.

Originating at Xi'an, the 4,000-mile (6,400-km) road, actually a caravan tract, followed the Great Wall of China to the north-west, bypassed the Takla Makan Desert, climbed the Pamirs (mountains), crossed Afghanistan, and went on to the Levant; from there, the merchandise was shipped across the Mediterranean Sea. Few persons travelled the entire route, and goods were handled in a staggered progression by middlemen. With the gradual loss of Roman territory in Asia and the rise of Arabian power in the Levant, the Silk Road became increasingly unsafe and untravelled.

The road now partially exists in the form of a paved highway connecting Pakistan and Xinjiang Uighur Autonomous Region, China. The old road has inspired a United Nations plan for a trans-Asian highway.

The Terracotta Army

About 20 miles (32 km) north-east of Xi'an lies the tomb of Shihuangdi (259–210/9 BCE), the early Chinese ruler famed, among other things, in connection with the Great Wall.

In March 1974 a work brigade of farmers drilling a well discovered a subterranean chamber that archaeologists later

found contained an army of more than 6,000 life-size terracotta soldiers (assembled from separately fired sections but
given individually detailed faces) and horses, along with richly
adorned chariots of wood (now disintegrated) and of bronze;
iron farm implements; bronze and leather bridles; objects of
silk, linen, jade, and bone; and such weapons as bows and
arrows, spears, and swords, cast from an unusual 13-element
alloy, which are still shiny and sharp today.

The clay figures, once brightly painted with mineral colours,
were grouped into a specific military formation—a configur-
ation of vanguard bowmen and crossbowmen, outer files of
archers, groups of infantrymen and charioteers, and an ar-
moured rear guard—that followed the military prescriptions
of the time. Three nearby chambers—one holding more than
1,400 ceramic figures representing a smaller, complementary
force of foot soldiers, chariots, and cavalry, one with 68
members of what probably represents an elite command unit,
and one that is empty—were also discovered in the 1970s.

The buried army faces east, poised for battle, about three-
quarters of a mile from the outer wall of the tomb proper,
guarding it from Shihuangdi's chief former adversaries, who
had come from that direction. In pits nearby have been found
the remains of seven humans (possibly the emperor's children),
a subterranean stable filled with horse skeletons, an assem-
blage of half-size bronze chariots, 70 individual burial sites, a
zoo for exotic animals, and other artefacts.

The tomb itself, which may have been looted shortly after its
completion, remains unexcavated. It lies within an inner wall
and beneath a four-sided pyramid mound that was originally
landscaped to appear as a low, wooded mountain. The interior
is reputedly a vast underground palace that took about
700,000 conscripted workmen more than 36 years to complete. The historian Sima Qian (c. 145–c. 85 BCE) wrote: "The

labourers dug through three subterranean streams, which they sealed off with bronze to construct the burial chamber. They built models of palaces, pavilions, and offices and filled the tomb with fine vessels, precious stones, and rarities. Artisans were ordered to instal mechanically triggered crossbows set to shoot any intruder. With quicksilver the various waterways of the empire, the Yangtze and Huang He (Yellow River), and even the great ocean itself were created and made to flow and circulate mechanically. With shining pearls the heavenly constellations were depicted above, and with figures of birds in gold and silver and of pine trees carved of jade the earth was laid out below. Lamps were fuelled with whale oil so that they might burn for the longest possible time."

The compound was declared a UNESCO World Heritage Site in 1987. After more than two decades of work on the site, archaeologists in the 1990s anticipated that it would take many more years, perhaps several generations, to unearth the remainder of the tomb complex. In the years since its discovery, the tomb of the terracotta warriors has become one of China's most important tourist destinations, drawing thousands of visitors to Xi'an each year.

Tibet

Tibet is often called "the roof of the world". It occupies about 471,700 square miles (1,221,600 square km) of the plateaus and mountains of Central Asia, including Mount Everest (Zhumulangma Feng). Before the 1950s Tibet was a unique entity that sought isolation from the rest of the world. It constituted a cultural and religious whole, marked by the Tibetan language and Tibetan Buddhism. Little effort was made to facilitate communication with other countries, and economic development was minimal. After official incorporation into China, fitful efforts at development took place in Tibet, disrupted by ethnic tension between the Han (Chinese) and Tibetans and Tibetan resistance to the imposition of Marxist values. Official policy since the early 1980s has been somewhat more conciliatory, resulting in slightly better Han–Tibetan relations and greater opportunities for economic development and tourism. The completion of the Qinghai–Tibet train line, the world's highest railway, in 2006 ushered in more tourists, but also provided a means for still more outsiders to enter the region, the population of which is increasingly less Tibetan and more Chinese.

History

According to legend the Tibetan people originated from the union of a monkey and a female demon. The Chinese Tang annals (tenth century) place the Tibetans' origin among the nomadic, pastoral Qiang tribes recorded about 200 BCE as inhabiting the great steppe north-west of China. That region, where diverse racial elements met and mingled for centuries, may be accepted as the original homeland of the Tibetans, but until at least the seventh century CE they continued to mix, by conquest or alliance, with other peoples. From that heritage two strains in particular stand out—the brachycephalic, or round-headed, peoples and the dolichocephalic, or long-headed, peoples. The former, which predominate in the cultivated valleys, may have derived from the Huang He basin and be akin to the early Chinese and Burmese; the latter, found mainly among the nomads of the north and in the noble families of Lhasa, seem to have affinities with the Turkic peoples, whose primitive wandering grounds were farther to the north. In addition, there are Dardic and Indian strains in the west, and along the eastern Himalayan border there are connections with a complex of tribal peoples known to the Tibetans as Mon.

From the seventh to the ninth century the Tibetan kingdom was a power to be reckoned with in Central Asia. When that kingdom disintegrated, Tibetans figured there from the tenth to the thirteenth century only casually as traders and raiders. The patronage of Tibetan Buddhism by the Yuan, or Mongol, dynasty of China made it a potential spiritual focus for the disunited tribes of Mongolia. This religious significance became of practical importance only in the eighteenth century when the Oyrat, who professed Tibetan Buddhism, threatened the authority of the Qing dynasty throughout Mongolia. In the nineteenth century Tibet was a buffer between Russian imperial expansion and India's frontier defence policy.

In the mid-nineteenth century the Tibetans repeatedly rebuffed overtures from the British, who at first saw Tibet as a trade route to China and later as countenancing Russian advances that might endanger India. Eventually, in 1903, after failure to get China to control its unruly vassal, a political mission was dispatched from India to secure understandings on frontier and trade relations. Tibetan resistance was overcome by force, the Dalai Lama fled to China, and the rough wooing ended in a treaty at Lhasa in 1904 between Britain and Tibet without Chinese adherence. In 1906, however, the Chinese achieved a treaty with Britain, without Tibetan participation, that recognized their suzerainty over Tibet. Success emboldened the Chinese to seek direct control of Tibet by using force against the Tibetans for the first time in 10 centuries. In 1910 the Dalai Lama again was forced to flee, this time to India.

That dying burst by the Manchu dynasty converted Tibetan indifference into enmity, and, after the Chinese Revolution in

1911–12, the Tibetans expelled all the Chinese and declared their independence of the new republic. Tibet functioned as an independent government until 1951 and defended its frontier against China in occasional fighting as late as 1931. In 1949, however, the "liberation" of Tibet was heralded, and in October 1950 the Chinese entered eastern Tibet, overwhelming the poorly equipped Tibetan troops. An appeal by the Dalai Lama to the United Nations was denied, and support from India and Britain was not forthcoming. A Tibetan delegation summoned to China in 1951 had to sign a treaty dictated by the Chinese. It professed to guarantee Tibetan autonomy and religion but also allowed the establishment at Lhasa of Chinese civil and military headquarters.

Smouldering resentment at the strain on the country's resources from the influx of Chinese soldiery and civilians was inflamed in 1956 by reports of savage fighting and oppression in districts east of the upper Yangtze, outside the administration of Lhasa but bound to it by race, language, and religion. Refugees from the fighting in the east carried guerrilla warfare against the Chinese into central Tibet, creating tensions that exploded in a popular rising at Lhasa in March 1959. The Dalai Lama, most of his ministers, and many followers escaped across the Himalayas, and the rising was suppressed.

The events of 1959 intensified China's disagreements with India, which had given asylum to the Dalai Lama, and in 1962 Chinese forces proved the efficiency of the new communications by invading north-east Assam.

In 1966 and 1967 the Chinese position was shaken by Red Guard excesses and internecine fighting when the Cultural Revolution reached Lhasa. Military control was restored by 1969, and in 1971 a new local government committee was announced. Between 1963 and 1971 no foreign visitor was allowed to enter Tibet. Persecution of Tibetans abated in the late 1970s with the end of the Cultural Revolution, but Chinese repression was resumed when the Tibetans renewed their claims for autonomy and even independence. However, China has invested in the economic development of Tibet and in the early 1980s took initiatives to repair diplomatic ties with the Dalai Lama. Despite China's efforts to restore some freedoms and ease its repressive posture, riots broke out in the late 1980s, and China imposed martial law in Tibet in 1988. Tibet continues to suffer from periodic unrest, and China's suppression of political and religious freedoms has led to Western criticism and protests by human rights organizations. The Dalai Lama, still unrecognized by the Chinese government, won the Nobel Peace Prize in 1989.

Although Tibetans refer to their country as Gangs-ljongs or Kha-ba-can ("Land of Snows"), the climate is generally dry, and most of Tibet receives only 18 inches (460 mm) of rain and snow annually. The Himalayas act as a barrier to the monsoon (rain-bearing) winds from the south, and precipitation decreases from south to north. The perpetual snow line lies at about 16,000 feet (4,850 m) in the Himalayas but rises to about 20,000 feet (6,060 m) in the northern mountains. Humidity is low, and fog is practically non-existent.

Temperatures in the higher altitudes are low, but the lower valleys and the south-east are mild and pleasant. Seasonal variation is minimal, and the greatest temperature differences occur during a 24-hour period. Lhasa, which lies at an elevation of 11,830 feet ((3,585 m), has a maximum daily temperature of 85°F (30°C) and a minimum of –2°F (–19°C). The bitterly cold temperatures of the early morning and night are aggravated by the gale-force winds that blow throughout most of the year. Because of the cool dry air, grain can be safely stored for 50 to 60 years, dried raw meat and butter can be preserved for more than one year, and epidemics are rare.

Government

Before the Chinese asserted control, Tibet had a theocratic government of which the Dalai Lama was the supreme religious and temporal head. After 1951 the Chinese relied on military control and a gradual establishment of regional autonomy, which was granted in 1965.

Since 1965, as part of the separation of religion and civil administration, Tibet has been an autonomous region (zizhiqu) of China. The region is divided into the municipality (*shi*) of Lhasa, directly under the jurisdiction of the regional government, and into prefectures (*diqu*), which are subdivided into counties (*xien*).

The army consists of regular Chinese troops under a Chinese military commander, who is stationed at Lhasa. There are military cantonments in major towns along the borders with India, Nepal, and Bhutan. Tibetans have been forcibly recruited into regular, security, and militia regiments.

Culture

Tibet is most renowned for its religious scroll paintings (tankas, or thang-ka), metal images, and wooden block prints. There are three categories of images—representing the peaceful, moderate, and angry deities—and three schools of painting—the Sman-thang, Gong-dkar Mkhan-bris, and Kar-ma sgar-bris—which are differentiated by colour tones and depicted facial expressions.

The rich and ancient culture is based on religion. The Gar and the 'cham are stylistic dances performed by monks; they re-enact the behaviour, attitudes, and gestures of the deities. Ancient legendary tales, historic events, classical solo songs, and musical debates are elaborately staged in the open air in the form of operas, operettas, and dramas. The folk songs and dances of local regions abound with colour, joy, and simplicity: the bro of the Khams region, the sgor-gzhas of the dbus-gtsang peasants, and the Kadra of the A-mdo area are spectacles that are performed in groups; on festive occasions they continue for several days. These cheerful performances tell of the people's loves and celebrate their faith in their religion, the beauty of their country, and the brave deeds of their ancestors.

Traditional marriage ceremonies involve consultations with both a lama and an astrologer in order to predict the compatibility of a couple. The signing of a marriage contract is followed by an official ceremony at the home of the bridegroom. Appearance in a temple or before a civil authority is not required. After a couple is officially wedded, prayer flags are hoisted from the bride's side of the family upon the rooftop of the bridegroom's house to symbolize the equality of the bride in her new home. Although polygamy was practised on a limited scale, monogamy is the predominant form of marriage.

When a death occurs, the family members make charitable contributions in the hope of ensuring a better reincarnation for the deceased. In the case of the death of an important religious figure, his corpse is preserved in a tomb. Otherwise, tradition calls for the corpse to be fed to the vultures, as a symbol of charity. The customs of burial and cremation exist but are seldom practised.

A white scarf (kha-btags) is offered during greetings, visits to shrines, marriage and death ceremonies, and other occasions. The tradition was derived from the ancient custom of offering clothes to adorn the statues of deities. Gradually, it evolved into a form of greeting, and the white scarf offering, symbolizing purity, became customary. Another tradition is the hoisting of prayer flags on rooftops, tents, hilltops, and almost anywhere a Tibetan can be found. These flags signify fortune and good luck.

The staple Tibetan food is barley flour (rtsam-pa), which is consumed daily. Other major foods include wheat flour, yak meat, mutton, and pork. Dairy products such as butter, milk, and cheese are also popular. The people in the higher altitudes generally consume more meat than those of the lower regions, where a variety of vegetables is available. Rice is generally restricted in consumption to the well-to-do families, southern border farmers, and monks.

Two beverages—tea and barley beer (chang)—are particularly noteworthy. Brick tea from China and local Tibetan tea leaves are boiled in soda water. The tea is then strained and poured into a churn, and salt and butter are added before the mixture is churned. The resulting tea is light reddish white and has a thick buttery surface. Chang, which is mildly intoxicating, is thick and white and has a sweet and pungent taste.

Festivals are both national and local in character. The many local celebrations are varied; national festivals, though fewer, are marked with a spirit of unity and lavishness.

The first day of the first month of the Tibetan calendar (February or March of the Gregorian calendar) is marked by New Year celebrations all over Tibet. Monasteries, temples, stupas (outdoor shrines), and home chapels are visited at dawn, and offerings are made before statues and relics of deities and saints. A special fried cookie known as kha-zas is prepared in every home. Either a real or an artificial head of a horned sheep adorns the offerings. A colourful container filled with barley flour and wheat grain and another container of chang are presented to all visitors, who take a pinch of the contents and make an offering to the deities by throwing it in the air.

The New Year celebrations are almost immediately followed by the Smom-lam ("prayer") festival, which begins three days after the New Year and is celebrated for 15 days.

The festival marks the victory of Buddha over his six religious opponents through debates and the performance of miracles. During this festival, special prayers are offered daily. Prayers, fasting, and charitable donations mark sa-ga zla-ba, the celebration of the anniversary of Buddha's birth, enlightenment, and death—three events that all occurred on the 15th day of the fourth month of the Tibetan calendar.

The death of Tsong-kha-pa, founder of the Dge-lugs-pa sect, is celebrated on the 25th day of the tenth month by the burning of butter lamps on the roofs and windowsills of every house. This festival is known as lnga-mchod. The dgu-gtor festival, or festival of the banishment of evil spirits, takes place on the 29th day of the last month of the Tibetan year. At night a bowl of flour soup and a bunch of burning straws are taken into every room of every house, and the evil spirits are called out. Outside, on a distant path, the soup and straws are thrown and left to burn.

Superstition has been prominent in Tibet. A traveller who encounters either a funeral procession, the source of running water, or a passer-by carrying a pitcher of water is considered to have good fortune awaiting him. If a vulture or an owl perches on a rooftop, it is believed that death or misfortune will soon befall the household. If snow falls during a marriage procession, it is believed that the newly-weds will face many misfortunes or difficulties. A snowfall during a funeral, however, symbolizes an impediment to death in the family for a long period of time.

INDEX

Britannica®

Since its birth in the Scottish Enlightenment Britannica's commitment to educated, reasoned, current, humane, and popular scholarship has never wavered. In 2008, Britannica celebrated its 240th anniversary.

Throughout its history, owners and users of *Encyclopædia Britannica* have drawn upon it for knowledge, understanding, answers, and inspiration. In the Internet age, Britannica, the first online encyclopædia, continues to deliver that fundamental requirement of reference, information and educational publishing—confidence in the material we read in it.

Readers of Britannica Guides are invited to take a FREE trial of Britannica's huge online database. Visit

https://china.britannicaguides.com

to find out more about this title and others in the series.